14⁰⁰
80E

Strategic Disarmament, Verification
and National Security

sipri

Stockholm International Peace Research Institute

SIPRI is an independent institute for research into problems of peace and conflict, with particular attention to the problems of disarmament and arms regulation. It was established in 1966 to commemorate Sweden's 150 years of unbroken peace.

The financing is provided by the Swedish Parliament. The staff, the Governing Board and the Scientific Council are international. As a consultative body, the Scientific Council is not responsible for the views expressed in the publications of the Institute.

Governing Board

Governor Rolf Edberg, Chairman (Sweden)
Professor Robert Neild, Vice Chairman (United Kingdom)
Mr Tim Greve (Norway)
Academician Ivan Málek (Czechoslovakia)
Professor Leo Mates (Yugoslavia)
Professor Gunnar Myrdal (Sweden)
Professor Bert Röling (Netherlands)
The Director

Director

Dr Frank Barnaby (United Kingdom)

sipri
Stockholm International Peace Research Institute
Sveavägen 166, S-113 46 Stockholm, Sweden
Cable: Peaceresearch, Stockholm
Telephone: 08-15 09 40

Strategic Disarmament, Verification and National Security

sipri

Stockholm International Peace Research Institute

Taylor & Francis Ltd
London

Crane, Russak & Company, Inc.
New York

1977

First published 1977 by Taylor & Francis Ltd., London
and Crane, Russak & Company, Inc., New York

Copyright © 1977 by SIPRI
Sveavägen 166, S-113 46 Stockholm

All rights reserved. No part of this publication may be
reproduced, stored in a retrieval system or transmitted,
in any form or by any means, electronic,
mechanical, photocopying, recording or otherwise,
without the prior permission of the copyright owner.

ISBN 0 8448 1227 7

Library of Congress Catalog Card Number 77-85318

Printed and bound in the United Kingdom by
Taylor & Francis (Printers) Ltd, Rankine Road,
Basingstoke, Hampshire RG24 0PR

Preface

Verification is a crucial but controversial issue in disarmament negotiations. On the one hand, states need adequate assurances of the compliance of others in any agreements reached. On the other hand, verification can be, and often is, used as an excuse for lack of progress in arms control and disarmament negotiations.

In the end, of course, the main factor determining the success or failure of disarmament efforts is the political will of the countries involved to obtain an agreement. But, even so, the importance of verification cannot be doubted. It is hoped that this book will assist discussion of the issues involved.

The book was written by Andrzej Karkoszka, who was a research fellow at SIPRI between August 1973 and December 1975, and is now working at the Polish Institute of International Affairs in Warsaw.

May 1977

Frank Barnaby
Director

Abbreviations and Acronyms

ABM	Anti-Ballistic Missile
ACDA	Arms Control and Disarmament Agency
ASW	Anti-Submarine Warfare
CBW	Chemical and Biological Warfare
CCA	Commission for Conventional Armaments
CEP	Circular Error Probability
FLR	Flexible Limited Response
GCD	General and Complete Disarmament
IAEA	International Atomic Energy Agency
ICBM	Intercontinental Ballistic Missile
K	Kill Potential
KN	Kill Offensive Potential
KS	Kill Defensive Potential
MAD	Mutually Assured Destruction
MARV	Manoeuvrable Re-entry Vehicle
MIRV	Multiple Independently targetable Re-entry Vehicle
MRV	Multiple Re-entry Vehicle
NPT	Non-Proliferation Treaty
OAR	Overall Reliability
PK	Probability of Kill
R&D	Research and Development
RV	Re-entry Vehicle
SALT	Strategic Arms Limitation Talks
SLBM	Submarine-Launched Ballistic Missile
SLCM	Submarine-Launched Cruise Missile
SSKP	Single Shot Kill Probability
SVR	Security Verification Requirement
TKP	Terminal Kill Probability

Contents

Introduction 1

Chapter 1. The impact of disarmament agreements 4

Chapter 2. Verification and its role in disarmament 10
I. The development of international control 10
II. The meaning of 'control' 11
III. Definition of the verification of disarmament 12
IV. Means, methods and types of disarmament verification 15
  Means and methods: a review of the literature – Means and methods in actual disarmament agreements – Means, methods and typology of verification: a proposal
V. The requirements for verification 28
VI. The functions of verification 33

Chapter 3. Conditions for implementation of disarmament agreements other than verification 40
I. Introduction 40
II. Factors acting against compliance with disarmament agreements 40
  Endangered balance of power – Deteriorating international relations – Military technology – 'Failure of expectations'
III. Factors acting for compliance with disarmament agreements 43
  International law – Public opinion – Bureaucratic restraints
IV. Cost and benefit evaluation of the violation 46

Chapter 4. National interests and national security in relation to disarmament 51
I. National interests: analysis of the concept 51
  Definitions – The formulation of national interests – The pursuit of national interests
II. National security in relation to disarmament 56
  Definitions – The rôle of security in national policy
III. The function of verification in safeguarding security 58

Chapter 5. Strategic military security through stable deterrence 61
I. Introduction 61
II. The concept of strategic deterrence 61
  MAD deterrence – FLR deterrence
III. The stability of deterrence in the arms race 64
  The structure of arsenals – Proportions in numbers of weapons – Deliverable megatonnage and throw weight/payload – Accuracy and reliability of weapons – Vulnerability of strategic weapons
IV. The stability of deterrence in disarmament 69

Chapter 6. Security and verification in strategic arms limitation—a case study 74
  I. Introduction 74
  II. The simplified concept of the relation between disarmament, security and verification 75
  III. The purpose and scope of the study 77
  IV. Terminology 78
    The notion of calculable security
  V. Verification and the preservation of security during strategic disarmament 80
    Scenario I: disarmament with frozen military technology – Strategic security and numerical violations – Strategic security and qualitative violations – The relation between verification and security in Scenario I – Scenario II: disarmament with unrestricted military technology – New strategic weapon systems – The relation between verification and security in Scenario II

Conclusions 98

Appendix 105
  I. The structure and characteristics of A and B's ICBM arsenals, 1974 .. 106
  II. Rules for carrying out ICBM reductions 106
    Discussion of the rules for reductions – The direct verification requirement – The security verification requirement
  III. Methods 114
    The concept of the residual second strike – Method I: The K method – Method II: the TKP method – Comparison of the two methods of calculation – The minimum deterrence threshold
  IV. Scenario I: numerical limitations of A and B's strategic forces accompanying a freeze in the qualitative arms race 128
    Calculation of the security verification requirements of A and B – ICBM reductions – SLBM reductions
  V. Scenario II: numerical limitations of A and B's strategic forces accompanying an unrestricted qualitative arms race 144
    Country A's ICBM conversions and replacements – Country B's ICBM conversions and replacements – Maximum limits of the K value – The minimum deterrence threshold – Calculation of the security verification requirements of A and B – ICBM reductions – SLBM reductions

Tables

Chapter 2. Verification and its role in disarmament

Table
1. Relation between the scope of a disarmament agreement and the type of verification 25

Appendix

Tables
1. ICBM forces of countries A and B at 1974, and their characteristics   106
2. Scenario I: ICBM reductions of countries A and B, 1974–1989   108
3. Calculation of the 'average' hardness of A's and B's silos (sample calculations)   121
4. Basic values used in sample calculations of the security verification requirement according to two different methods   121
5. Comparison of the security verification requirement values resulting from the two different methods of sample calculation   122
6. K' required to destroy a given silo with the probability $P_k = 0.95$....   128
7. K per warhead of the missiles of reliability ρ reduced in Scenario I...   128
8. Total KN and $K'S$ values represented by A's and B's arsenals in 1974   129
9. Scenario I: the residual second strikes of A and B during ICBM reductions, 1974–1989, given in $K'S$ values   129
10. Scenario I: values of security verification requirements for countries A and B during ICBM reductions, 1974–1989   131
11. Scenario I: levels of required verification for countries A and B during ICBM reductions, 1974–1987   137
12. Country A: diagram of simultaneous ICBM reductions, replacements and improvements   145
13. Characteristics of the new ICBMs introduced by countries A and B during the reductions in Scenario II..........................   147
14. K per warhead of the missiles of reliability ρ reduced in Scenario II..   147
15. Scenario II: Hardness (H) and K' values of the reduced silos........   147
16. Country B: diagram of simultaneous ICBM reductions and improvements   148
17. Fluctuation of the minimum deterrence threshold of A during ICBM reductions in Scenario II, given in $K'S$ values and in numbers of the opponent's best missiles needed to overcome these $K'S$ values......   153
18. Fluctuation of the minimum deterrence threshold of B during ICBM reductions in Scenario II, given in $K'S$ values and in numbers of the opponent's best missiles needed to overcome these $K'S$ values......   153
19. Scenario II: the residual second strikes of A and B during ICBM reductions concomitant with an unrestricted qualitative arms race 1974–1989, given in $K'S$ values..............................   156

20. Scenario II: the security verification requirements of A and B during ICBM reductions concomitant with an unrestricted qualitative arms race, 1974–1989 156
21. Scenario II: levels of required verification for countries A and B during ICBM reductions concomitant with an unrestricted qualitative arms race, 1974–1989 164

Graphs

Chapter 6. Security and verification in strategic arms limitation—a case study
Graph
1. The Wiesner curve... 76

Appendix
Graphs
1. Scenario I: countries A and B's reductions of missiles and warheads, 1974–89 111
2. Scenarios I and II: number of ICBMs reduced by A and B during disarmament, 1974–89 113
3. Scenario I: country A's security verification requirement and minimum deterrence threshold during ICBM reductions, 1974–89 126
4. Scenario I: B's security verification requirements and minimum deterrence threshold during ICBM reductions, 1974–89................. 127
5. Scenario I: security verification requirements of countries A and B during ICBM reductions, 1974–89. A's requirement is indicated in numbers of MIII warheads and missiles, B's in numbers of SS9s 130
6. Scenario I: three phases of change in A's security during ICBM reductions, 1974–89.. 132
7. Scenario I: three phases of change in B's security during ICBM reductions, 1974–89.. 133
8. Scenario I: relation between disarmament and security of country A during 15 stages of ICBM reductions........................... 134
9. Scenario I: relation between disarmament and security of country B during 15 stages of ICBM reductions........................... 136
10. Scenario I: level of required verification of countries A and B during ICBM reductions, 1974–89..................................... 138
11. Scenario I: Relation between disarmament, security and verification for country A, ICBM reductions................................. 139
12. Scenario I: the relation between disarmament, security and verification for country B, ICBM reductions, 1974–89................... 140
13. Scenario II: illustration of A and B's reductions of missiles and warheads, 1974–89, concomitant with an unrestricted qualitative arms race... 150
14. Scenario II: Fluctuations of A and B's minimum deterrence threshold during ICBM reductions, 1974–89, concomitant with an unrestricted qualitative arms race 154
15. Scenario II: country A's security verification requirement during ICBM reductions, 1974–89, concomitant with an unrestricted qualitative arms race, and A's minimum deterrence threshold during these reductions 157

16. Scenario II: country B's security verification requirement during ICBM reductions, 1974–89, concomitant with an unrestricted qualitative arms race, and B's minimum deterrence threshold during these reductions 158
17. Scenario II: Phases of change in A's security during ICBM reductions, 1974–89, concomitant with an unrestricted qualitative arms race 160
18. Scenario II: three phases of change in B's security during ICBM reductions, 1974–89, concomitant with an unrestricted qualitative arms race... 161
19. Relation between disarmament concomitant with an unrestricted qualitative arms race and the security of country A during ICBM reductions 163
20. Scenario II: levels of required verification for countries A and B during ICBM reductions concomitant with an unrestricted qualitative arms race, 1974–89... 165
21. Relation between disarmament, concomitant with an unrestricted qualitative arms race, and the security of country B during ICBM reductions 166
22. Scenario II: comparison between the required level of verification of countries A and B in Scenarios I and II (Level 1 is equal to verification's efficiency at points α_A and α_B in Scenario I, where the security of both countries has been completely satisfied.................. 167

Introduction

The purpose of this book is to undertake an analysis of the relationship between the security of two states mutually undergoing strategic disarmament and the need for safeguarding their security by means of a verification system. The study thus intends to take up one of the basic problems in the disarmament debate; in the past, an issue of great political controversy[1], and still something of a hot potato even today.

A number of studies have already been made on the problem. These were, however, mainly descriptive or historical, lacking in objective political analysis, and rather tending to exhibit some political bias, depending on the political school of the author. There is thus some justification for the statement made by some outstanding authorities in the field that 'to date, no systematic analysis has been attempted to determine what different disarmament measures would optimally require of verification methods . . .'.[2] This book cannot claim to be a complete answer to this criticism, although our ambition is to respond in part to it, at least so far as the strategic context of disarmament is concerned.

The first impulse for this book was the widespread and often-quoted belief that verification is the best remedy against states' reluctance to enter into disarmament agreements, caused by the fear that disarmament will jeopardize their security and undermine their chances of survival. Even in this book the assumption of a close relationship existing between states' security and disarmament verification was initially taken as a serious working assumption. Using it as a basis, a case study of strategic disarmament between two states was made, leading to a number of calculations, now constituting the appendix to this book. And though these calculations were simplified and limited in scope, they gave rise to serious scepticism as to the validity of the concept of a direct relationship between the security of states carrying out strategic disarmament, and verification, as understood conventionally (that is, that verification functions as a 'watchdog' of complete compliance of states with the terms of a treaty).

This scepticism seemed to demand a more comprehensive study of the basic terms used in the analysis, that is, the concepts of 'security' and 'verification'. Such additional analysis was deemed necessary because of the difficulty of making a quantified analysis based on such unquantifiable concepts as 'security'. To avoid, as far as was possible, all factors which might make our calculations invalid, we had to discuss such concepts, to be able to extract those which were quantifiable and those which were not. If we had not done so, our conclusions might have been misleading. This is the reason for discussing theoretically matters which might otherwise seem far removed from the main purpose of the book.

The chapters of the book may be grouped into three parts. Part 1 (Chapter 1) consists of an introduction. Part 2 discusses and analyses separately the two basic notions of the book: 'security' and 'verification' (Chapters 2, 3, 4 and 5). Here an attempt has been made to find definitions for these concepts, and to analyse their rôles as a function of disarmament. Finally, Part 3, constituting Chapter 6 and the Appendix, attempts to relate these two basic notions in the context of strategic disarmament, first in a general way, drawing from the experience gained from the arms race, and later in a specific model of disarmament, where the relationship is measured in a quantified way. The third part of the book gives rise to numerous conclusions, some of them novel, and others already known, although hitherto in a rather intuitive way.

Chapter 1 introduces us to the enormous range of repercussions caused by a disarmament agreement. Disarmament, it is clear, is a weighty business, influencing both the domestic political situation of the participants to an agreement, and international relations as a whole. And this is even more so in the case of strategic disarmament because of the specific worldwide dimensions of the weaponry involved and the extraordinary influence that the states possessing strategic weapons are able to exert on the international political situation. It is this knowledge of the consequences of a disarmament measure that makes any decision to enter it so politically complicated and difficult. A state must take into account a whole host of different interests, tuning them together, both nationally and internationally. And having once entered into an agreement, with all the political weight committed behind it, it is understandable that states are so eager to gain the assurance that the agreement will be mutually upheld by all the parties to it.

One of the mechanisms set up in disarmament agreements that is intended to safeguard the interests of the states disarming is verification. In Chapter 2 we examine this concept of verification, analysing the meaning of the term, presenting various definitions of what verification is and attempting to systematize the concept. The basic aim of this chapter is to establish the functions of, and the extent of the need for verification, seen from different angles, especially that of a state's security.

It has been noted on many occasions that the verification set up in a disarmament treaty is only one of a number of factors working towards compliance with a treaty. In fact the rôle of verification in preserving the treaty, and therefore the security of its participants, is to a large extent limited. Without all the other conditions, described in Chapter 3, verification on its own can do little to preserve the treaty régime.

Fundamental concern about its security is one of the chief factors determining the way in which a state will participate in a disarmament treaty. Chapter 4 gives a brief analysis of this concept of national interests in general, and the concept of national security in particular. It can be seen how far these concepts, while being extremely imprecise and volatile on the one hand, are of great political importance on the other.

Among all the elements of 'security', it is military security that plays by far the largest rôle. Because of this, Chapter 5 considers a specific case of strategic military security, in which security, defined as stable strategic deterrence between two states, is analysed. The effects on that security of the fluctuations in the countries' respective military potentials in the context of the ongoing arms race, are also considered.

At this stage, it must be mentioned that the use of deterrence theory and a number of concepts associated with the strategic deterrence doctrine does not at all mean that the author associates himself with it in any way. It is used here only as an analytical tool, and so far, the most convenient one in the context, even though it is at the same time unacceptable in practical political terms.

Finally in Chapter 6 the question is analysed of what happens to security based on strategic deterrence when states enter into the disarmament process. More specifically, the rôle of verification in preserving security in such circumstances is analysed, thereby answering the main problem of the book: what is the relationship between verification and security during strategic disarmament. This relationship is analysed according to hypotheses partly based on current experience of arms race stability, partly on the theoretical studies of deterrence considered in Chapter 5 and partly on the author's own calculations of the Appendix. All these data indicate clearly that in the case of strategic disarmament, the real factor bearing upon the ability of a state to preserve its security during the process of disarmament is military technology and not verification of full compliance with the injunctions of the treaty. Verification of developments in military technology, whether related directly or indirectly to the stipulations of the strategic disarmament treaty is thus the main task of verification, if it is to preserve the security of the states concerned.

1. See, for example: Bogdanov, O. B., *Jadiernoje Razoruzhenije* (*Nuclear Disarmament*). Izdatielstvo IMO, Moskva 1961, pp. 136–142; Wright, M., *Disarm and Verify. An Explanation of the Central Difficulties and of National Policies.* Chatto and Windus, London 1964; Towpik, A., *Bezpieczenstwo Miedzynarodowe a Rozbrojenie* (*International Security and Disarmament*), PISM, Warszawa 1970, pp. 111–126.
2. Myrdal, A.,The International Control of Disarmament, *Scientific American*, Vol. 231, No. 4, p. 23.

1. The impact of disarmament agreements

In a world in which a strong military capability and the preparedness to meet any external threat are traditionally believed to be the main bulwark of a state's security, the act of signing a disarmament agreement is undoubtedly of great national significance to the country concerned. A voluntary disarmament measure, broadly conceived, is an act of self-restraint imposed upon the free expansion of military power, and may possibly lead to a curtailment of that power. To a nation-state, the effects of disarmament on its security – the security of its independence and sovereignty, the integrity of its national territory and its well-being – and on its ability to maintain its position and influence internationally are of fundamental importance. Thus, on signing and implementing a treaty, a state has to be continually appraising the implications of the treaty *vis-à-vis* its security.[1]

In accepting a disarmament measure, a state makes at the same time a decision on its armaments policy, as well as its future military strategy and posture. It is relatively easy to assess quantitatively and qualitatively what changes the measure will bring about in a state's own military structure. It is much more difficult to predict the net effect of a disarmament agreement on the relative balance of military power internationally. A state may feel militarily better or worse off after fulfilling the letter of an agreement without necessarily being aware of its objective situation. The optimal situation is, of course, one where states are – or their governments think they are – in the same balance of military power after the realization of an agreement as they were before signing it, although at a lower level of military preparedness and expenditure. It is, however, always extremely difficult to assess the balance of military power of states *vis-à-vis* that of other countries. How does one measure it? One can, for example, compare the numbers of different complexes of weapon systems in each country; or one can try to assess the overall military balance, not by single systems, but by due consideration of them all. Evaluations of military balance are always subjective and depend on the individual making the assessment; nevertheless they are extremely important factors in the internal discussions of governments contemplating disarmament agreements, and externally on those governments' assessments of the position of their opponents.

In general, one can say that the net result of an agreement largely depends on the number of states adhering to it. The greater the participation in a given disarmament measure, the greater the stabilizing effect on the international situation. The stabilizing effect of such broader participation results from the fact that more states act on the international scene according to agreed rules of behaviour, and thus the military situation can be expected to be more stable. States which lie outside the framework of the treaty and which are not restricted and controlled by such rules tend to be less predictable, thereby increasing the margin of contingencies to which states can be dangerously exposed. This is, of course, a generalization. A comprehensive agreement which is not well balanced in content or in its results could bring about less stability than other, more limited measures. In general, however, an agreement which is more comprehensive in scope will have a positive influence on military stability, at least so far as the following three factors are concerned: (*a*) by excluding from the qualitative and quantitative arms race more weapon systems, and thus diminishing the fear of technological surprise; (*b*) by covering wider geographical areas, and hence lessening the arms competition there; and (*c*) by making it easier to compare remaining military capabilities. By the same token, a limited disarmament agreement may have precisely the opposite effect; it may cover a weapon or activity to which the military do not attach much importance in any case, and thereby release funds which may be diverted to the development of more advanced and dangerous weapons,[2] creating the possibility of a shift in the military balance, and hence a shift in the security of the parties to the agreement.

Quite apart from such considerations of the effects of a disarmament measure on the balance of military power, a state contemplating signing an agreement is bound to consider the implications of such an agreement for the military and political alliances of which it is a member. Ideally, of course, an agreement would consolidate an alliance and enhance the possibilities for cooperation; on the other hand an agreement concluded between members of ideologically opposite alliances could appear to be in contravention of the basic premises of those alliances. In the worst possible case, where only some members of an alliance are involved in a disarmament agreement and not others, states could find themselves in a situation of conflicting loyalties. All these factors have to be weighed up by the states concerned.

Again, a comprehensive disarmament agreement would naturally entail some loss of its military power by a state party, and hence somewhat weaken its ability to use that power as a factor supporting its foreign policy.[3] In the long run, this would generally be a positive development in that a reduced rôle of the military would imply that states would be obliged to find other, more peaceful ways of gaining influence. In the short run, states are likely to consider the implications of this loss of their ultimate sanction when they enter into a commitment to disarm.

Apart from these military and political considerations, any disarmament agreement has to be seen in its economic context as well. Armaments industries habitually play a major rôle in the economy of industrialized countries, so that any change in the pattern of arms production will have widespread repercussions on the whole economy. Some factories will have to change their arms production or may even close down, whereas others might benefit from the inevitable redistribution of resources away from armaments industries. In addition, the effect of disarmament on the national labour market would be considerable; large numbers of workers in the armaments industry, as well as a number of highly trained and specialized research and development (R&D) scientists, would have to be diverted into the civilian sector of the economy. If the resources released from the military sector were directed into the service industries or were used to augment the public sector and to solve grave social problems, a disarmament agreement might be expected to receive widespread public support, which would help the government to gain acceptance for an agreement from its voters; on the other hand any change in arms procurement policy causing widespread unemployment would inevitably meet with considerable opposition and result in loss of popularity for the government concerned. This is quite apart from the inevitable hostility from all the other vested interests in the armaments industry.

The relationship between disarmament and international economic development has been emphasized on a number of occasions. In the well-known UN Report on the Economic and Social Consequences of Disarmament[4] it was noted that the international suspicions and fears caused by the arms race impede a natural exchange between countries in respect of trade, flow of capital and transfer of knowledge and technical know-how. On the other hand some developed countries obtain substantial profits from their arms trade, which enable them to meet their external balance of payments.[5] A specific disarmament agreement which might preclude the production, and hence export of a given weapon system, can be expected to come under considerable scrutiny both in terms of its effects on the industry concerned and on the balance-of-payments position of the state in question.

A disarmament treaty always has an influence on the international political atmosphere, as has been observed on a number of occasions. Disarmament is normally considered to be a tension-relaxing, confidence-building and threat-reducing act. In a world so strongly polarized and heavily equipped with nuclear weapons, any political act which reduces – globally or regionally – the danger of war by easing international tension and the likelihood of military confrontation, is of undeniable value. By reducing, even partially, reliance on military power, a disarmament agreement encourages the development of positive interactions between states which lead to social and economic cooperation, and to the universal acceptance of the rules of international law as the supreme code of a state's behaviour.

The conclusion of a disarmament agreement can be regarded as an important indication of change in the main lines of a state's foreign policy, or as a reaffirmation of the continuity of that policy. Irrespective of either, however, negotiation of an agreement will require some degree of information exchange and cooperation, even between states which hold basically antagonistic positions. Still more collaboration is necessary when an agreement establishes a body to institutionalize such cooperation, such as a consultative committee, as, for example, the Standing Consultative Commission established by the SALT I agreement, or verification machinery to supervise compliance with an agreement. Ideally one could hope that a successful agreement would in the long run do much to remove some of the animosities existing today, and to create room for more intensive cooperation, even in fields not related to the initial agreement. Ultimately a new world order might be envisaged; one in which former enemies and adversaries have common interests, cold-war type propaganda is modified, and emphasis is shifted away from preoccupation with military confrontation and preparations, to cooperation, mutual understanding and confidence.

This is the ideal situation. In the meantime governments embarking on disarmament measures have to solve all sorts of short-term problems, and in the process may come under considerable attack from the many vested interests involved. Changes will occur in the relative power of different groups, such as the armed services and armaments industries. Parliamentary politics will be affected, as occurred, for example, during the ABM and SALT I debates in the US Congress. There will be pressures from individual deputies who are responding to the threat of unemployment in their own constituencies and who themselves are under pressure from their local armaments industries. Similarly if a disarmament measure establishes some kind of verification machinery, especially one involving more intrusive processes, a certain amount of opposition is inevitable, both from groups which fear that the country will lose some of its sovereignty, and from interests concerned with possible infringements of the rights of free commercial enterprise. All these power conflicts will have to be resolved by the government if it is to have support for any agreement. Some groups may be played off against each other, internal alliances may be shifted, and other interests may have to be appeased. Generally speaking, a government seriously interested in a genuine disarmament effort would be obliged for its own sake to give moral leadership in the question. In the long run these developments could produce an irreversible mood in the political, social and even cultural life of the country.

This short description, though rather philosophical, of some of the possible effects of a disarmament treaty, gives some idea of the magnitude and variety of those effects on the entire life of a country. For obvious reasons the more comprehensive and far-reaching the disarmament measure, the deeper will those effects be. Such is the case with strategic disarmament. Without going into great detail the implications of strategic disarmament can be summarized in the following way.

Strategic disarmament, the subject matter of this study, affects the most powerful weapons existing – weapons of mass destruction which can be effective over continents. Their possession confers the highest status on nations, and their presence since World War II has revolutionized international relations. This is epitomized in the shift away from the 'balance of power' approach to that of the 'balance of fear'.[6] These weapon systems overshadow the politics of every single nation-state, linking them all by the common menace of mass destruction. Although possessed by very few states, they affect the security, not only of those states, but of the entire world. Any strategic disarmament agreement will therefore inevitably have widespread repercussions throughout the international community, namely, (*a*) in that it would imply a change in the relations between the most powerful countries in the world, and hence in all other international relations; (*b*) in that strategic disarmament, if successful, could open the way for other, more comprehensive measures, embracing a larger number of states and a broader range of prohibited weapons; and (*c*) in that the cost of R&D, production and maintenance of strategic arsenals represents the major item in military budgets, so that any reduction in strategic weapons is likely to have an enormous effect on the economy of the states concerned, and on the international economy as a whole.

Turning back to general considerations of the national and international consequences of any disarmament agreement including strategic agreements, it should be noted that a government makes, or appears to make, a decision to disarm on the basis of its assessment of the sum total of all the possible gains and losses to itself and to the other parties. In other words, only when a state is convinced that an agreement would be in its own national interests will it commit itself to signing. And of these interests the most important are those relating to its security.

At this point it is apparent that deliberations of this kind, and especially anything related to such a diffuse concept as 'national security', are no easy matter. Firstly, some of the effects of a disarmament agreement will, for example, counteract others – yet all might be equally important. Secondly, even if a government is able to judge the net advantages of a treaty at a certain moment in time, there is no guarantee that the conditions then prevailing will continue indefinitely. This uncertainty is, of course, one of the reasons for the slow progress of disarmament. Thirdly, one can envisage a situation in which it is difficult, if not impossible, for governments to make a clear assessment of their security *vis-à-vis* others; thus they may decide to sign a treaty on the basis of one or two of their more salient objectives. In this case the net balance of all minor gains and losses would not then count. This occurred, for example, in the case of the Partial Test Ban Treaty. Concluded only one year after the Cuban missile crisis, the treaty marked the wish of the two great powers to put an end to their previous confrontation-orientated and cold-war relationship. An additional factor was the desire to eliminate the burden, on both sides, of public pressure generated by the increase in radioactivity from nuclear tests carried out mainly by the United States and the Soviet Union.

However, it is not only prior to the agreement that security considerations are decisive. Even at later stages, during the implementation of a treaty, a state will continue to appraise it in the light of its security interests in order to ensure that the balance of power envisaged at the time of the treaty's inception is being maintained even after weapons have been reduced in quantity. The state's most serious concern will be to have assurance that the terms of the treaty are being adhered to by all parties. Only then will the state feel satisfied that the outcome of a treaty will be close to that envisaged at the start of negotiations and that its calculations and assessments were correct. States tend to be extremely anxious on this point, both because they cannot tolerate loss of security and because of their deep distrust of other states. It is because of this lack of security that states seek to control the actions of other state-parties *vis-à-vis* the provisions of a treaty, usually by establishing some system of verification. Hence there is a direct link between the supreme national interests of states and the verification of disarmament. The aim of this book is to consider this link in detail.

References and Notes to Chapter 1

1. See, for example, Jansen, L., *Return from the Nuclear Brink, National Interest and the Nuclear Proliferation Treaty* (Lexington Books, Mass., 1974), p. 1.
2. This is also called the 'displacement' effect of arms control. See, on this point, Rathjens, G. W. et al., *Nuclear Arms Control Agreements: Process and Impact* (Washington, Carnegie Endowment for International Peace, 1974), pp. 21–24.
3. Although the acceptability of the use of military force is at present a matter of increasing debate, its existence is still regarded as having a function in contemporary international relations. See, for example, *Force in Modern Societies: Its Place in International Politics*, Adelphi Paper No. 102 (London, International Institute for Strategic Studies, 1973).
4. *Economic and Social Consequences of Disarmament*, United Nations Publication (New York, United Nations, 1962).
5. For example, the total value of US weapons, equipment and related services exported in 1975 was $9 511 million (total value of orders). See *World Armaments and Disarmament, SIPRI Yearbook 1976* (Stockholm, Almqvist & Wiksell, 1976, Stockholm International Peace Research Institute), p. 138.
6. Snyder, G. H., *Deterrence and Defense, Toward a Theory of National Security* (Princeton, N. J., Princeton University Press, 1961), pp. 46–51; Towpik, A., *Bezpieczenstwo Miedzynarodowe a Rozbrojenie* [*International Security and Disarmament*] (Warsaw, 1970, Polish Institute of International Affairs), p. 73; and especially Nash, H. T., *Nuclear Weapons and International Behaviour*, Atlantic Series No. 9 (Leyden, A. W. Sijthoff, 1975).

2. Verification and its rôle in disarmament

I. The development of international control

International control of the relations between states is no new thing. Even at the very beginning of the 19th century control was instituted in agreements regulating the navigation of international rivers, and since then the spheres of control have widened to include financial matters between states, international communication and transport, trade in agricultural and other goods, cooperation in the protection of labour, international anti-narcotic efforts and fishing in international waters, to name only a few.

Apart from these regulations of an economic, administrative and humanitarian character, a wide range of international control was established by peace treaties after World War I, both in connection with territorial changes stipulated by the Paris Peace Conference of 1919 and with the restrictions imposed on the armaments of the defeated nations. Later on, together with the inception and work of the United Nations after World War II, the institution of international control was broadened to cover many other fields. It was during the post-war period that the first institutions of international control in the field of arms limitation were established. Historically, therefore, the concept of disarmament verification is a fairly recent one, not more than half a century old.

A wide variety of types of international control exists, ranging from more non-institutionalized, mutual control based on the exchange of relevant information between the contracting parties, to highly systematized control with specific control organizations and a large number of control procedures. In general the trend is towards the development of more of these latter types of control in response to the rapid development and growing number of international organizations.

There are two other, to some degree contradictory trends in the development of international control. The first, connected with the increasing internationalization of control through the expansion of interorganizational links all over the world, may be characterized as coordinative control. This kind of control covering an increasing area of the activities of states does not subordinate the sovereignty of states to the international authority, although states adhering to an agreement may mutually agree to forgo some of their rights. International control of this type seems to be orientated more towards cooperation, and in apprehending the mutual interests of states participating in international agreements in order to coordinate these interests into a mutually beneficial compromise. The other type of international control is represented by institutions which perform certain functions usually reserved for the sovereign state. This does not mean that the state gives up its sovereignty, but that only in certain fields it delegates some of its functions to an international controlling body. Such is the case with, for example, a number of regional organizations in Western Europe. This type of control is obviously less common, and where it has been achieved, it has clearly only been possible because the parties to an agreement were largely homogeneous politically, and because the areas in which the control was to operate were of a less vital nature. States are naturally reluctant to delegate certain of their functions to such an international body in the more important spheres of life, and even less so, to a politically heterogeneous body.

II. The meaning of 'control'

The difficulty in establishing an unambiguous definition for the word 'control' is only too well known. Not only does the word have different meanings in different languages, but even within individual languages, it may have a range of meanings.

One definition of the verb, usually referred to as the 'French', describes it as 'to check, test or verify by evidence or experiments', and in its noun form as 'the act or instance of controlling'. The English connotations of the word are 'to exercise restraining or directing influence over', hence to 'regulate', and to 'have power over', hence to rule. The noun form is therefore defined as 'the skill in the use of a tool, instrument or technique', or alternatively, as 'direction, regulation, coordination', or 'restraint or reserve'. It may also be defined as the 'means or methods of controlling, as (*a*) the subject of a control experiment, or (*b*) a mechanism used to regulate or guide the operation of a machine or system'.[1]

This variety of meaning has given rise to considerable confusion, not least in the field of disarmament negotiation. Thus, because of the predominance of English as an international language, the term has come to denote a specific type of disarmament, in which states restrain their armaments in order to rationalize their defence efforts, or to curb their most dangerous military activities. In this sense of the word, control has come to be synonymous with arms limitation, but the word is also used in its French sense, as meaning the act of checking or verifying the actions of states implementing disarmament. It is this latter meaning of the word that will be used and analysed here.

From the legal point of view, international control is a regulatory action of an international body, established by international agreement, which is designed to determine, so far as it is able, whether states that are parties to an agreement are complying with the obligations undertaken in the agreement. It implies that a comparison is made of the legal, technical and political norms as set up by the treaty against the actual legal, technical and political situation created by the implementation of that treaty; and the function of the body of international control is to verify the degree of fulfilment of those norms.[2]

This is more complex than it may seem at first glance, however, and depends on the character of the agreement and the object being controlled. Theoretically

11

where an agreement is mainly of a technical nature, and legal and political issues are of secondary importance, it would be a simple case of checking that the technical stipulations of a treaty are being put into effect. In theory an agreement of a more strictly legal character could be regulated by the rules of international law, or if the agreement allows it, by the laws of an individual state. The problem arises when the political element of an agreement is predominant, so that fulfilment of an agreement is defined not only by legal rules or by international customary law, but by political expedience, that is, national interests. For this reason some international agreements concluded in recent years, and particularly those related to disarmament and hence to the security of states, have contained clauses permitting states under certain conditions to withdraw from agreements and from the fulfilment of the norms established by them. In such a case of withdrawal, international control cannot be exercised.

III. Definition of the verification of disarmament

In this study, the term 'verification of disarmament' is used in preference to the term 'control of disarmament' or other terms less frequently used such as 'disarmament safeguards' and 'international supervision of disarmament'. Although at first sight this may appear to be a mere substitution of synonyms, there are political, psychological and linguistic justifications for doing so.

The linguistic problems involved with the definition of control were mentioned above, not least of which is the fact that the term is increasingly being used in connection with 'arms control', in the sense of arms limitation, arms freezes, geographical restrictions and so on. The application of the same term in the sense of verification, supervision or checking would therefore be confusing.

However, even in its latter sense, the interpretation of the word control has been one of the major stumbling blocks in the history of disarmament negotiations. In fact some authors would argue that it has been used as a stumbling block in order to avoid the real political issues at stake; that is, that it is easier to quibble over words and definitions than to 'lay the cards on the table'. Whatever the motives it is a fact that the word control has been used at different stages in a number of different ways. In the early post-World War II disarmament discussions it was almost without exception associated with comprehensive and highly intrusive inspection to be carried out on national territories,[3] and as such, ran into a great deal of difficulty because of the political atmosphere at that time. In fact problems over the type of control to be carried out have been one of the reasons for the slow progress of post-war disarmament negotiations, and even today the negative overtones of the word still persist. Hence, because the word 'control' still has the historical connotations of 'inspection', there is reason to favour replacing it by another one.

According to Webster's Dictionary, verification is the 'act or process of verifying or the state of being verified; the authentication of truth or accuracy by such means as facts, statements, citations, measurements, or attendant circumstances, confirmation by evidence in law, confirmation by oath or affidavit, the procedure required for the establishment of the truth or falsity of a statement...'.[4]

The term as used in general science, where the verification of theories, hypotheses, logical statements or propositions is used as a basic tool, is not very applicable to disarmament, although one of its elements, the idea of positive and negative verification, could be extracted and applied to this field. Basically this consists of measuring the degree of correspondence between an unverified proposition and the empirical observation of the facts to which the proposition refers. These degrees of correspondence form a continuum from no correspondence, slight correspondence, and so on (constituting rejection of the proposition, or negative verification) to moderate, great, up to perfect correspondence (constituting positive verification of the proposition).[5]

Verification of disarmament has been defined in a number of ways at different times; so it might be useful to compare some of these definitions, especially those of the early and mid-1960s with the more recent ones.

At the preliminary stages of disarmament discussions on issues related to the regulation and reduction of nuclear and conventional arms, verification was referred to under the term 'safeguards'. For example, a resolution of the Commission for Conventional Armaments of 1948 defines it as follows: 'an adequate system of safeguards, which by including an agreed system of international supervision will ensure the observance of the provisions of the treaty or convention by all parties thereto'.[6]

The Woods Hole Summer Study of 1962 defines verification of disarmament as 'the totality of means, of which inspection is just one, by which one nation can determine whether another nation is complying with obligations under an arms control or disarmament agreement'.[7] Another definition, that of the US Joint Chiefs of Staff, reads as follows: 'Verification. In arms control, any action, including inspection, detection and identification, taken to ascertain compliance with agreed measures.'[8] That of the Institute of Defence Analysis taken from the same source as the latter gives: 'Verification. Any action ascertaining that agreed measures are in fact being taken and the provisions complied with by the parties to the agreement.'

As an example of contemporary definitions we may cite the following, prepared on the occasion of the SALT negotiations: 'Verification. The process of determining the degree to which parties to an agreement are complying with the provisions of the agreement.'[9]

All the definitions quoted above are designed to meet the needs of a given time, and although basically correct they lack the generality required to cover all present and future agreements, whatever their institutional and procedural type, and whatever the parties to the agreement.

A proposal for such a comprehensive definition could be the following:

Verification of disarmament. A process, specifically established or approved by a disarmament agreement, carried out by individual state parties to the agreement, either reciprocally or not, or by an international body established or empowered to carry out the process, by personnel or by technical means, in order to determine the degree to which the parties to the agreement have implemented its provisions and thereby observed or discharged their obligations under the treaty.

Let us clarify the elements of this rather complex definition. First, because disarmament is always a process requiring, even in the case of a small, isolated disarmament measure, a sequence of actions in time, it follows that verification of disarmament will also be a process, possibly consisting of separate acts. Second, that process may be 'established' or 'approved' by an agreement. The distinction here lies in the fact that verification may either be established from scratch, that is, new procedures may be set up specifically for the agreement as in the case of the Antarctic Treaty of 1959, or it may take advantage of the verification or observation procedures already in existence, and merely give them a formal legal sanction to verify the terms of the agreement. One type of such solution would be the approval of International Atomic Energy Agency (IAEA) safeguards for the purposes of the Non-Proliferation Treaty (NPT). Another could be the acceptance of national technical means of observation in the SALT I agreements. At this point it must be stressed that, because only such legally sanctioned means come into the category of verification, intelligence and other similar unilateral methods of gathering information would not be covered by the definition of verification considered here. Third, the 'subject' carrying out the process of verification may be either an individual state, an international body comprising a number of states, or a 'supernational' organization, with a certain amount of sovereignty of its own. The definition thus encompasses both bilateral and multilateral verification. Fourth, it is usual to think of verification as being reciprocal, namely, that all parties to an agreement will be equally subject to verification and have equal powers to verify. However, reciprocity does not always apply. It is possible, for example, to have a disarmament agreement between two or more countries being verified by a third party, signatory or not to the agreement. The troop withdrawal and ceasefire between Egypt and Israel in the Sinai, in which the United States was the verifying party, is a case in point.[10] Again, reciprocity 'in kind' (that is, identical techniques) is not necessary for the system of verification. If the verification of an agreement is based on the individual national capabilities of states, then they may use quite different but satisfactory equipment for the purpose. Absolute equality and reciprocity is therefore not an essential precondition for verification. Fifth, the body carrying out the verification may be established specifically by the agreement, such as the agency established by the Treaty of Tlatelolco, or it may be an existing organization empowered to take over the role of verification, such as the International Atomic Energy Agency for the Non-Proliferation Treaty. In the latter case, the Agency had been in existence and had established its system of safeguards long before the NPT was signed. After the treaty had been signed, the safeguards were extended geographically and amended to meet the more stringent requirements of the treaty (although some scholars argue that after the NPT, safeguards became less stringent in order to secure their acceptance by some Western states). Sixth, the expression 'by personnel or technical means' covers the many different means and methods that can be used to verify. Finally, the general purpose of verification, as defined in our proposal, is to ascertain the degree to which the parties implement the provisions of a treaty. The data provided by the verification should give the states an opportunity to decide whether the activities of the other parties are tantamount to compliance with or breach of the treaty. The definition differs on this point from the definitions given earlier, which underlined the necessity for complete or ideal fulfilment of the letter and spirit of a treaty. In our definition it is considered sufficient to allow the state concerned to decide whether it is satisfied with the fulfilment of the treaty by the other parties. Verification should therefore merely provide states with the possibility of determining whether they can rest assured that their security interests are not endangered while a treaty is in force.

IV. Means, methods and types of disarmament verification

Means and methods: a review of the literature

Post-World War II literature on disarmament verification uses an enormous variety of terms and concepts to describe the means, methods and types of information gathering used to determine the degree of compliance with disarmament agreements. Many of these terms are used synonymously, and are defined in a very subjective way, causing frequent confusion where they overlap and contradict. This review comprises material from a wide variety of sources: official and unofficial, scientific and political, texts of treaties in force and proposals for such treaties. In describing the proposals and findings of authors the terms will be used as they appear in the texts, thereby giving a simple but instructive insight into the evolution of the terminology.

In a report of the US Atomic Energy Commission of 11 September 1947,[11] the following methods for the verification of a treaty on the control of atomic energy were proposed: explorations, ground or aerial surveys, inspections and formal enquiries. Exploration was defined as a particular type of investigation for the purposes of discovering and determining the nature and extent of deposits of source material, as well as obtaining and testing samples of ores. Ground or aerial surveys were defined as any systematic investigation of an area by a party on the ground, or from aircraft flying over it using visual and photographic observational equipment. Inspections were to detect clandestine activities and to check authorized facilities. This meant a close scrutiny of areas, mines and facilities to discover, confirm, or disprove possible evasions or violations of a treaty or convention in the form of unreported, prohibited and hidden activities. Moreover, inspections were to verify reports and to put all relevant facilities under close scrutiny in order to detect possible evasions or violations of proscribed means or operations, or to discover possible diversions of material.

Accounting of materials, examination of records, observation of points of ingress and egress and of other activities were to serve as the means of carrying out these inspections.

Before verification began, states were obliged to furnish the control agency with detailed reports about locations, levels and types of production, and so on. These surveys were to be either routine or *ad hoc*, but subject to the objections and modifications of the state concerned.

According to Protocol No. IV of the Paris Agreements of 23 October 1954,[12] the Agency of the Western European Union for the Control of Armaments could carry out its functions by scrutinizing statistical and budgetary information supplied by states, and by undertaking test checks, visits and inspections at production plants, depots and places of deployment of forces. These inspections were to be at regular intervals.

In its proposal introduced in the Disarmament Subcommittee on the Reduction of Armaments, Prohibition of Atomic Weapons and the Elimination of the Threat of a New War, of 10 May 1955,[13] the Soviet Union foresaw: the establishment of permanent control posts at large ports, at railway junctions, on main motorways, and at aerodromes; submission by states to the controlling body of any necessary information important for the execution of the agreed measures as well as unimpeded access of the body to budgetary records. During subsequent stages of the envisaged reductions the Soviet Union proposed the inclusion of inspection on a continuing basis to the extent 'necessary to ensure implementation of the agreement and within the bounds of the control functions of the organ'.

Another idea was introduced in the 'open skies' proposal submitted by President Eisenhower during the Geneva Conference of Heads of Government of 21 July 1955.[14] It was proposed that bilateral exchange of complete blueprints of all military establishments take place, including their examination by aerial inspection. During subsequent discussions[15], on 30 April 1957, the Soviet Union modified the Eisenhower idea by proposing zonal photographic observation carried out together with the establishment of regional fixed observation posts (located on the peripheries of the United States and the Soviet Union). The United States subsequently added mobile ground teams to the proposal.[16]

An important development in this respect was the creation of the International Atomic Energy Agency in Vienna on 26 October 1956.[17] Its statutes included several means and methods of verification, such as exchange of information with and through the Agency, examination of the designs of new nuclear facilities, submission of records, and inspections carried out with free access to all reactors and other facilities after consultation with the relevant state.

One of the first comprehensive studies on the problems of verification, prepared by S. Melman,[18] lists six general and three additional methods of verification: aerial inspection, fiscal inspection, detection of bomb testing, radiation inspection (sampling), checking of scientific personnel, detection of missile testing, inspection of military plans, inspection of military records and inspection 'by people'. Some of these methods were incorporated in the report, of 21 August 1958,[19] of the conference of experts to study the possibility of detecting violations of an agreement on the suspension of nuclear tests.

A new element in the procedural issues regarding inspection was introduced in discussions initiated by the US proposal, of 11 February 1960,[20] on quotas of inspections carried out to verify an agreement on the discontinuance of nuclear tests.[21]

Another comprehensive design for verification may be found in B. Feld's paper,[22] in which three basic groups of inspection are listed: (*a*) physical inspection, comprising all techniques of direct surveillance, and verification of specific activities which depend on physical contact with the action in question, (*b*) records inspection, which involves detailed analysis of documents concerning industrial and government activities, and (*c*) non-physical inspection using those techniques which primarily involve the use of human agencies.

In the first group Feld places general (ground) surveillance, inspection of known facilities, aerial and space reconnaissance and surveillance to discover illegal activities, special techniques for the detection of radioactivity and observation of the maintenance of weapon stockpiles. To the second group belong budget and expenditure inspection, as well as checking of production and inventory records. Finally in the third group he includes psychological inspection, utilization of the general population for gathering information, utilization of key people for the same purpose, a census of the activities of specialists and the establishment of an international intelligence network.

In yet another paper L. C. Bohn[23] elaborates on non-physical inspection techniques. All physical inspection, like instrumental detection, fixed and mobile inspection teams, records monitoring and investigation of suspicious events, is focused on the discovery of the violation itself and is regarded by Bohn as conventional inspection. Apart from these methods Bohn proposes a non-conventional approach based on knowledge about secret physical violation which is 'a mental phenomenon in the heads of individual human beings'. This approach he calls 'knowledge-detection' inspection, and it would act through the volunteered knowledge, supplied on the basis of patriotism, obedience to the law, or fear of penalty. In addition it would be directed at withheld knowledge, detected by lie detectors applied to the highest ranking persons in politics and science.

The Woods Hole Summer Study on verification and response, published in 1962, lists as means of verification: inspection, intelligence, examination of open sources, voluntary self-disclosure and 'common knowledge'.[24]

Among proposals for General and Complete Disarmament (GCD), only some few add to the list of means and methods which could be envisaged in the verification of disarmament, as they are concerned more with procedural and administrative matters. However, in the US proposal for GCD on 18 April 1962[25] fresh concepts were forwarded. These were the prelaunch inspection of all objects to be fired into outer space; extensive exchange of military missions; registration and serialization of nuclear weapons and fissionable materials; as verification of the destruction and conversion of armaments; verification of the declared locations, levels and nature of armaments; verification of observance of agreed levels and of the non-existence of other clandestine activities. All these measures would be applied zonally. Similar types of verification (called requirements) are described by M. Wright[26], who classifies them as verification

17

of 'bonfires', verification of non-replacement (and non-production), verification of remainders, and verification of non-concealment.

According to the scale of 'intrusiveness', that is, the degree of access to the internal affairs of a state, L. P. Bloomfield and L. Henkin[27] list seven types of inspection. These are:

1. External verification – unilateral, by personnel or instruments located outside the territorial limits of a state, without necessarily having the cooperation or even the acquiescence on the part of the state to be verified.

2. External verification – cooperative, by similarly located means as those above which, to be effective, require a certain amount of cooperation or acquiescence on the part of the state to be verified. To this type belong, for example, transmission of adequate budgetary data to an international body, and verification of 'bonfires' outside the boundaries of the states concerned.

3. Existing internal verification, by personnel such as attachés, journalists, visiting scientists and travellers.

4. Invitation to witness destruction or divestment of declared items, by personnel specifically invited to observe the prescribed activity.

5. Significantly increased internal verification, by personnel on the ground or in the air, but still not on a large scale.

6. Access to the declared facilities, performed through visits, interrogation and examination of records.

7. Full access (inspection) of undeclared facilities, where sites for inspections are selected by an inspectorate.

C. B. Marshall[28] calls types (1) and (2) above 'monitoring', types (3) and (4) 'persuasive authentication', type (5) 'permissive investigation', and the rest, 'inspection'.

Similar methods of verification are discussed in D. W. Wainhouse's book.[29] The criterion used is the level of internationalization of the verification system. According to Wainhouse there are four types of verification:

1. External verification, using any means short of those requiring physical intrusion.

2. Reciprocal systems (bilateral or multilateral), where a state or group of states inspects each other, on their respective territories.

3. Mixed systems, where, in addition to the existence of reciprocal systems, there is also a small number of international personnel.

4. International systems, of four kinds: (*a*) those set up for a specific operation, (*b*) those for regional arms control, (*c*) those limited international disarmament organizations set up to monitor partial-measure agreements, and (*d*) an international disarmament organization at the first stage of general and complete disarmament.

Means and methods in actual disarmament agreements

In practice three disarmament agreements should be mentioned as introducing new methods of verification. The first, the Biological Weapons Convention,[30] approves the institution of complaint to the UN Security Council as a means of ensuring the implementation of the agreement. The means and methods of actual observation of the activities of states in the field of biological weapons which could provide the evidence for complaints are, however, not specified. The second, the Sea-Bed Treaty[31] of 11 February 1971, mentions as the means of verification the observation of activities by states, consultations with the party responsible for the actions which raise doubt, notification to the other parties if the doubts persist, and finally inspection decided upon, and carried out by the other parties concerned. This verification may be carried out unilaterally, or with the assistance of the other parties, or by the United Nations. In the third case, and perhaps most importantly, the SALT agreements of 1972[32] for the first time explicitly mention the national technical means as an approved type of verification, together with provisions for non-interference with their action. They do not, however, go into any detail as to what precisely constitutes these national technical means.

Even this short review of the theory and practice of verification illustrates the difficulties in defining the terms used. The greatest subjectivity exists in the usage of the term 'inspection', and it is indicative that the further one goes back into the past, the more extended is the scope of meaning of this term. On many occasions the word inspection seems to have been used almost synonymously with that of verification, to cover many different methods of gathering information, from technical monitoring to the examination of records and on-the-spot investigations. Such an approach was less a matter of ambiguous terminology than of a rational and politically meaningful emphasis on a certain method of verification. As the authors of the Woods Hole Summer Study note:

> Inspection, which has often been used synonymously with verification, has appeared to be a key principle of US disarmament policy and the focus of Soviet resistance to the Western position. However, inspection is not a principle but a particular method of obtaining information necessary for verification.[33]

Means, methods and typology of verification: a proposal

According to the dictionary the words 'means' and 'methods' may overlap in meaning. For the purposes of this study, however, this ambiguity will be avoided as much as possible. Thus, 'means' will be used in the sense of an intermediary agent or instrument, or that by which some object is or may be obtained, or which is concerned in bringing about some result. 'Method', in turn, will be used as meaning the procedure for obtaining an object, that is, the special form of procedure adopted in any branch of human activity for achieving an end. Underlying this definition of method are the connotations of orderliness and regularity.[34]

Means of verification

Means of disarmament verification will be classified as technical or non-technical. Among the technical means will be included all sensing, sampling, recording, communicating, storing and interpreting devices and their associated equipment which may find application in the verification of disarmament, that is, in acquiring information relevant to determining the compliance of states with their obligations.

The other, non-technical means consist of, *inter alia*, written or oral information (both official and private), studies, questionnaires, complaints, petitions and reports, including reports of on-the-spot investigations by authorized personnel.

The means of verification can be further classified according to the owner or controller of them and the beneficiary of the information that they give. Roughly speaking, there are three categories of means: national, international and 'mixed'. This division is quite superficial. There exist no means, either technical or non-technical, which are only of use nationally. Even reconnaissance satellites and the equipment carried by them will probably be made available to international bodies for verification of multilateral agreements in the future. At present, however, the ownership of such means is strictly national, and countries are not even required to have the permission of the states being verified so long as they do not infringe on their sovereignty. All information gathered by satellites is relayed directly and exclusively to the state possessing them; but this does not completely preclude the possibility of states releasing that information to others. Moreover, in a sense, even though they are owned and manned by an individual state, national means of disarmament verification always play an international rôle, in that any disarmament treaty and its implementation is of international significance with an influence on the interests of the whole international community. In addition their operational feature, namely their universality in gathering information over the territories of all states, gives them an international character.

The term 'mixed' means of verification may apply either to the composition of international organizations, where people of different nationalities cooperate, or to situations in which the means of verification of one country are used in the interests of another.

Methods of verification

The methods of verification run parallel to the means they use, hence there is a similar division into technical and non-technical methods. The first can be defined as any method using technical equipment, that is, monitoring, surveying or observing largely with the use of sensing devices to photograph, listen to, measure and compare the objects being verified. Non-technical methods can include collecting data by individuals, collating, interpreting and evaluating the data, and finally, visiting and inspecting relevant areas, facilities and equipment.

It is clear that, to be effective, verification systems would not be confined to one specific method of gathering information, but would rather cover a number of different means and methods in order to gain the widest possible coverage of the object being verified, and the maximum objectivity.

Types of verification

It is evident from the above review of the literature on disarmament verification that verification can take many different forms involving a wide variety of means and covering vastly differing fields. For the purpose of this study we propose to classify verification according to the following four criteria: (*a*) the degree of internationalization of the verification; (*b*) the degree and kind of access to the territory of the state being verified; (*c*) the object and scope of a disarmament measure, and (*d*) the stage of the disarmament agreement at which verification is applied. Each of these criteria will be discussed in turn.

Degree of internationalization. As mentioned above, three levels of internationalization can be determined: (*a*) verification on a national basis, (*b*) mixed basis, and (*c*) international basis.

Verification on a national basis uses means, both technical and non-technical, possessed by a state operating in accordance with the rules of international law (that is, the state does not encroach upon the sovereignty of other states). We have seen from experience of a number of treaties, such as the Partial Test Ban Treaty,[35] that formal provisions for this type of verification do not necessarily need to be included in the text of the treaty. Nor is national verification a static concept. Just as technology is continually developing improved and new weapons, so the capabilities and effectiveness of the means of verification are constantly being expanded, though it is clear that as no resources are directed specifically towards disarmament verification, there is always a time-lag before this function is noticed. The introduction of new and more efficient means has already considerably facilitated a number of disarmament negotiations, especially those requiring verification of numerical limitations of large weapons, or restrictions on certain military activities, such as tests on weapons, large movements of troops and weapons, deployment of weapons, and so on. Such verification requires, however, very sophisticated equipment, and although world-wide technological progress will steadily expand the number of states able to apply such means of verification, it is possible that the high cost of the equipment and the rapidity of development may, unless appropriate preventive measures are taken, cause a distinction to emerge between states according to whether they possess the technical resources or not. In the long run such a development could impede disarmament negotiations; so it is to be hoped that broader international cooperation in this field will prevent this.

National verification can be divided theoretically into unilateral verification – that is, without the acquiescence of the verified state – and cooperative verification. In practice, however, some form of cooperation will always exist. The Partial Test Ban Treaty, for example, does not provide for any form of cooperation in connection with its verification; nevertheless, international seismological cooperation has undoubtedly enhanced the efficiency and reliability of the national means of verifying compliance with this treaty. Where agreements contain provisions prohibiting countermeasures aimed at disturbing or inactivating the verification system, such as jamming or camouflage and so on, there must similarly be some form of cooperation, though in this case it will be 'negative' cooperation. Another form of national verification would be arrangements based on bilateral or multilateral treaties, in which verification would be carried out mutually by the parties concerned, either on an individual basis as adversaries, or reciprocally.

Verification on a mixed basis exists when various national and international elements are involved in the verification. In its simplest form it consists of delegating the information gathered by national means to an international body for examination and evaluation. Such a solution of mixed national and international verification was proposed for the chemical disarmament convention at the Conference of the Committee on Disarmament (CCD). Mixed verification also occurs when the international verification body is composed of both national and international personnel operating in various capacities and with various rights. A special case of mixed verification arises when treaties are verified by one state, party or not to the agreement, on behalf of the other parties. A case in point was the troop withdrawal in Sinai where, because neither of the parties possessed adequate resources for verification and because of the mutual suspicion between them, they relied on information transferred to them by the United States, and in fact, they continue to do so.

In the case of international verification a multitude of organizational solutions can be envisaged. Some of these have already been described in the various disarmament propositions, such as those on general and complete disarmament. Some treaties already concluded make provision for international verification, as in the case of the Non-Proliferation Treaty where verification is carried out by the IAEA. International verification is usually connected with the existence of special international bodies to which the task of verification is entrusted.

The three types of verification described above may be applied individually, or the agreement may provide for their common application. In the latter case, as in the Sea-Bed Treaty, the basic form of verification is national, but the provisions of the treaty also allow other states and the UN Security Council to be included in the verification process.

Degree and kind of access. The second criterion proposed for the systematization of types of verification was the degree and kind of access to the territory of the verified parties that are permitted by the agreement. Here again, one can talk of three subtypes: (*a*) verification with no direct physical access, (*b*) verification with some kind of access to the territory and (*c*) verification in areas without national sovereignty.

In practice all kinds of verification require some degree of access to the national affairs or to the territory of the state being verified. Even a report or questionnaire answered by a state in connection with the implementation of a treaty constitutes some form of access to a state's internal affairs. In addition their territories are constantly being photographed from outer space by high resolution cameras; radio and other telecommunications are monitored from abroad; movements of weapons and personnel are watched; levels of production are measured; the construction of fresh installations is established and so forth. All such monitoring encroaches deeply into a state's affairs and the information gained by it is extremely detailed and comprehensive. However, because such activities are not covered by any specific rules of international law, they cannot be prohibited by the states which are subjected to them. What is remarkable is that this type of verification is often termed 'non-intrusive'. The only explanation for the term is that direct personal access to sovereign territory, waters, or airspace is not required.

The second subtype, verification with some kind of physical access, may also vary according to a number of factors. These are:

1. The characteristics of the means and methods used in the verification. As discussed above on page 20, a wide range of possibilities could be involved.

2. The duration of the access, whether permanent, *ad hoc*, occasional (that is, requested by a party or verification body when circumstances require it), and periodic verification.

3. The number of entries into the territory of a state can be specifically established by agreement, or left open for the parties to decide. There may be provisions in a treaty permitting entry into a state at any time, if the majority of parties to it require it, or should the international body responsible for verification decide to do so in accordance with the powers given to it by the treaty.

4. The area covered by verification may extend to the whole territory, or to some parts of it; it may be zonal or peripheral, or it may be established at fixed points.

5. The freedom of action in the verified territory. In some cases the international body may have very wide powers in the fulfilment of its obligations in respect of verification, whereas in other cases, these powers may be limited by the conditions imposed by the state which is subject to verification, and may even be vetoed.

6. The degree and kind of cooperation by the host country. Here again it may be predetermined by the agreement itself; left to the verifying body to decide; or left entirely to the state which is subject to verification.

The third subtype is verification where no national sovereignty exists. This occurs specifically in agreements concerning areas or environments which, because they became accessible to man only in recent years, are either not subject to national sovereign rights, or are of ambiguous legal status, as in the case of large regions of the sea-bed. Examples of such agreements are the Antarctic Treaty,[36] the Outer Space Treaty covering the Moon and other celestial bodies,[37] and the Sea-Bed Treaty.

In each case different solutions to the problem of verification have been found. In the Antarctic Treaty, for example, provisions for verification allow complete freedom of access to or, in other words, inspection of, all the areas concerned, and to all installations and equipment manned by the states operating there. More limited verification is provided for in the other agreements, where verification is allowed with partially qualified freedom of access to installations and equipment, although there is no absolute right of veto. So far as the Outer Space Treaty is concerned the limitation consists in the requirement for reciprocity, and the demand for advanced notice of a projected visit, necessitated by the unavoidability of maximum safety precautions. In the Sea-Bed Treaty 'appropriate' procedures for verification, including inspection of installations, must be agreed upon by the contracting parties after other methods, such as outside observation and consultation, have failed to clarify an issue of suspected violation. A further variation in treaties on areas without national sovereignty is to provide for verification, but without access to the installations. Such is the case with the supervision covered by Article IV of the Outer Space Treaty, which article prohibits the placing of weapons of mass destruction in the Earth's orbit. Verification is then left implicitly either to national means, or to such methods as external observation, international scientific cooperation, exchange of information and so on.

At this point it is worth mentioning that even without the differences in degree of access granted to the different verification systems, there will also be substantial differences in the types of channels through which the information passes and in the processes by which it is analysed. Nevertheless, human involvement is always unavoidable, whether it be on the spot, or at a central office to which remotely gathered information is relayed and subsequently evaluated.

The object and scope of an agreement. Our third criterion of the types of disarmament verification depends on the object and scope of an agreement.

The obligations to be undertaken in a disarmament agreement are of two main types: (*a*) actions to be carried out in pursuance of a treaty; and (*b*) actions forbidden by the treaty. These actions may be straight stipulations for certain actions to be taken (such as destruction of stockpiles), or for prohibited actions (such as nuclear tests in the atmosphere). Or they may involve quantitative and qualitative stipulations, such as limitations in numbers of weapons, or restrictions on R&D. In each case the verification will be closely related to the kind of stipulations contained in the treaty.

The relation of the type of verification to the variety of possible disarmament measures is illustrated in Table 2.1.

As can be seen from the Table the object and scope of the agreement logically seem to prescribe the kind of verification that is required. Verification cannot go beyond the terms of reference prescribed by an agreement without losing its legal and logical connection with it. However, this simple statement meets with surprisingly controversial interpretations in the context of disarmament negotiations and entails enormous political difficulties. To illustrate this let us consider two simple cases of disarmament and try to ascertain what the minimum and maximum demand for verification might be.

Case 1: Complete prohibition of a single-purpose chemical-warfare agent Z.

Minimum verification

(*a*) Providing proof that agent Z is not being produced at previous production sites.

Table 2.1. Relation between the scope of a disarmament agreement and the type of verification

Scope of disarmament measure	Type of verification
Action agreed upon	
Destruction	Verification of destruction
Redeployment/replacement	Verification of actual deployment or replacement
Conversion into peaceful uses	Verification of conversion
Quantitative stipulations	
Freeze of numbers	Verification of actual deployment
Reduction in numbers	Verification of actual deployment or reduction
Zero numbers	Verification of non-existence
Qualitative stipulations	
Reduction in capabilities	Verification of actual capabilities
Freeze of qualities	Verification of actual capabilities
Action forbidden	
Deployment	Verification of actual deployment or non-existence
Redeployment/replacement	Verification of actual deployment or non-existence
Conversion into different kind of weapon	Verification of non-conversion
Production	Verification of non-production
Stockpiling	Verification of stockpiles
Testing	Verification of non-testing
R&D	Verification of R&D or non-existence
Export/import of weapons, materials, facilities, etc.	Verification of trade, imports and exports etc.
Quantitative prohibitions	
Increase in numbers	Verification of actual deployment
Same or increased levels	Verification of actual deployment
Possession of any weapon	Verification of non-existence
Qualitative prohibitions	
Same or increased capabilities	Verification of actual capabilities
Improvement in quality	Verification of actual capabilities

(b) Providing proof that known stocks of Z in containers and in ammunition have been destroyed.

Maximum verification

(a) Providing proof that agent Z is not being produced at previous production sites; is not being produced in *any other factory* in the country concerned, and is not being obtained in any way from outside sources.

(b) Providing proof that known stocks of agent Z have been destroyed, and that no other military depot in the country contains this agent.

Case 2: Reduction in number of weapons XYZ.

Minimum verification

(a) Providing proof that the prescribed number of weapons XYZ has been destroyed, converted, etc.

Maximum verification

(a) Providing proof that the number of weapons XYZ has been destroyed, together with the assurance that the remaining number of weapons XYZ is actually smaller by the reduced number, thus requiring complete information as to the remaining stocks and their locations all over the country. In addition providing proof that the remaining stocks do not increase anywhere in the country.

In fact, minimum demands for verification may be even more remote, from maximum demands. The above two cases serve only to demonstrate the problem of interpretation of the 'terms of reference prescribed by an agreement'. It may be said that there always exists the possibility of a minimum and maximum demand for the verification of disarmament, both of which may be justified in legal terms, though not necessarily acceptable politically, nor from the point of view of a state's security.[38]

Presumably influenced by their concern with the effects of disarmament on their national interests, states have sometimes demanded 'maximum' verification, and in certain cases, even verification covering more areas than the actual disarmament measure. Such was the case with the US proposal on General and Complete Disarmament of 18 April 1962,[39] in which verification of the non-existence of clandestine activities in zones of reduction was proposed. This approach is reflected in M. Wright's typology of verification, where he lists among other 'requirements' the verification of non-concealment of forbidden arms.[40] Such a demand would, if interpreted in its extreme form, mean the right of the verifying state or international body to enter every part of the territory involved, and to check all aspects of a state's affairs in its search for potential clandestine activity, and as such would entail a substantial encroachment on the sovereign right of states. This possible encroachment was the main reason for strong opposition to such proposals from other states.

For obvious reasons the problem of different interpretations of required verification would be much simpler in the case of very comprehensive disarmament, and especially so in the case of general and complete disarmament. Verification would then be required to make sure that disarmament obligations were being completely fulfilled, and verification of the non-existence of clandestine activities in any of the countries undertaking disarmament would be in full accordance with the letter and the spirit of the measures of complete disarmament It would then be technically easier to verify because nothing would be omitted (all weapons excluded, no areas reserved for armaments, security based on means other than military power), and also politically quite feasible (bearing in mind that general and complete disarmament is likely only to take place in a peaceful world which is free from the sharply antagonistic positions existing today).

Stage of disarmament

Finally the criterion of the time factor has to be discussed, namely, the stage of disarmament at which verification is applied. Two elements are involved. First one needs to examine verification in the disarmament agreement itself, that is, at which stages of the disarmament agreement the verification is applied. Secondly, one needs to examine the relation of the disarmament agreement, and the verification it contains, in the context of the general development of disarmament as a whole. These are two distinct ideas.

Turning to the first, verification can be seen to act at several different stages of an agreement. Pre-agreement verification concerns activities planned under an agreement, or before the agreement enters into the phase of execution. It may consist of the examination of such information as declarations, blueprints of inventions, information about plans or designs, and examination of places and activities. Simultaneous verification, on the other hand, is that which starts functioning at the same time as the disarmament agreement. In a sense it could be termed 'real' verification because it is this which controls the actual implementation of the agreement, namely, to see that its terms are being observed by the parties. Finally there may be successive verification or follow-up verification, that is, verification of actions after they have been carried out according to the substance of the disarmament treaty.

It may be worth recalling at this point that the different emphases on these three phases of verification, and especially the West's strong requirement for pre-agreement verification, has characterized post-war disarmament discussions and has in fact been the main source of contention between states. It is symbolized by the question: Which comes first, control or disarmament? and indicates the degree of mistrust existing at the time.

According to the second aspect of the time factor, that is, the general relation of verification to the disarmament treaty in the broad context of the history of disarmament, three degrees of verification can again be discerned. They may be: (*a*) verification of a particular partial measure; (*b*) verification of a number of partial or collateral measures, constituting a kind of limited disarmament scheme; and (*c*) verification of general and complete disarmament. Obviously the type of verification system in operation will be largely a function of the extent and scope of the disarmament agreement, with the most comprehensive set of verification methods and the highest level of access being found in the final stages of general and complete disarmament.

V. *The requirements for verification*

Having discussed the kind of factors that will have a bearing on the type of verification applied to the different disarmament agreements we now turn to the essential conditions which verification should be able to fulfil and the demands to which it should be able to respond. These we shall call the requirements for verification. An early definition of these requirements is given by the UN Commission for Conventional Armaments in 1948 in the following form:

> A system of safeguards cannot be adequate unless it possess the following characteristics
> (*a*) it is technically feasible and practical;
> (*b*) it is capable of detecting promptly the occurrence of violations;
> (*c*) it causes the minimum interference with, and imposes the minimum burdens on any aspect of the life of individual nations.[41]

(It may be observed that point (*c*) of the above definition gives a quite strong and clear description of the 'non-intrusiveness' of verification, and moreover, makes it one of the most important conditions for adequate verification.)

A verification system should respond primarily to the requirements created by the subject and scope of the treaty itself. In addition the specific military and political circumstances which brought the treaty into being, and the expectations of states signing the treaty will place certain demands on the verification system.

Four principle groups of requirements can be discerned:[42] (*a*) technical, (*b*) legal, (*c*) military and (*d*) political.

Among the technical requirements belong, first, what we shall term the *detectability* requirement. This corresponds to the 'visibility' of the object of the agreement, in other words, before any kind of verification system can be set up, the object of the agreement must be considered technically verifiable.

The second technical requirement is that of *feasibility*. It concerns the relation between the desired capability of verification and the actual technical potential possessed by states. This actual capacity of states sets the upper technical limits for the design of the verification system. It may be that the verification system is technically feasible only for some parties to an agreement and not for others, in which case merely granting to states the right to verify will be meaningless unless assistance to those less well-equipped is given by those parties which are technically more advanced.[43]

Thirdly, the verification system is limited by the requirement of technical *sufficiency*, which sets up the lower technical limits to efficient verification below which a verification system can not function effectively. In other words the bounds of verification will be set, first by what is technically possible for the states themselves, and secondly by what the verification system is required to do. Some disarmament measures may pose such high technical requirements that what may otherwise have been considered an adequate system does not prove to be technically feasible.[44] Such may be the case with an agreement on military R&D or chemical and biological warfare (CBW) restrictions. However technically advanced a verification system may be, disarmament agreements in these fields may be extremely difficult to verify. Assessment of the technical feasibility and adequacy of verification depends on the degree of detectability required, and this, of course, is mainly a political issue. It was exemplified by the discussions on verification of the ban on underground nuclear explosions, where the means which the Soviet Union regarded as feasible and adequate were considered by the United States to be inadequate, and those that the latter regarded as adequate were not considered feasible by the Soviet Union. Again, the concept of adequacy is not a static one, but changes with the object of the agreement. What may be considered appropriate for general supervision of an agreement may not be efficient enough if a high degree of detail is needed.

The fourth technical requirement is that of *continuity*, meaning a need for uninterrupted flow of information from a verification system. This requirement is of special importance to any system using means which are susceptible to jamming, screening, camouflaging and so on, and applies both to means and to methods, that is, to technical as well as to procedural arrangements necessary for carrying out the provisions on verification.

The fifth requirement is for *timeliness*, that is, the necessity for prompt verification. Irrespective of how complicated the procedural arrangements may be, or of the kind of technological processes involved in gathering, relaying and interpreting the information, the verification system must be able to ensure a rapid response by the parties to an agreement. This naturally becomes more difficult the more multinational and technologically sophisticated the verification machinery happens to be.

In some cases a requirement for *confidentiality* has been considered an important precondition for successful verification. This applies only to verification based on national means, and obviously is of no relevance to a system of verification where the procedures for supervision of compliance are international, by and large determined in the agreement and therefore known to all the parties. Confidentiality consists in the exclusive knowledge by the state possessing the means of verification so far as their efficiency, accuracy, resolution and so on are concerned. The theory behind this requirement is that the prospective violator, being verified by unknown means, is likely to ascribe to those means capabilities greater than they may possess, and is thus deterred to a greater extent from violating the agreement. The extreme case, and the one thought to be the best from the point of view of enforcement of agreements, is that where verification takes place completely undetected by the state subject to verification. This requirement for confidentiality (also called the secrecy requirement) is linked to the deterrent function of verification discussed below on page 34, and its importance must be assessed along the same lines.

The requirement for secrecy of verification may raise the problem of the legitimacy of intelligence as a means of disarmament verification. Undoubtedly in considering the whole range of factors involved in the discovery of a violation, intelligence of different kinds plays a rôle which is by no means insignificant. However, as the definition of disarmament verification excludes all activities undertaken by states without the legal sanction of a mutually agreed treaty and which are therefore incompatible with international law, intelligence in many of its forms, and especially espionage, must also be excluded. Moreover, any attempt to include such activities in the framework of disarmament would be bound to add to the serious difficulties already inherent in discussions on verification procedures.

A further important requirement for verification is *flexibility*, that is, the verification system should be able to cope with technical changes. This requirement is two-edged; on the one hand technology causes changes in the arsenals of states by producing more diverse and sophisticated weapons, thereby making the task of verification more difficult (sometimes even insurmountable); on the other hand technological change can benefit the verification techniques themselves and enhance their capabilities. A verification system should therefore possess some flexibility in acquiring new means and procedures and applying them to new military situations. This requirement of adaptability is similar to the necessity of 'phasing in' verification techniques at different stages of a disarmament treaty, so that the verification system can keep pace with the new needs of the treaty.

Linked to the technical arrangements is the requirement of *economic acceptability* of verification. The cost-effectiveness of verification is a subjective matter and depends on the resources possessed by the various countries as well as on the importance attached to verification. Generally this requirement stresses the point that the cost of verification should not impede the conclusion and implementation of a treaty, nor should it restrict the access of less technically advanced states to the verification machinery.

All these technical requirements can be said to set up the relevant parameters of the verification system, and to some degree to provide a measure of the extent to which it is likely to be effective. However, the actual perception of the level of efficiency required, and hence the degree to which these technical requirements will be fulfilled, are matters for the subjective judgements of governments, and as such become political questions. Thus, no matter how feasible and flexible a verification system may be, unless there is the political will to implement it, and confidence that one's security will not be jeopardized by it, the system will stand no chance of being included in a treaty. Technical requirements are therefore always subordinate to political decisions.

Apart from the requirements of a purely technical nature, which have a bearing on the type of verification system set up in any particular instance, there will also be a number of legal parameters within which verification is bound to operate. These legal requirements may also be called direct requirements, seeing that they are linked specifically to the function of verification based on confirmation or repudiation of the complete fulfilment of the legal norms as set up by the treaty. In short, the legal requirement simply means that all the injunctions of the treaty, namely, that states really reduce prescribed numbers of weapons, restrain themselves from certain actions, and follow prescribed procedures to the letter, are implemented.

This is, of course, ideal in theory. In practice, however, verification designed solely according to legal requirements, no matter how sophisticated, will still be unable to provide a complete check on all the activities of states, and will therefore not be completely watertight. Complete fulfilment of the legal requirement of verification seems therefore highly improbable in some cases of disarmament even if the provisions of the treaty are actually carried out in the smallest technical detail; in fact one can say that it is not always necessary anyway.

Such weak emphasis of the legal requirement of verification does not imply diminution in the necessity for complete fulfilment of a legal obligation undertaken by a state in a disarmament treaty. Our point is only that the evidence provided by a verification system need not necessarily give complete data in order to prove compliance; rather the verification system needs to provide sufficient evidence that compliance may be proved with an acceptably small margin of error (and this margin of error is measured subjectively by a state through its political and military security requirements).

The third type of requirement, which we have called the military requirement, consists of the demand on the verification system to detect any violation which would have a bearing on the military security of states. It is not concerned, like the legal requirement, with creating mechanisms able to register every conceivable violation that takes place. Petty administrative, and other kinds of minor, violations, often with little danger to security, fall within the realm of the legal mechanisms of verification, at least initially; although once they start to be of military security significance, then they need to be dealt with in other ways.

It is such matters pertaining to military security that dictate the military requirement of verification, and for this reason, we shall subsequently call this requirement the security verification requirement. The term will therefore apply to a general evaluation of the necessity for any verification system to be able to check all the possible surreptitious breaches of disarmament treaties that seriously undermine the military security of the parties to those treaties.[45] Because security, even though it may be measured with military yardsticks, is always a political matter, the military security verification requirement is also subordinate to political factors.

The military security requirement, thus conceived, can be concretely expressed in the need of the verification system to detect those violations which could bring a decisive military advantage to the violator, and indisputable insecurity to the other parties to an agreement. The requirement would also be orientated on preservation of the capability of a timely military response to a violation of this size. To put it more simply, in the case of strategic disarmament where security is based on strategic deterrence between states, the security requirement would mean the need for the verification system to be able to protect the deterrent of each side that could be threatened by a violation. The security verification requirement, as it is used subsequently here, answers the question: What is the maximum extent of evasion that could indisputably endanger the security (that is, the second strike) of a complying state in strategic disarmament?

Finally, the fourth type of requirement for verification, the political requirement, originates from the internal political needs of nation states, which in turn are a response to the international political situation.

Domestic political demands for verification may be of two kinds – they may be an opportunistic response to the political struggles of different pressure groups, or they may have their basis in the more deeply rooted attitudes of the general public to disarmament treaties as a whole, and to the other parties to those treaties. In general these attitudes are based on people's perceptions of the intentions of other states, and of the threats that they seem to represent. And these are continually shifting. For example, what appeared to the US public as a threat of communist attack on the United States in the 1950s was by the 1970s no longer an issue. This change in attitudes was in turn to remove some of the pressure connected with enforcement provisions in treaties concluded with communist governments.

Undoubtedly, the rôle of public opinion, and especially its fears and prejudices, may be a handy tool for political manipulation, the more so when strong interests opposing an agreement wish to use it. In this case even excessive demands for verification may receive support, especially when disarmament agreements are to be concluded with traditional and powerful enemies. Then there is never too much security. In general one can say that a tradition of suspicion reinforces the demand for strong verification and conversely that the same tradition obliges states to treat such demands as sinister, whereas one consisting of cooperation and friendship gives the verification of disarmament the character of an expensive luxury. For example, no verification machinery has ever been established to monitor the demilitarization of the border between Norway and Sweden, nor did the Rush-Bagot agreement on the demilitarization of the Great Lakes require it.

The political requirement of verification is also a function of the actual external political conditions existing at the time of the treaty's formulation. At an early stage of disarmament, especially when international relations are polarized and tormented by crises, a state's position on verification may be expected to be rigid and cautious. With increasing mutual confidence the political requirement of verification is bound to lessen. As we have shown in earlier discussion, the political requirement of verification, like everything connected with security considerations, is a matter for the subjective assessment of governments, and is in fact related as much to the internal social interplay within countries as to actual international situations.

An historical examination of post-war disarmament negotiations indicates that political demands on and requirements of verification systems are always of primary importance and that legal, technical and military factors always play a subordinate rôle in the design of provisions on verification procedures. For example during the negotiations on the Nuclear Test Ban Treaty in 1958 the verification of underground nuclear tests was deemed technically feasible within certain limits of uncertainty, providing that adequate organizational and scientific effort had been made. Subsequently, however, the politicians omitted these tests from the treaty. Technical problems were given as the main excuse for the omission, although the real reasons were political and military. What therefore was deemed to be technically feasible, turned out to be unacceptable politically. Nevertheless, it is continually maintained by governments that their main consideration in disarmament agreements is to safeguard the security (largely the military security) of their states through verification. It is the purpose of this study to demonstrate that the real barrier to progress in disarmament, especially strategic disarmament, is not the difficulty over technical requirements, nor even military security requirements, but rather the lack of political consensus among the participants of disarmament discussions. It is our aim in Chapter 6 and the appendix to analyse the intricacies of the relationship between verification and military security in disarmament, and by so doing to show that the true obstacles to disarmament lie not in verification as a purely technical or bureaucratic arrangement, but in other factors, whether political or technological.

VI. *The functions of verification*

It is important that the verification of disarmament should be seen as just one of many different types of general international control. However, because of the specific content of disarmament treaties and their close relevance to national security and other vital national interests, the function of disarmament verification has acquired much greater importance and a larger political dimension than other types of international control.

The basic function of verification is to gather information.[46] The uses to which this information is to be put is, however, a matter of opinion. Usually, and in closer accord with the definition of the term, it is held that the information supplied by verification should serve as a basis for conclusions about the observance of treaty obligations by different states, that is, their compliance (or not) with an agreement. This understanding of the function of verification is expressed and underlined in all official disarmament proposals and is embodied in operating disarmament treaties. It is also reflected in the general definition of disarmament verification proposed for this study (see pages 13–19.

However, the function of verification has also been defined more broadly to cover more than mere monitoring of the terms of a treaty. In this case information is gathered about the capabilities, and even the intentions of states, in order to provide the other parties to an agreement with some sort of assurance that their security is not being endangered.[47] Thus it is believed that verification should be able to provide information about such events as significant military developments in order to allow states to make modifications to agreements, or to give them ample time to deal with potential military threats. Connected with this is the idea that verification should ensure the timely opportunity for response in the case of non-compliance with the treaty. Some see the function of verification as furnishing all 'necessary' information, that is, any information that is of relevance to the scope of the treaty and to the security of the parties. Obviously then the functions of verification will have a much broader scope.

It is interesting when analysing the relevant literature to observe how these two concepts of the function of verification have developed, and especially to see how, the further one goes back into the past, the broader the function of verification that was foreseen.

Until quite recently a scale of the functions of verification, placed in descending order of importance, might look as follows:

1. Deterrence of violation, inducing or enforcing compliance by the threat of discovery of violations.[48]

2. Reassurance for the security of states through confirmation that a treaty is being implemented, or through a high probability of detecting violations if they occur; thus the function of confidence-building.

3. Channel of communication.

4. Precedent for subsequent, more advanced stages of disarmament.

5. Mechanism for distinguishing between major and minor violations.

Let us now discuss these functions and their place in the scale of importance.

Several writers, among them Schelling and Halperin,[49] believe that deterrence as the main function of verification is implicit in any desire to monitor compliance of a state with the terms of a disarmament agreement. In this view detection and deterrence are closely related, because the expectation of detection is an important deterrent. This would seem to be an oversimplification of the question, primarily because it seems to overestimate the capabilities of verification systems. Detection of violations is not an absolute certainty, and therefore its value as a deterrent cannot be called absolute either. The strongest voice against this approach has been raised by R. Barnett:

> No inspection system is capable of deterring a nation with a high incentive to cheat. The simple assumption that any capability for evasion will be automatically translated into violation strikes me as highly dubious, but it lies at the heart of US thinking on inspection...[50]

Elsewhere he goes on to say, 'If compliance depends to any significant extent upon deterrence through exposure, compliance cannot be assured at low armament levels...'.

The real value of the deterrent function of verification may be assessed against the background of the possible gains and losses involved in a violation. These may vary, as is illustrated in Chapter 3 (see pages 46–49). In general it is concluded there that in most cases any profits from a small, minor violation would be counteracted by the negative consequences of such a detectable breach of a treaty. This would be especially so if, despite its minor violation, a state were still interested in its own or another state's participation in a treaty. Moreover, if a state feels that a major action against a treaty is necessary for its security, there are a number of legitimate ways of doing so, including open withdrawal, rather than choosing clandestine, less expedient alternatives. Thus, although the deterrent function of verification cannot be denied, it cannot be regarded as the most important and fundamental one. Excessive belief in this function of verification is bound to cause political and technical difficulties, because it presupposes a verification system so advanced technically, and with such extreme capacity for detection as to be well-nigh impossible.

The most rational approach to the function of verification seems to lie in the second item listed above. Here the function of verification is seen mainly as a positive concept; the idea that verification is not merely a deterrent against violations in a negative sense, but that it is a means of establishing a positive environment within which a treaty can function by giving states the reassurance that their security is not being jeopardized by the implementation of the treaty.

The confidence-building function of verification is double-edged: it may be regarded in the narrower sense as creating and preserving confidence in the fulfilment of a treaty; or in a broader sense as giving states confidence in a general, long-term security policy, and in the intentions and good faith of the other parties. Both help to keep the treaty régime in force against possible domestic opposition to it, and to create a basis for a more optimistic assessment of the behaviour and attitude of other states.

A third and important function of verification is to provide a convenient channel of communication through which states may identify and deal with potential disputes before they become too serious. This channel allows states to query the dubious actions of other parties, and to clarify issues that are not unequivocally solved by the treaty, without giving them the character of accusations to be submitted to the full blaze of publicity. Related to this function is the ability of the verification system to act as a kind of 'hot line' between states, in which 'signals', that is, information about specific violations of a treaty, or activities close to violation, are relayed from one state to another. Such signals may not be intended to terminate the treaty as a whole, but may only give notice of the intentions of a state.

The importance of verification as a channel of communication has already been recognized and formalized in a number of treaties, among which can be counted SALT I, which provides for the establishment of the Standing Consultative Committee to carry out precisely this function. Where such formalized machinery does not exist, diplomatic channels may be used instead.

The fourth function of verification, that of establishing precedents, is important in the sense that the verification procedures used in some treaties may prepare the ground, politically and psychologically for the more extensive verification procedures that may be necessary in the future. In addition the practical experience gained may be applied to future agreements.

The fifth function on the list, that of being a mechanism for distinguishing between major and minor violations, is important for the simple reason that countries must be able to make a response to the misconduct of another state, that is to say, in proportion to the magnitude and gravity of the violation. R. Barnett distinguishes between three types of violation, according to the three different areas in which a disarmament treaty is bound to impose constraints on its parties.[51] These are: (*a*) substantive violations; (*b*) procedural violations; and (*c*) non-disarmament conduct.

Substantive violations concern the contents of a treaty, ranging from a massive and decisive breach of an agreement through an overt, but less than all-out challenge to its stipulations, down to real or alleged misinterpretations of the disarmament obligations. Only in the last case would a state responsible for the violation probably try to justify it.

35

Procedural violations would be mainly connected with the mechanism of the verification machinery, consisting mainly of legal or procedural disputes over the right of access, timing of verification, and composition of verification teams.

Finally, 'non-disarmament conduct' would be the action of a state outside the actual stipulations of an agreement, and would contradict the 'spirit' of the agreement to such an extent that it would influence the implementation of the agreement by other parties to it.

As Barnett emphasizes, a violation should be considered as a signal of the intentions of the violator, and often the motives behind the violation are more important to the other parties than the actual consequences of the violation itself. From this aspect several cases can be discerned. The most serious from the point of view of the disarmament agreement are those government-inspired violations which represent a political position *vis-à-vis* the entire complex of the disarmament agreement. On the other hand, violations may be unintentional – usually caused by an error on the part of government officials, or of the personnel carrying out the terms of the treaty. There may be ambiguous violations, that is, cases where it is difficult to ascertain whether violations were made with or without the acquiescence of the government. Furthermore, violations may be unauthorized, committed clearly by an individual or small group in violation of the internal legal norms and clearly against the government's will. Then, there is the case of gradual violations, consisting of a series of minor covert acts designed gradually to ensure an improved military position. Finally, there are selective violations, when governments, in order to effect a *de facto* renegotiation of an agreement, and not having any other means of doing so, ignore certain of the terms of the agreement whilst respecting the remainder.

Knowledge of the nature of the violation and of the motives behind it may be gathered by the contracting parties from a number of sources, one of which is verification. Though verification may not be regarded as the best or most efficient means, it has the advantage of being completely legal, giving unbiased, factual data through an agreed channel of communication. This method of gathering information is useful, especially when the data are controversial. It also obliges states to take common action in response to the ambiguous conduct of the erring party, and so will tend to deter the prospective violator.

Furthermore, the verification machinery itself often makes provision for the possibility of minor and rather unimportant violations, together with actions belonging to the 'grey' or 'penumbra' areas of a treaty.[52] Many treaties actually contain provisions for consultations, review conferences and additional interpretive protocols, presumably in expectation of eventual ambiguities. Such is, at least in part, the function of the consultative body set up by the SALT I Treaties, the Review Conferences for the Non-Proliferation Treaty and the Sea-Bed Treaty, and the provisions on consultation in other disarmament treaties and their protocols. In some cases, such as the treaty on the limitation of underground nuclear tests between the USSR and the USA, the parties even admitted the possibility of slight, unintentional breaches of a 150-kt threshold, and agreed that one or two such cases would not be regarded as violations, though they would be a matter of concern and consultation.[53]

A thorough understanding of the different functions of verification, or of the purpose for which verification is established, is an important political matter.[54] The different national positions on the interpretation of this function have created difficulties from the outset of disarmament negotiations. This is so because the way in which the function is conceived determines the whole structure of the verification system, the means and methods it will use, as well as the whole political and legal setting in which it will operate.

References and Notes to Chapter 2

1. *Webster's Seventh New Collegiate Dictionary* (Springfield, Mass., G. and C. Merriam, 1969).
2. Symonides, J., *Kontrola mied Zynarodowa* [*International Control*] (Warszawa, PWN, 1964).
3. As an example of how these questions can be confused the following observations may be given: 'Inspection. The establishment of machinery to verify compliance with or to detect violations of a disarmament treaty . . . Inspection is a key ingredient of any disarmament agreeement because the security of each participant depends on the compliance of all to the terms of the accord'. See Plato, J. C., *The International Relations Dictionary* (Roy Olton, 1969) p. 233. And another: 'The key to the control issue is inspection – that is to say, verifying to one's own satisfaction that agreed measures in fact have been carried out by the other side'. See Bloomfield, L. P., The Politics of Administering Disarmament, *Disarmament and Arms Control*, Vol. I, No. 2, Autumn 1963, p. 120.
4. *Webster's Third New International Dictionary* (Springfield, Mass., G. and C. Merriam, 1966,) p. 2543.
5. See, for example, Roberts, G. K., *A Dictionary of Political Analysis* (London, Longman, 1971), p. 223; J. Gould and W. L. Kolb, eds., *A Dictionary of the Social Sciences* (Norwich, Tavistock Publ., 1964), p. 748.
6. Resolution of the Commission for Conventional Armaments: Formulation of Proposals for Regulation and Reduction of Armaments and Armed Forces, 12 August 1948, in *Documents on Disarmament, 1945–1959*, Vol. I, 1945–1956, p. 175.
7. *Verification and Response in Disarmament Agreements*, Woods Hole Summer Study, 1962 (Washington, Institute of Defense Analyses, 1962), p. 2.
8. Dougherty, J. E., *Arms Control and Disarmament. The Critical Issues* (Washington, Center for Strategic Studies, Georgetown University, Special Report Series, 1966), p. 87.
9. *SALT Lexicon*, ACDA Publication No. 74 (Washington, Arms Control and Disarmament Agency, 1974).
10. See the text of the Sinai Agreement in: *The Times, Le Monde*, 3 September 1975.
11. Dupuy, T. N. and Hammerman, G. M., eds., *A Documentary History of Arms Control and Disarmament* (New York, London, R. R. Bowker Co., 1973), p. 320.
12. *Ibid.*, p. 365.
13. *Ibid.*, pp. 376–78.
14. *Ibid.*, pp. 379–81.
15. *Ibid.*, pp. 417–18.
16. *Ibid.*, p. 424.
17. *Ibid.*, pp. 402–406.

18. Melman, S., ed., *Inspection for Disarmament* (New York, Columbia University Press, 1958).
19. *Report of the Conference of Experts to Study the Possibility of Detecting Violations of a Possible Agreement on the Suspension of Nuclear Tests* in *A Documentary History of Arms Control and Disarmament, op. cit.*, pp. 428–31.
20. *A Documentary History of Arms Control and Disarmament, op. cit.*, p. 465.
21. At one point in the history of disarmament the positions of the two great powers were quite close on this matter (USA, 7 inspections, USSR, 3).
22. Feld, B. F., Inspection Techniques of Arms Control in: D. G. Brennan, ed., *Arms Control, Disarmament and National Security* (New York, George Braziller, 1969), pp. 321–24.
23. Bohn, L. C., Non-Physical Inspection Techniques in: *Arms Control and National Security, op. cit.*, pp. 347–64.
24. *Verification and Response in Disarmament Agreements, op. cit.*, p. 8.
25. *A Documentary History of Arms Control and Disarmament, op. cit.*, pp. 502–503.
26. Wright, M., *Disarm and Verify. An Explanation of the Central Difficulties and of National Policies* (London, 1964), p. 46.
27. Bloomfield, L. P. and Henkin, L., Inspection and the Problem of Access in R. J. Barnett and R. A. Falk, eds., *Security in Disarmament* (Princeton, N.J., Princeton University Press, 1965), pp. 111–21.
28. Marshall, C. B., *Assurance, Inspection and Verification. What Needs to be Inspected.* Paper for the 4th International Arms Control Symposium, 17–19 October 1969, Philadelphia, p. 1.
29. Wainhouse, D. W., et al., *Arms Control Agreements. Designs for Verification and Organization* (Baltimore, Maryland, The Johns Hopkins Press, 1968), pp. 107–116.
30. For the text of the Convention see *A Documentary History of Arms Control and Disarmament, op. cit.*, pp. 599–602.
31. For the text of the treaty see *ibid.*, pp. 580–83.
32. For the texts of the agreements see *World Armaments and Disarmament, SIPRI Yearbook 1973* (Stockholm, Almqvist & Wiksell, 1973, Stockholm International Peace Research Institute), pp. 20–27.
33. *Verification and Response in Disarmament Agreements, op. cit.*, p. 8.
34. *The Shorter Oxford English Dictionary*, Vol. 1, 3rd ed., revised, p. 1223.
35. *A Documentary History of Arms Control and Disarmament, op. cit.*, pp. 525–26.
36. *Ibid.*, pp. 455–59.
37. *Ibid.*, pp. 531–35.
38. Myrdal, A., The International Control of Disarmament, *Scientific American*, Vol. 231, No. 4, p. 23.
39. *Ibid.*, p. 494.
40. See footnote 24.
41. Resolution of the Commission for Conventional Armaments: Formulation of Proposals for Regulation and Reduction of Armaments and Armed Forces, 12 August 1948, in *Documents of Disarmament, 1945–1959*, Volume I, 1945–1956, p. 175.
42. Finkelstein, L. S., Arms Inspection, *International Conciliation*, No. 540, Nov '62; *International Organizational Arrangements to Verify Compliance with Arms Control and Disarmament Agreements*, Report prepared for the Arms Control and Disarmament Agency, G.C. 70, June 1966, p. 140; Linde, H. A., Verification Requirements for a Production Cut-off of Weapons-Grade Fissionable Materials in: *Security in Disarmament, op. cit.*, p. 84; Schelling, T. C., and Halperin, M. H., Strategy and

Arms Control, American Academy of Arts and Sciences, *Summer Study on Arms Control*, New York, 1961.
43. This point has been underlined especially by Barnett, R. J., Inspection, Shadow and Substance in: *Security in Disarmament, op. cit.*, p. 32; *Verification and Response in Disarmament Agreements, op. cit.*, Annex to Vol. I, p. 60, and Schelling, T. C. and Halperin, M. H., *op. cit.*, p. 93.
44. See, for example, Bloomfield, L. P., The Politics of Administering Disarmament in: *Security in Disarmament, op. cit.*, p. 125; Finkelstein, L. S., *op. cit.*, p. 16.
45. Schelling, T. C. and Halperin, M. H., *op. cit.*, p. 99.
46. Falk, R. A., Inspection, Trust and Security During Disarmament in: *Security in Disarmament, op. cit.*, p. 27 and 32.
47. See especially on this subject *Verification and Response in Disarmament Agreements, op. cit.*, pp. 4–8; Annex Vol. I, Part I, pp. 2–86.
48. Stein, E., Impact of New Weapons Technology on International Law: Selected Aspects in: *Collected Courses of the Hague Academy of International Law*, 1971-II, Tome 133 de la collection (Leyde, A. W. Sijthoff, 1972), pp. 351–52.
49. See, for example, Rodberg, L. S., The Rationale for Inspection in: S. Melman, ed. *Disarmament, its Politics and Economics*, American Academy of Arts and Science, Boston, 1962.
50. Scoville, H. Jr., Verification of Nuclear Arms Limitations: An analysis, *Bull. Atom. Sci.* Vol. XXVI, No. 8, October 1970, p. 6.
51. Barnett, R., Disarmament Violations in: *Verification and Response in Disarmament Agreements*, Woods Hole Summer Study, ACDA Contract ST–5 (Washington, Institute for Defense Analyses, 1962), Annex Vol. II, Appendix A, pp. 18–34.
52. On this 'penumbra' issue see Rathjens, G. W. *et al.*, *Nuclear Arms Control Agreements: Process and Impact* (Washington, Carnegie Endowment for International Peace, 1974), pp. 46–48. See also Chapter 3, pp. 47–48 and Footnote 18.
53. Treaties with the Union of Soviet Socialist Republics on the Limitation of Underground Nuclear Tests and on Underground Nuclear Explosions for Peaceful Purposes, with Protocols. Message from the President of the United States, US Senate, 94th Congress, 2nd Session, Washington, 1976.
54. See on this point Myrdal, A., *op. cit.*, p. 24.

3. Conditions for implementation of disarmament agreements other than verification

I. Introduction

The conclusion of voluntary disarmament agreements by states presupposes that at a certain point in time they were confident that an act of disarmament was in the interests of all parties, and that the mutual obligations of the treaty would be advantageous, both single and collectively.[1]

The advantage of an agreement, as seen by each country, may well vary, but in the final assessment by all parties, there is bound to be some acceptable balance, at least initially. However, the possibility of a subsequent change in circumstances and political attitudes is not excluded, so that later there may be an attempt on the part of states to renounce the treaty, or even to violate it.

To meet this contingency different kinds of safeguards are usually incorporated into the body of the treaty. The safeguards aim at establishing mechanisms to warn states about changes in the other parties' intentions, and at discovering acts specifically forbidden under the treaty. These safeguards usually consist of provisions for verification and control, as well as for due notice of intention to withdraw from the treaty prior to doing so.

However, there are some factors, other than those embodied in the disarmament agreement itself, which govern the way in which a state handles the agreement. To have a proper understanding of the importance of verification in the context of disarmament agreements it is necessary to analyse some of these factors.

II. Factors acting against compliance with disarmament agreements

Endangered balance of power

This has already been mentioned as an important preoccupation of governments. The question here is, how much does a disarmament treaty influence the existing balance of power. We have established that if a disarmament treaty is to be concluded at all, then states must *apprehend* it as preserving the existing balance of military power (regardless of the *actual* state of balance). Yet whilst the treaty is in force the situation may change in two areas: between parties to the treaty, and between parties and non-parties.

Taking the latter case first, it is conceivable that non-parties to a treaty might take advantage of the fact that other countries were disarming, and so accumulate military power themselves, either by a conscious build-up of arms, or merely by not disarming. Consequently it would not be long before such third parties would begin to undermine the security of those parties to the agreement, either in reality, or in their perception. Such a situation can of course be foreseen by the contracting sides before the conclusion of a treaty, but not in every case. If the only way to redress the endangered balance of power is by repudiating the treaty, then the incentive to do so may override the obligations to keep it in force (especially in the case where an agreement lacks the appropriate provisions for abrogation).

Therefore, the probability of compliance with a treaty is greater the greater the number of participating states, especially those which, because of the character of their arsenals, location or economic importance, can have appreciable influence on the balance of power. In the next best analysis a treaty has a relatively favourable chance of survival even if some states do not participate, provided that their capabilities and policies are known when the treaty is concluded. The greatest threat to compliance with a treaty is the unknown factor, such as the emergence of a completely new power, either technologically or geographically, which makes all former calculations invalid.

The balance of power may even be shifted between parties to an agreement. It may well be that the scope of the treaty is too narrow, so that developments in areas outside its framework begin to threaten the equilibrium on which the treaty was founded. In this case the only way of stopping the process and redressing the imbalance may be by weakening the agreement.

In short, whether or not the balance of power is maintained during and after an agreement seems to depend on the kind of disarmament covered by the agreement, and the degree to which the agreement influences the international balance of power. Thus, conditions for full and long-term compliance with agreements are better the greater the number of relevant countries that participate, and the broader the scope of the agreement. Even in the best case, that is, with far-reaching and comprehensive disarmament, where the resulting balance of power exists at a very low level of military capabilities, a minor change in the relative equilibrium of states could have serious repercussions which might open the possibility of repudiating or evading the agreement.

Deteriorating international relations

In practice this factor would seem to play a greater rôle during negotiation of a treaty rather than after the treaty has been signed. Nevertheless, one could conceive of a critical situation occurring somewhere in the world, even very far away, which would cause the parties to an agreement to re-evaluate their position vis-à-vis the treaty. This could be, for example, the result of promilitaristic pressures within a country, opening the way for violations of the treaty; and such a situation in one country could be a signal to the other – perhaps already suspicious – to take pre-emptive measures of the same kind.

Military technology[2]

Efforts in military as well as civilian R&D are so intensive and diverse that it is extremely difficult to predict what kind of changes will occur in military technology. In general, however, the length of time for procurement of new weapons, the so-called long-lead time, permits governments to observe developments in the arsenals of their rivals, and to react in kind. (This is actually one of the forces behind the present arms race, in which no country gains a decisive advantage, especially in the field of strategic weapons.)

However, states tend to be prepared for any contingency and to organize militarily orientated scientific efforts in every promising field. This situation may result in technological breakthroughs which could not in any way be predicted at the time of conclusion of a disarmament agreement. Such a breakthrough could make the introduction of a completely new weapon system possible, and even a new method of warfare, with unpredictable effects on the overall military situation. Moreover, as the new weapon would be, at least for a time, an unknown factor for other countries, they might tend to overrate its value, and even exaggerate its threat. In the worst case it might be easier for those countries to meet the threat by expanding their potentials in the weapons they have already available, even if these weapons are prohibited by the treaty to which they are a party.

In fact the history of the development of weapons shows that real technological breakthroughs of this kind are rare, but evolve rather slowly over a long period of time. Their danger may therefore be treated as remote. However, there is another means of technological expansion of military arsenals which could cause a change in the positive attitude of countries towards their disarmament obligations: namely, the gradual qualitative improvement of existing weapon systems and the introduction of new generations of them in the arsenals. Unless controlled by a treaty this technological progress could alter the whole military basis on which a treaty was built.[3] Again, a country unable to respond in kind, or in any other legitimate way, might resort to concealed, or even open violations of the treaty.

'Failure of expectations'

This seems an extremely speculative reason for repudiating a disarmament agreement, but it may have some justification. The intention of one party to an agreement could conceivably be not to preserve military stability, but to gain from it unilaterally, that is, to benefit from the specific provisions of the treaty: and if this hope proves unfounded, it is possible that a state might prefer to break the provisions of a treaty rather than fulfil them. It is a fact that disarmament negotiations take years, and over this period, states have ample opportunity to assess their expectations, which may prove to be too optimistic. One can imagine a situation in which governments, foreseeing difficulty in fully implementing an agreement, but wishing to avoid loss of face by withdrawing from a treaty ready for signature, might prefer to wait until the treaty is in force. If then the situation were still not amended as they expected, they could decide not to adhere to the treaty. A variation of such a situation may be found in the history of the NPT's signatures and ratifications.

III. *Factors acting for compliance with disarmament agreements*

International law

It is difficult to measure the real influence of international law on the practical conduct of a state's foreign policy. What can be observed, however, is the growing importance of legal rules in international life, necessitated by the increased internationalization of many of the world's problems, and the need for international laws formulated so as to regulate interaction between states.

The fundamental principle of the law of treaties states that treaties should be fulfilled – *pacta sunt servanda*. According to the Vienna Convention of 1969, 'Every treaty in force is binding upon the parties to it and must be performed by them in good faith'.[4] This rule was for centuries a norm of customary law, being the basis for the conclusion of treaties between states. It was expressed as a norm of the law of treaties in the London Declaration on the Sanctity of Treaties (1871), and afterwards in numerous documents, among them the Convenant of the League of Nations (Article I, paragraph 2), and the Preamble to the UN Charter.

Breaches of treaties seem to be characteristic of states pursuing aggressive and imperialist policies, and have always met with strong condemnation from the international community.[5] In general, international laws are negative towards the treaty breaker. In any case most disarmament treaties contain legal provisions enabling the state-parties to renounce or suspend the treaty when they consider their 'supreme national interests' or their security endangered by it. Even the additional requirement for notifying and explaining the reasons for intended withdrawal, though it complicates matters, need not deter states from taking advantage of such provisions.[6] Thus states already have the opportunity of withdrawing from a treaty without necessarily abrogating it.

When a treaty contains no other specific provisions there are two main grounds for renunciation or suspension of a treaty, namely, the case of a fundamental change in circumstances (*rebus sic stantibus*), and the case of a breach by another party. In both cases the law tends to be restrictive. Thus Lauterpacht in discussing the 'fundamental change in circumstances' acknowledges that

> every treaty implies a condition that, if by an unforeseen change of circumstances an obligation provided for in the treaty should imperil the existence or vital development of one of the parties, it should have the right to demand to be released from the obligation concerned.

He goes on to qualify this by noting that *'rebus sic stantibus* does not give a state the right, immediately upon the happening of a vital change of circumstances to declare itself free from the obligations of a treaty, but only *entitles it to claim to be released from them by the other party or parties to the treaty'*.[7] Similarly the Vienna Convention defines this fundamental change in circumstances as applying only when two conditions are met, namely, (*a*) the existence of those circumstances constitutes an essential basis of the consent of the parties as bound by the treaty; and (*b*) the effect of the change radically transforms the scope of the obligations still to be performed under the treaty.[8]

In practice, therefore, operation of this principle has been extremely limited, as evidenced in several cases invoked before such international tribunals as the International Court of Justice where, although the principle itself was upheld, its application was rejected in the majority of specific cases.[9]

Similarly the rules about breaches are equally confined. Although in principle, 'violation of a treaty by one of the contracting states does not *ipso facto* cancel the treaty; but it is within the discretion of the other party to cancel it on this ground',[10] in practice there are a number of limitations to this rule laid down by the Vienna Conventions of 1969.[11]

In sum, therefore, it can be concluded that international law may in general act as a restraint against the violation of disarmament agreements. The basic rule of international law enforces the fulfilment of treaties – *pacta sunt servanda*. Those rules which theoretically could be used as an excuse for the unlawful suspension or termination of a treaty are very restrictive and tend to be interpreted likewise. In addition, to be invoked as grounds for termination of a treaty, the fact of a breach as well as evidence of a fundamental change in circumstances must first be assessed and revealed by governments invoking them, as well as by all other parties. To guard against groundless accusations, and to protect the legitimate and lawful behaviour of states in the framework of a treaty, an efficient mechanism is needed to clarify the issue. Thus to a certain degree the actual functioning of international law depends on the existence of verification machinery which supplies evidence supporting or refuting such invocations.

An additional rôle for international law is its possible ability to impose sanctions on the transgressor. Hitherto, no disarmament agreement has ever contained explicit provisions for such sanctions, although the possibility has been under discussion.

Public opinion

It has already been said in Chapter 1 that whether an agreement is fulfilled or not is to some extent a function of the amount of public support it received initially. A disarmament agreement is more likely to be accepted as a permanent feature of national life if it is widely accepted, so that only a serious change in circumstances, such as preparations for war by other parties to a treaty, or open violations of the terms of a treaty, are likely to cause a change of heart. Thus, when governments lack such convenient justifications for violating a treaty, it will be very difficult for them to ignore the pressures and disapproval of their own people. Of course public opinion can be changed; but having once created public support for a treaty and ridden on the wave of approval, governments tend to avoid the complete about turn in policy that this would necessitate. This difficulty in retreating from a policy once established can be regarded as one of the conditions making it more difficult for a government to violate a treaty.

The influence of international public opinion on the behaviour of governments is more subtle. No theory of international morality exists, and there are no rules of international conduct other than those pertaining to international law. Certainly then in theory, so long as they do not trespass on the legitimate right of other countries, states are free to pursue their own interests unhindered, even if these seem to be contrary to the interests of the international community as a whole. However, one can conceive of international opinion condemning the unlawful action of a state, and although it is unlikely to have a substantial influence on a government's actions, it may not be entirely disregarded.[12] This is demonstrated by the fact that quite often governments find it necessary publicly to justify their decisions; and although the arguments used on such occasions may be merely *ex post* justifications, and even deceptive, their value cannot be totally neglected.

Bureaucratic restraints

The process of decision-making leading to the conclusion of disarmament agreements varies enormously according to the socio-economic system. In the capitalist system it is the industrial interests and the institutions representing them which play a major rôle, followed by the military and scientific/technical circles. This interlinkage between the three groups of interest has given rise to the concept of a military-industrial-scientific complex as the main driving force behind decisions on the military and security policy of capitalist states. In the socialist systems, on the other hand, the main feature of the decision-making process is that political considerations are always the dominant factor, even on highly technical issues. Even though the military play at least as important a rôle as their counterparts in the West, they are more clearly subordinate to the ideological and political leadership.[13] These differences, coupled with the more obvious distinctions between the two systems, such as the rôle of parliamentary politics, mass media and the organization of their respective administrative structures, are fundamental. However, the very existence of the vast bureaucratic machinery characteristic of every developed state makes it possible to generalize and draw similar conclusions about the impact of these bureaucratic processes on the implementation of disarmament treaties.

A common feature of any bureaucratic system is that it tends to preserve decisions or rules of action once they have been established.[14] One can even go so far as to say that the typical weakness of a bureaucracy, which makes it so unwieldy and time-consuming during the process of reaching a decision on disarmament, works in favour of compliance with a treaty once the decision has been made. This is so for a number of reasons. First, decisions are never made by one group on its own, but are the result of the laborious participation of numerous governmental departments, institutions and pressure groups thrashing out their differences in order to come to a final compromise or consensus. These groups in turn interact with many external groups and individuals whose policies are the result of the same kind of compromise and consensus. Thus, when the final consensus is achieved, many individuals among those taking part in the whole process will identify themselves with the result, and have an interest in defending the decision until its completion.

Violation of a treaty would constitute a reversal of the previous decision-making process. It would necessitate the same administrative steps, but in reverse, and in many cases involve the same institutions and individuals who were involved in the creation of the treaty.[15] These would all tend to work against the reversal of a decision with which they had been personally involved. In the worst case internal argument among the bureaucracy could break out in public and thus widen the sphere of decision and end the secrecy surrounding the intended violation.

Secondly, administrative decisions are such that before there were any question of a treaty being abrogated, the provisions of the treaty would already be in the process of implementation. New internal legislation would have appeared, institutional changes would already be in effect, thereby shifting the relative administrative strength among the departments, and financial resources would already be redistributed to new purposes. Laboratories and production facilities may have been closed down, and their personnel moved to new administrative units and interests. In the areas covered by the treaty the prospects for careers and other advantages would have become fewer and unattractive. As a result of all these developments, the individuals favouring violation of a treaty would probably not find the administrative and other support needed to carry such a proposal through the bureaucaratic machinery.[16]

IV. Cost and benefit evaluation of the violation

The basic though trivial assumption here is that to enter into a disarmament treaty a state must have been convinced at a given time that conclusion of the agreement was more advantageous than not. By the same token, to violate a treaty a government must believe that the possible gains from this act definitely outweigh all the known benefits derivable from adhering to the treaty. Putting it in another way, the cost of keeping the agreement in force must be unacceptable from the point of view of a state's security and be considered as less than the disadvantages resulting from the violation.

One motive for violating a disarmament agreement could be the possibility of gaining some political or military advantage over the other participants in a legal contract. This could be an attempt to gain military superiority over the whole range of weapons, or a simple predominance in one kind of weapon. In both cases states may justify such attempts politically, that is, to use such force as a political lever; or militarily, that is, to enable a swift and successful attack. However, to gain any real advantage the violation would need to be numerically substantial, rapid and decisive; and this in itself would detract from its value, because the more substantial the clandestine activities the sooner they would be discovered and countered by the other side. Any military advantage gained would thus be quickly lost. Whether a violation could bring any military advantage at all would depend on the character of the treaty and its stage of implementation. It may be assumed that in the majority of partial arms-limitation measures, the security of states is based on factors lying outside the limited range of such treaties, so that violation of a treaty would not threaten the overall security of states. It would be much more serious if a violation occurred at a very advanced stage of a comprehensive disarmament agreement, when even very small violations could drastically shift the balance of power. (The question of how serious the violation should be to bring about a decisive change in the relationship of two parties to a treaty on strategic disarmament is discussed further in Chapter 6 and the Appendix.) Against such a possibility, however, there would be a number of general political circumstances; substantial, long-term, comprehensive disarmament seems possible only in a peaceful and stable international environment based on mutual cooperation and confidence. In such circumstances it appears doubtful, though it is theoretically possible, that a state would resort to violation, with all the attendant risks, not only of destroying the treaty régime but also of dramatically reversing a stable and peaceful international climate.

The other motive for violation could be the desire to invalidate an agreement which turned out, despite expectations to the contrary, to be detrimental to a state's security, either because of developments in states which are not parties, or because of developments in fields not covered by the agreement. In both cases the violating state would have to be convinced that it is forced to redress the political and military imbalance, and that this is feasible only through a violation.

Leaving aside the question of why a state chooses to violate rather than to use other politically and legally valid means available to stop unwelcome developments, it is still doubtful if a violation to redress an imbalance could really achieve its purpose. The difficulty would lie in the fact that to catch up with developments, a state would have to act in secret, but in order to be able to compete with the open, dynamic and legitimate armament of the other party, its clandestine activities would have to be of such magnitude that in the long run they would inevitably be discovered. Only in some specific areas of armaments such as biological warfare, or military R&D could a violator hope to escape discovery of clandestine activities for any length of time.

In some cases, without breaking the agreement as a whole, one can envisage a violation, probably only a minor one, being used as an intentional signal to the other parties in order to influence their attitude. This kind of signalling is risky, even though feasible, because the other side might interpret the signal quite contrary to the way it was intended. The intentional minor violation used as a signal is similar, incidentally, to cases of action within the so-called 'grey area' of a treaty, where – on account of ambiguity, such as unclear definitions and omissions of unforeseen technological developments – the actions of states may be interpreted as being very close to violations. Such is the case in the provisions of the SALT I treaty where there is some dispute as to the meaning of the characteristics of radar, or the size of ICBM silos.

Three kinds of reasoning may underlie the dubious conduct of a state in the 'grey area' and the intended minor violation used as a signal. In the first place, in the absence of special communication channels a signal may be unnoticed or misinterpreted, and thereby lose its rationale. Secondly, such an act may undermine the confidence of the other parties, who may suspend further implementation of the treaty, or may even consider reciprocal action of some kind. Thirdly, the act may be disregarded by the other parties. Seeing that the treaty establishes a kind of 'signal-noise threshold',[17] other parties may treat reports about a dubious act as just another 'noise', and will prefer for the sake of preserving the treaty to abstain from serious reaction, at least until more substantial breaches occur.

Another cause of violation may be the difficulty of legitimate withdrawal from a treaty using the clausulae of 'endangered security interests' that are embodied in most disarmament treaties.[18] The difficulty lies in the possible reluctance on the part of states to give advance notification to other parties, and thereby expose themselves to international criticism. Because an announcement of intention to withdraw would probably be treated as greatly undermining the treaty, and could even mean its ultimate collapse, states might prefer to conceal their actions, and so gain time before other states react. In the final analysis, whether a state withdraws legally, or whether it violates the terms of the treaty, there is bound to be strong international reaction in either case. At all events, the cooperative atmosphere between states will have been damaged, 'détente' threatened; and in the worst case the conditions for an adversary's overreaction, in the form of a new and costly arms race, will have been created. All this would destroy the treaty régime which 'would require a major adjustment of relations with an adversary'.[19] In most cases this would not only nullify any possible gain from the violation, but could even worsen the violator's position in comparison with that which existed before the violation took place. The reaction would not only be international. Domestically there would be hostile repercussions inside the violating country. Those who opposed the agreement in the beginning would have an axe to grind against the government for having failed in its policy. Leaders who had staked their political careers on creating the treaty would be discredited. All this would have grave consequences for the domestic balance of power and for a country's whole domestic and foreign policy.[20]

To summarize, the net balance of the cost and benefits of violation appears to be clearly in favour of the implementation of a treaty once it has been concluded. There are several powerful factors which force a state to fulfil its obligations, and discourage it from violating a treaty. The existence of these factors indicates that the incentives for choosing to evade an agreement surreptitiously, rather than to take other legitimate action are weak. All in all it can be assumed that the political commitment to a treaty, once it has been negotiated and is therefore legally binding, is the most reliable guarantee of compliance.[21] The lack of strong incentives to 'cheat' may be additionally reinforced by the existence of verification machinery embodied in the disarmament treaty. Nevertheless, the verification machinery itself is not enough to ensure successful implementation of disarmament without the simultaneous pressures of all these other factors.

References and Notes to Chapter 3

1. F. A. Long's observations on this occasion were: 'Political and military imbalances between nations are often great, and mutual suspicion is commonplace. Only occasionally, then, will there be the confluence of interests that makes substantial arms-control agreements possible, i.e., a situation where governments will be of *mutual benefit* [his italics], where, in other words, a "non-zero sum game" is at least conceivable'. Long, F. A., Arms Control in the Nineteen-Seventies in: *Arms, Defense Policy, and Arms Control* (Daedalus, Summer 1975), Vol. 104, No. 3, p. 5.
2. See on this subject, among other sources: Feld, B. T. *et al.*, eds., *The Impact of New Technologies on the Arms Race*, a Pugwash Monograph (Cambridge, Mass., MIT, 1971), pp. 271–99 and 316–22; Leitenberg, M., The Dynamics of Military Technology Today, *International Society of Science Journal*, Vol. XXV, No. 3, 1973; Possony, S. T. and Pournelle, J. E., *The Strategy of Technology, Winning the Decisive War* (Cambridge, Mass., Dunellen, 1970).
3. On the impact of technology upon the military situation, see: Kahn, H. and Weiner, A. J., *The Year 2000. A Framework for Speculation on the Next Thirty-Three Years* (New York, The Macmillan Company, 1968), pp. 75–78.
4. Sinclair, I. M., *The Vienna Convention on the Law of Treaties* (Manchester, University of Manchester Press, 1973), p. 53.
5. As in the case of Nazi Germany which was accused at the Nuremberg Tribunal of the breach of 24 international agreements. See in addition Klafkowski, A., Prawo Miedzynarodowe Publiczne [International Public Law] (Warszawa, PWN, 1964), p. 75.
6. Rathjens, G. W. *et al.*, *Nuclear Arms Control Agreements: Process and Impact* (Washington, Carnegie Endowment for International Peace, 1974), pp. 57–59.
7. Oppenheim, L., *Internationl Law. A Treatise. 8th edition, Vol. I, Peace*, H. Lauterpacht, ed. (Longmans, 1955), p. 941.
8. Sinclair, I. M., *The Vienna Convention on the Law of Treaties, op. cit.*, p. 106.
9. For a list of cases in which the rule was considered see: Oppenheim, L., *International Law, op. cit.*, p. 940, footnote 2; and also: Briggs, H. W., Unilateral Denunciation of Treaties: The Vienna Convention and the International Court of Justice, *American Journal of International Law*, Vol. 68, No. 1, January 1974.
10. Oppenheim, L., *International Law, op. cit.*, p. 106.
11. Sinclair, I. M., *The Vienna Convention on the Law of Treaties, op. cit.*, p. 103.:
    'a/ A material breach of a bilateral treaty by one of the parties entitles the other to invoke the breach as a ground for terminating the treaty or suspending its operation in whole or in part.
    b/ A material breach of a multilateral treaty by sone of the parties entitles the other parties by unanimous agreement to suspend the operation of the treaty in

whole or in part or to terminate it either in relations between them and the defaulting State or generally.

c/ A material breach of a multilateral treaty by one of the parties entitles a party especially affected by the breach to invoke it as ground for suspending operation of the treaty as a whole or in part in relations between itself and the defaulting State.

d/ A material breach of a multilateral treaty by one of the parties entitles any party other than the defaulting State to invoke the breach as a ground for suspending the operation of the treaty in whole or in part with respect to itself if the treaty is of such a character that a material breach of its provisions by one party radically changes the position of every party with respect to the performance of its obligations under the treaty.'

12. See for example: Brennan, D. G., ed., *Arms Control, Disarmament, and National Security* (New York, 1961), p. 58–59.
13. Gallagher, M. P. *et al.*, *The Politics of Power: Soviet Decision making for Defense* (Arlington, Virginia, Institute for Defense Analyses, October 1971), p. 103.
14. Rathjens, G. W. *et al.*, *Nuclear Arms Control Agreements: Process and Impact*, *op. cit.*, pp. 45–50.
15. Newhouse observed: 'in choosing to sign the Moscow agreements himself, Brezhnev was proclaiming his identification with SALT, which has become an instrument of his foreign policy, for now, a very much detente-oriented policy'. Newhouse, J., *Cold Dawn. The Story of SALT* (New York, Holt, Reinhart and Winston, 1973), p. 269.
16. Rathjens, G. W. *et al.*, *Nuclear Arms Control Agreements. Process and Impact*, *op. cit.*, p. 46: 'With a treaty in effect, there is simply no occasion for gearing up the elaborate paraphernalia of national security decision-making to consider these issues (that is, courses of action involving the violation)'.
17. *Ibid.*, p. 48.
18. For example: Treaty Banning Nuclear Tests in the Atmosphere, Outer Space and Under Water, Art. IV; Treaty for the Prohibition of Nuclear Weapons in Latin America, Art. 30, p. 1; Treaty on the Non-Proliferation of Nuclear Weapons, Art. X, p. 1; Sea-Bed Treaty, Art. VIII; Convention on the Ban of the Development, Production and Stockpiling of Bacteriological (Biological) and Toxin Weapons and on Their Destruction, Art. XIII, p. 2; and also the SALT Treaties between the USSR and the USA.
19. Rathjens, G. W. *et al.*, *Nuclear Arms Control Agreement: Process and Impact*, *op. cit.*, pp. 48 and 53.
20. *Ibid.*, p. 62–63.
21. See on this point Myrdal, A., The International Control of Disarmament, *Scientific American*, October 1974, Vol. 231, No. 4, p. 22.

4. National interests and national security in relation to disarmament

I. National interests: analysis of the concept

Definitions

Like many other basic concepts used in international relations the term 'national interests' is difficult to define in a clear and unequivocal way. Different attempts to define the scope and meaning of the term, however extensive, give no clear-cut definition, nor any substantial explanation of how it can be used. Writing a whole book on the subject Frankel reserves judgement: 'The vagueness of the concept, the complete lack of agreement about its definition and the absence of any empirical indicators, have precluded its rigorous use. It is possible to argue, as Professor Rosenau does, that we cannot useful employ it analytically and must merely take cognizance of its employment in political action, use it as a datum requiring analysis'.[1]

Different categories of national interests are used in the literature on the subject.[2] These are based on (a) the degree of importance of the interests ('criticality') to a state; (b) the degree of permanence ('durability'), thus introducing the time dimension; (c) the degree of generality; and (d) the spatial element of such interests. Thus Frankel divides interests broadly into two categories, vital (critical) and secondary interests; whereas Holsti uses 'core' and other interests;[3] and Robinson enumerates them according to three corresponding pairs of variables: primary–secondary, permanent–variable, and specific–general, thus obtaining eight possible categories of national interest.[4] Many of the categories used in the literature are synonymous, so that 'primary' interests are interchangeable with 'vital', 'critical', 'core' or 'supreme' interests; and similarly, specific interests may be called 'material' or 'limited' interests. In this context the term 'primary' will be used henceforth.

Basically, primary interests could be defined as those which are linked to a state's national survival or the protection of its physical, political, ethnic, religious or cultural existence. In short, primary national interests are those concerned with the preservation of the territorial integrity of a state, the inviolability of its boundaries, and the protection of its so-called 'vital core' – that is, its capital and its major concentrations of population and industry. They can thus be defined in terms of the self-preservation of a state as a political unit and of the perpetuation of its socio-economic system. All these elements of the primary interests of a state are of a more permanent character. To defend these interests the citizens of a state are said to be prepared to make the ultimate sacrifice, and governments are unwilling to make concessions or compromises on them. An important observation, though apparently a truism, is the fact that all states have basically the same primary national interests and construct their policies accordingly.

Having established that some national interests are of greater importance than others brings us no closer to a clear legal or political definition of what these primary interests really are. The nature of these interests, it is true, is mainly of a strategic-political character, but it can also be economic and ideological. The strategic-political sphere is strictly connected with the notion of military power deemed necessary for national survival in a dangerous international environment, and for the attainment of all other national goals. So it follows that disarmament will fundamentally affect the primary interests of a state undertaking it.

Terms such as 'territory', 'boundaries', 'capital', and 'industrial centres' are inherent in the definition of primary national interests. All of them are spatial notions, playing an important rôle in defining national interests. The link is of a direct character – that which is closer to the boundaries of a state is more important as a national interest than that far from those borders. Thus a conflict between distant states could be expected to affect the national interests of a state less than one taking place between its neighbours. Even this statement must be qualified in that it is not distance as such which determines the sphere of national interests; it is the technical and economic capabilities of a state which determine the extent of that sphere. Thus the larger the capabilities the smaller the impact of distance on a state's foreign policy. The best example here is the global extent of the interests of the most powerful states.

Again a state's national interests have to be seen in relation to time. That which may at a given moment appear to be a permanent primary interest may over a long period lose its significance, either because a state acquires increased capabilities *vis-à-vis* other states, or because other states change in relation to the former. An example of such a change is the evolution of the relationship between Australia and the United Kingdom before 1942 in comparison with US-Australian relations since 1942. The changeability of even these primary interests strongly underlines the generally subjective character of any kind of national interest. An example of national interests changing with time is provided by the history of British imperial policy. The present interests connected with Britain's former colonial possessions are now quite different from those of a century ago, and though still important cannot be described as 'vital'. States seem to measure their supreme national interests against their 'net achievement capability', that is, they define the realm of their national interests according to their capabilities and constraints.

Generally speaking the greater the capabilities and the higher the status of a state in the international community the broader is the scope of its national interests.[5] This permanent extension of primary interests expanding alongside capabilities is described by J. Burton as self-destructive:

> Each successive extension can be promoted only by further extension, and the cost of each successive extension is higher than the previous one. At some point, the cost must exhaust capability, the process of extention is necessarily halted, and the widespread structure begins to crumble.[6]

This somewhat mechanistic model seems rather too simple because it does not take account of a more or less rational subject, who calculates every extension of national interests in relation to his capabilities, and who may in some cases even refrain from certain actions to achieve more long-term goals.

By introducing the time factor national interests may be put into three categories: short-term, medium-term and long-term. Short-term interests can be defined as an outgrowth from a specific situation within a state, such as reaction to a special public demand, or the personal interests of the leadership, or the results of an interplay among political factions. In dealing with such interests governments attempt to meet actual public and private demands and needs through immediate national and international action. These are very specific interests, and are rather well-defined in time and subject. Medium-range interests, on the other hand, are related to an increase in a state's prestige, more often than not as the result of an increase in military capability. In this category lie all possible forms of self-extension, such as establishing colonies, protectorates, 'satellites' or spheres of influence.[7] Finally come the long-term interests, most aptly described as 'those plans, dreams and visions concerning the ultimate political and/or ideological organization of the international system, rules governing relations in that system, and the rôle of particular nations within it'.[8]

Moreover there are three levels at which the term 'national interest' is used; these can be termed as the aspirational, operational and explanatory/polemical levels.[9]

The first, the aspirational level, is linked with the vision of the good life, which sets the goal for the nation-state. National interests of this kind are usually long-term, being rooted in history and ideology, and so providing purpose or direction for a state's policy, although they may not be clearly expressed and relate rather to political will than to real capabilities.

National interests at the operational level are those actually pursued by the state's policy. They are characterized by being short-term as the concern of a government or a political party actually in power; they have descriptive rather than normative form, and are determined more by a state's capabilities than by political inclination. They are easier to change than the former.

The third level of national interest, the explanatory/polemical, relates to the political arguments in which 'national interests' are used to explain, evaluate, rationalize or criticize the foreign policy of another state. In this case statements about national interests serve not so much normative or descriptive purposes, but rather as a means of political struggle. At this level, divergent opinions held by individuals or groups as to the nature of the national interests find expression. In view of the importance of such debate for the process of defining and redefining the nation's greatest and immediate ambitions, it should be pointed out that the arguments put forward may serve different selfish, as well as broad, social aims. As Frankel writes; 'It may be a case of trying to sell "the right case" for the wrong, but most appealing reasons, as well as that of trying to find the "right" reasons to explain away a "bad case" '.[10] Here it is obvious that the concept of national interests being used by a particular government is not necessarily that shared by its people as a whole, but may be a notion only of its most influential groups, possible even of only its most eminent individuals. At this point it may be of value to discuss the processes underlying the formulation of national interests, that is, who defines the national interests and in what way.

The formulation of national interests

The way in which national interests are formulated within a nation-state seems to be a function of a number of continually changing factors, such as the structure of the international system, the internal situation of the country, the interests of various classes, the interests of the political élite, and the perceptions and personalities of that élite. Formulation of the national interests is based not so much on the real state of affairs as on people's subjective ideas. These ideas are in turn reflections of a particular culture and historical experience. Definition of national interests also depends on the accuracy of the information reaching the decision-makers. The perception of threats, the degree of urgency given to particular problems, and the perception of alternatives depend on all these factors.

An important and at the same time unpredictable factor is the rôle played by public opinion. National leaders may define and propagate such national interests as they think will attract the broadest support for themselves, but they may not necessarily be the legitimate objective interests of the country as a whole. In this case the public will be subjected to a considerable amount of pressure to change its ideas of the national interest, through, for example, indoctrination and other types of propaganda. However, such efforts may not always be necessary, as for example in a case of national emergency, where the group defining the national interest may be very small, and may have no need to gain the broad support of the population. Although there are no data to support such a thesis, it may perhaps be said that when a matter of national policy requires long-term and broadly based support its formulation reflects to a greater degree the needs and values of a majority of the population, and to a less degree the desires of the ruling élite. In general, therefore, one could pose the hypothesis that the legitimacy and scope of national interests at a given moment is a function of the time available for formulating those interests.

If one accepts that the formulation of national interests is to a large extent the net result of competition between various power groups, each with diverse interests, then the final result depends much more on the relative power of these groups than on the consistency and substance of the arguments they present. The same can be said of the interplay between different government agencies and departments. Despite the diversity of these particular interests, however, to legitimatize them as national interests requires that they must fall in an area politically, culturally and ideologically acceptable to a broad sector of the population.

The next important question to be clarified is: which area, domestic or international, in the life of a nation-state plays the decisive rôle in the formulation of national interests?

Explaining his predisposition to consider the national interest mainly in connection with foreign policy, and basing his judgement on the assumption that individuals are mainly interested in their material well-being and everyday problems, J. Frankel, for example, states that 'the individuals and the subgroups are here in foreign policy generally more ignorant and powerless, and less directly concerned'.[11] He agrees to take the rôle of the national situation partly into account only because it is more calculable and predictable than the international situation. This seems to be a gross simplification of the matter, because national and international politics are so closely intertwined, and 'a well-conceived foreign policy is not only related to, but is necessarily subordinate to, domestic needs and aspirations'.[12]

The pursuit of national interests

In protecting or furthering its national interests a state will inevitably be forced to interact with other states in the international system. This interaction can be either competitive, collaborative or conflicting.[13]

Collaboration occurs when the interests, values or objectives of states coincide and can be satisfied simultaneously by all the parties. In general such cooperation concentrates mainly on questions of the international milieu, with states trying in cooperation with other countries to create a better and more peaceful international system. This requires the concerted action of a number of states, and is much more difficult to achieve than a more nationally orientated, self-centred policy.

Conflict arises when the objective or the interests of two or more states are incompatible, and pursuit of them by one state deprives the other of its own interests. In this respect it is worth noting that a conflict-generating, self-centred policy seems much easier to define, and is more likely to gain public support, than a more long-term and internationally orientated policy. Of course conflicting interests in some areas, even quite fundamental ones, do not entirely preclude cooperation between states, when they stand to benefit. This situation is well illustrated by the history of post-war disarmament negotiations in which states with antagonistic ideologies and conflicting strategic objectives have been able to cooperate despite their differences.

Competition, on the other hand, arises when the objectives or values pursued in parallel by states do not interact with each other, that is, their fulfilment does not depend upon the behaviour of other states.

To sum up the rôle of national interests in relation to disarmament, it can be seen that the concept of national interests as used to justify a particular foreign policy is not a static one, but is continually shifting, depending upon which governing class or ruling élite is in power at a given moment, and according to the international situation. Formulation of the national interest is the result of an aggregate of pressure groups acting with or without the broad support of the population. At the end of the process a mass of conflicting information is reduced to one, more or less cohesive policy. It is at this stage that the rôle of the leadership, and of the leading groups they represent, must be emphasized. Because of the numerous sources and kinds of information they have to handle, the number of demands to which they have to respond, and the diversity of their own private attitudes and biases, it would be easy to reject any attempt to define the national interests as a meaningful concept (as some outstanding scholars in fact do). Indeed some writers would go so far as to refute any notion that the actions of states are governed by 'rational considerations of national interests' at all.[14] Nevertheless, one has to accept that this term, however vague, is of major political attractiveness, being used universally to explain and justify the policies of states. Therefore it cannot be left out of any discussion of the policies leading to the conclusion, fulfilment and abrogation of disarmament agreements.

II. National security in relation to disarmament

Definitions

'National security', like the term 'national interests', when used singly or in combination with the latter, is equally vague and undefined, with the result that it is often misused.

'Security' is described as the quality of feeling secure, that is, feeling free from danger, fear and uncertainty.[15] When referring to a nation-state it seems to be related to the likelihood of survival, to confidence in the maintenance of the state's boundaries, to the nation's well-being and its ability to preserve its territorial, cultural or ideological integrity. Two elements seem to be embodied in the concept: (*a*) a subjective awareness of an absence of danger to the vital interests of a state,[16] and (*b*) the existence of means which seem to be sufficient to meet such a danger should it occur. The two terms 'security' and 'interests' are therefore inextricably linked.

Generally speaking, 'national security' may be defined as the probability of survival of a nation-state.[17] Since this probability depends on the continually changing situation, both within the state and in its relations *vis-à-vis* other states, the concept of what national security is will also be continually changing. It is important to observe at this point that what is called 'security' is always a subjective assessment. In theory one can visualize also the existence of such a thing as actual, objective security; but in practice security is only that which some individuals or groups *ascribe* to the state's probability of survival, according to their own beliefs and access to information.

Factors bearing upon the security of a state are either permanent or unstable. The permanent factors, such as a state's location or its resources, may at a certain time be decisive for its security. For example, Britain was relatively secure for centuries because of its insularity. However, many continually changing factors are of far greater importance for the security of states than the more permanent ones. Among these can be mentioned real changes, such as progress in science and technology, especially in the military field. To use Britain as an example again, the fact of its being an island is now no longer of particular relevance in an age of intercontinental missiles; Britain is now vulnerable to an increasing variety of weapons. In addition, a country's security may also be affected by more subjective changes, that is, changes in its own awareness of its rôle *vis-à-vis* other countries, whether unfounded or not.

The rôle of security in national policy

Historically states have customarily tried to maximize their security in two ways. The first, and that most widely used, is orientated towards maximizing protective measures; or in other words, towards making military preparations to withstand external and internal threats to a state's security. Such a policy is obviously connected with the current emphasis on states' military power. The other way of achieving and preserving the security of a state is by influencing its international environment.[18] This in turn can take two forms. It can be collaborative, in which case all participants increase their security, and no state relinquishes anything; or it can be conflicting, in which case some of the states may be deprived of some of their security. Substituting the word security for that of 'autonomy', O. Berg puts the case very aptly:

> One system can influence another system unilaterally, i.e. without relinquishing its own autonomy, or reciprocally, i.e. by relinquishing its autonomy as well. In the first instance, the high autonomy and security of one denotes the low autonomy and security of the other. In the second instance, the reduced autonomy of both can come to mean the increased security of both.[19]

So far it may safely be said that the latter type of approach to security – that is, a policy based on mutually agreed advantages and restraints, involving ideas of détente, arms control and disarmament and other forms of cooperation – is evolving only slowly. When it does occur, the fact that it takes place alongside the traditional approach – involving expansion of military power and self-reliance – detracts from its effectiveness.

However, there may still be room for optimism. It is clear that the traditional emphasis on military power has proved to be both inefficient, expensive and dangerous. States are now no more secure after the post-World War II arms race than they were before it, and they may be less so. Moreover, there are increasing signs internationally of the need for new approaches to security: among these are the dangerous potentialities of nuclear weapons and their increasingly deadly delivery vehicles; the enormous economic and social costs of modern armaments; the increase in the number of states actively participating in international affairs, and the growing economic interdependence of states. In addition there is a growing internationalization of many vital problems: such as environmental destruction; the population explosion together with the deteriorating food situation; the shortage of raw materials; and the expansion of the international organizational structure; to mention only the most important. All these factors diminish the rôle of individual nation-states and force them to give up some of their sovereignty and autonomy, and to cooperate with others. Whether this cooperation will be based on a 'positive' strategy in which states attempt to realize an idealistic model of the world according to a general plan to which all states adhere, or be based on a 'negative' strategy in which states attempt to reduce their insecurity merely by amending those aspects of international life which are the most likely to create insecurity and tension,[20] remains to be seen. So far, even those 'negative' attempts such as disarmament, arms control and development aid have been far from successful.

To summarize, the security of a state is the ability of that state to resist both immediate and long-term threats to its survival as a political and administrative unit. This ability depends on a number of factors among which military power is usually considered to be of primary importance. Because of the dynamic character of the environment in which a state exists, internally and externally, this ability varies with time, and has to be continually asserted.[21] The crux of a state's domestic and foreign policy is its preoccupation with its security. Of course, a state entering into a disarmament agreement will consider it in the light of its interests; but in the final analysis, it is its security requirements which determine whether or not it becomes party to a treaty (with the aforementioned reservations regarding the objectivity of these requirements). These security considerations are continually coming into play, even while the treaty is being implemented. It is for this reason that verification of disarmament has assumed such importance – rightly or wrongly, it is considered that verification provides states with adequate safeguards that their security is not being undermined by others.

IV. The function of verification in safeguarding security

On theoretical grounds the importance of verification as a safeguard should always be weighed against the substance of the agreement and according to the impact of the agreement on a state's defence capabilities and its economic and social life.

The question of compliance with an agreement (and therefore also its verification) is directly related to the security of the parties to the agreement. Thus, if country A clandestinely evades the agreement, it can be assumed that sooner or later country B will find out. Country B, considering that its security has been endangered, will then seek to rectify the situation by taking countermeasures which in turn will be regarded by country A as endangering its own security. This mutual interaction creates a situation in which every country, cheating or being cheated alike, ultimately loses its security. The existence of technically efficient verification machinery, which ensures that the time-lag between the evasion and its discovery is very small, means that the mutual loss of security of both the complying and the non-complying nations is very nearly simultaneous. In other words, verification machinery makes evasions of the treaty not worth while from the point of view of security.

However, verification has a function other than mere monitoring of the terms of a treaty. It has been argued earlier that to be successful any agreement must be in line with the long-range ideological and general strategic-political interests and values of the most influential groups in a state, and hence of the general public as a whole. Moreover, an agreement falling into the aspirational rather than the operational sphere of the national interest has a much greater chance of being supported by society and fulfilled by governments. This is because the aspirational level of interest being more fundamental, long-term and stable is less exposed to the shorter-term more selfish interests of competing pressure groups. So it may be expected that unless there is a change in external circumstances which could alter the focus of national interests and change the direction of security policy, a treaty, once it has been signed, will be fulfilled. In such a situation, where treaties have a broad base of popular support from all sectors of the public, it could be argued that a unanimously accepted treaty can hardly be violated in a substantial manner without severe social and political repercussions within a country. In this case countries might be expected to put less emphasis on formal verification of the terms of the treaty and more on the checks and balances of public opinion in order to ensure compliance.

Now suppose that there were a fundamental change in attitude, so that a state, for example, replaced its cooperative, milieu-orientated foreign policy by a more self-centred policy, obsessed by military security and preparations. In this case it would be important for the verification machinery to be orientated not only to the specific provisions of the treaty, but also to those changes occurring externally. Those changes, when noticed – and one would expect this to be the obvious product of any verification system gathering information on the factual details relevant to the merits of an agreement – could give a first sign of negative attitudes towards the agreement, indicating that a country is reexamining its interests in standing by the letter and spirit of an agreement.[22]

References and Notes to Chapter 4

1. Frankel, J., *National Interest* (London, Pall Mall, 1970), p. 22; similarly W. Fulbright writes: 'As formulated by men of power, the national interest is a subjective and even capricious potpourri, with ingredients of strategic advantage, economic aspiration, national pride, group emotion, and the personal vanity of the leaders themselves. This is not to suggest that the concept of "national interest" is false but that it is elusive and far from self-evident . . .' Fulbright, J. W., What is the National Interest? *The Center Magazine*, Vol. VII, No. 1, January-February, 1974, p. 40.
2. In addition to the sources quoted in subsequent notes see also: Sonderman, *et al.*, *The Theory and Practice of International Relations*, 3rd ed. (Englewood Cliffs, N.J., Prentice-Hall Inc., 1970); Neuchterlein, D. E., *US National Interests in a*

Changing World (Lexington, The University Press of Kentucky, 1973); Padelford, N. J. and Lincoln, G. A., *International Politics. Foundations of International Relations* (New York, The Macmillan Company, 1954).
3. Holsti, K. J., *International Politics. A Framework for Analysis* (Englewood Cliffs, N.J., Prentice Hall Inc., 1967).
4. Robinson, T. W., The National Interest in: Sonderman, *et al.*, *The Theory and Practice of International Relations. op. cit.*
5. Frankel, J., *National Interest, op. cit.*, p. 69.
6. Burton, J. W., *Systems, States, Diplomacy and Rules* (1968) quoted in Frankel, J., *National Interest, op. cit.*, p. 76.
7. Holsti, K. J., *International Politics, op. cit.*, p. 137.
8. *Ibid.*, p. 138.
9. Frankel, J., *National Interest, op. cit.*, p. 31 ff.
10. *Ibid.*, p. 69.
11. *Ibid.*, p. 39.
12. Fulbright, J. W., *What is the National Interest?*, *op. cit.*, p. 41.
13. Holsti, K. J., *International Politics, op. cit.*, p. 146–50.
14. Rathjens, G. W., *et al.*, *Nuclear Arms Control Agreements: Process and Impact*, *op. cit.*, p. 1.
15. *Webster's Third New International Dictionary* (Springfield, Mass., G. and C. Merriam, 1966), p. 1178.
16. Orvik, N., The Threat: Problems of Analysis, *International Journal*, Vol. XXVI, No. 4, Autumn 1974, p. 675–85.
17. Berg, O., Security Policy Consideration, *Cooperation and Conflict*, No. 1, 1971; Andren, N., In Search of Security, *Cooperation and Conflict*, No. 4, 1968.
18. See on this point: Schulman, M. D., Arms Control in the International Context in: *Arms, Defense Policy, and Arms Control* (Daedalus, Summer 1975), Vol. 104, No. 3, pp. 59–61.
19. Berg, O., Security Policy Considerations, *op. cit.*, p. 35.
20. *Ibid.*, p. 35–37.
21. Padelford, N. J. and Lincoln, A. G., *International Politics, op. cit.*, p. 296–98.
22. Rathjens, G. W. *et al.*, *Nuclear Arms Control Agreements: Process and Impact*, *op. cit.*, p. 57, characterized this issue in the following way: 'We conclude that the explanation of compliance with existing strategic arms control agreements is not to be found in any technical process of verification or inspection. We believe that the most important inducement to compliance are bureaucratic and political forces in the governments of the parties, operating in the context of extensive, though incomplete knowledge of the other's military programmes and posture'.

5. Strategic military security through stable deterrence

I. Introduction

The difficulty with a clear and unequivocal definition of the notion of national security has been underlined in the preceding chapter. It has also been stressed that in an assessment of national security the military element of the overall security of a state is usually the most important criterion. Despite the obvious distortion inherent in such a restricted approach, we have in this study limited our calculations to military security, because this is the element, of all the other components of national security, whether geographical, economic or social, most amenable to calculation.

Among all the possible variations in military security, a special case is that based, or believed to be based, on strategic nuclear deterrence. It is this type of security that will be discussed here.

II. The concept of strategic deterrence

In general terms a military force capable of deterrence is (*a*) a force able to discourage the enemy from taking military action because the cost and risks would outweigh any gains made by the enemy; and (*b*) a force able to carry out a war should (*a*) fail.[1] The second element does not seem logically to belong to the pure meaning of deterrence. However, without it deterrence lacks credibility and hence cannot function. More explicitly no one could call the first 'deterrence proper', whereas the second might be termed 'defence'. The difference between the two is that deterrence influences the intentions of the enemy and diminishes the probability that he will attack, whilst defence enables a state to reduce the potential damage that would be caused by an attack, and prevents the enemy from making those gains on which he reckoned in waging the war.

Although the idea of strategic deterrence is very deeply rooted in military thinking, and is used as a basic concept in analysing the current military situation, it is by no means proved that nuclear deterrence really provides the great nuclear powers with security. This is precisely because of the two-edged nature of deterrence. On the one hand, nuclear forces are so large that they discourage any enemy from waging war; on the other, the defence element of deterrence, or its war-fighting capability must be seen as a real possibility. This capability is subject to continual and intensive expansion, which if not put under control may ultimately cause deterrence to fail.[2] This fact is the contradiction in the concept of nuclear deterrence, and gives security based on nuclear deterrence its dialectical or dubious character.

Bearing this in mind one has, however, to accept the concept of deterrence as a convenient model for analysis. Apart from its functional benefits, this approach gives us a chance of finding a common language with those who strongly believe that only nuclear deterrence based on powerful military hardware can save the world.

In the context of nuclear deterrence as considered here, countries A and B deter each other through a threat to inflict a punitive nuclear response in retaliation for the other's nuclear aggression. Two basic kinds of nuclear deterrence strategy will be discussed. The first is deterrence through the threat of mutually assured destruction (MAD), and the second is deterrence based on the ability for flexible limited response (FLR).

MAD deterrence

The theory behind MAD is that states are able to inflict, through a countervalue retaliatory strike, an unacceptable degree of damage on the aggressor, even in the worst case of an all-out attack on the strategic forces of the state which is attacked.[3] A countervalue strike means a strike against the major urban and industrial centres of the opponent. It is also sometimes termed a counter-city or punitive strike. A retaliatory strike, also called the second strike, carried out by those forces that have survived an attack, is the ability to strike back in response to the attack. Unacceptable damage is the amount of destruction caused by the retaliatory strike that would be unacceptable to the aggressor. According to McNamara's estimates unacceptable damage in the case of the Soviet Union would probably be the destruction of one-fourth to one-fifth of its population and one-half to two-thirds of its industrial capacity. However, what constitutes unacceptable damage is largely a matter of subjective judgement, and is extremely difficult to define quantitatively. If one accepts McNamara's assessment, it would be tantamount to complete destruction of the state making the first attack. The actual damage caused by the second strike of the arsenals analysed here may vary; even in the worst case, where the attacked state's weapons have been heavily hit, some weapons would survive to cause this unacceptable damage (1/4 to 1/5 and 1/2 to 1/3) and to ensure destruction, and where the attack had not been so heavy, then the second strike by the attacked country could cause damage many times larger than 'unacceptable'. Even this degree of minimum retaliation capability equal to McNamara's estimates would be sufficient to ensure mutual deterrence through the threat of total destruction. Military potential of which the retaliatory destructive power is equal to 'unacceptable damage' will in future be called the minimum deterrent threshold.

The concept of a 'minimum deterrent' is again a subjective matter. Afheldt and Sonntag assumed its numerical threshold to be over 100 1-Mt warheads.[4] In the present study an even higher threshold, the most conservative estimate of those that appeared to be reasonable, has been calculated to be the number of nuclear warheads able to destroy 200 of the opponent's major cities. Although the thresholds are usually assumed to be equal for the two sides, they could in reality obviously differ.[5]

The definition of MAD deterrence adopted here presupposes that the aggression will be directed against the strategic forces of the attacked state. Such an attack is called a counterforce strike. This military potential must be characterized by the ability to destroy military targets, especially the well-protected, so-called 'hard targets'.

MAD deterrence ceases as soon as one of the states has acquired a first strike capability against the opponent's arsenal. This first strike capability arises when a state is able to destroy the other side's forces to the extent that it cannot retaliate at all, or in retaliating cannot inflict an unacceptable degree of damage (destruction below the minimum deterrent threshold) upon the attacking state.

The concept of aggression underlying the above definition of MAD deterrence, in which only a single 'all-out' counterforce attack is foreseen, is obviously a considerable simplification. In any realistic scenario of strategic exchange no country will use all its offensive weapons at once, and deplete its strategic arsenals in one go. Furthermore, the characteristics of nuclear weapons would not make such an attack technically feasible. However, despite the surrealism of such an occurrence, we shall for the sake of simplicity of argument, assume the worst case of an all-out strategic strike.

The security of states A and B, engaged in strategic disarmament, defined in terms of the stability of MAD deterrence will thus be based on the preservation by both states of the residual second strike capability, despite the reductions in their respective strategic arsenals.

FLR deterrence

FLR deterrence will be defined here as the ability of a state to retaliate in kind to any form and to any extent of nuclear aggression on its territory.[6] According to the extent of aggression, even after sustaining an all-out attack, the retaliation may range from the local, limited and single counterforce strike up to the massive, full-scale countervalue strike causing unacceptable damage to the territory of the aggressor state.

It is apparent from the above definition that FLR deterrence is basically an extension of the defensive, war-fighting element in the general definition of strategic nuclear deterrence. With FLR deterrence the ability to make retaliation in kind for any degree of aggression[7] is believed to enhance the credibility of deterrence, because countries exposed to a limited attack are no longer confronted with the horrifying choice of either making retaliation for the enemy's limited attack with all available means directed at the enemy's urban centres as well as military targets, or not retaliating at all, and so submitting to the enemy's dictate. It is assumed that possession of the FRL deterrent will deter all degrees of aggression. Moreover, the flexibility of the available means and the targeting doctrine are believed to provide the means for encouraging negotiations during the early stages of a nuclear war, or in possible 'fire-breaks' during its subsequent stages, thereby giving states a chance to prevent further escalation of the conflict.

At this point it should be stressed again that the definition of FLR deterrence also contains an element of MAD, although the eventuality of cities being attacked is treated as the last resort, which all the interim stages of FLR deterrence should be able to prevent.

In the case of FLR deterrence the strategic military security of states A and B during the process of strategic disarmament will consist in retaining the ability of flexible limited retaliation in kind to any contingency of nuclear aggression by the other state, despite the reductions and constraints imposed on their arsenals by the disarmament agreement.

III. The stability of deterrence in the arms race

It is clear from the various analyses that have been made of our nearly three-decade long nuclear deterrence in relation to the dynamic strategic arms race, that there are several factors working either to stabilize or to destabilize that deterrence.[8] In particular some quantitative theoretical studies have been made which have analysed deterrence in the light of all possible variations and modifications in the make-up of strategic arsenals.[9] The present study will draw for the most part from one of these studies, namely, Afheldt and Sonntag's *Stability and Strategic Nuclear Arms*.[10]

Strategic stability, or the stability of nuclear deterrence, is obviously a quite specific form of 'stability' or 'balance'. The arsenals on both sides of the balance are composed of a great variety of different weapon-systems, varying in numbers and of different qualities. However, when discussing the strategic balance we compare only the overall military potential resulting from the interaction of quantitative and qualitative elements constituting a kind of equilibrium or 'essential equivalence'. Thus it is usual in talking about strategic balance to use a kind of systems analysis in which the aggregate balance is seen in terms of the sum of its parts interacting with each other.

In the present study, however, it seems appropriate to use the opposite approach. Here we are interested in understanding not so much the overall balance as the effect of a change in one of the components of the balance, which would be caused by violation of a disarmament agreement. Seeing that drafters of treaties tend to be restricted to simple terms and measures, such as numbers, sizes, weights and so on, and are rarely able to use even simplified aggregates of such measures, our analysis must be similarly restricted. Simple individual measures and terms constitute the language of legal obligations and serve as the basis for verification. Our focus of interest is therefore on these individual measures in order to determine the effect of their violation on the whole strategic balance.

The following factors bearing on the overall strategic potential and the stability of deterrence will be discussed here: the structure of arsenals; proportions of numbers; deliverable megatonnage and throw-weight; accuracy and reliability; and invulnerability.

The structure of arsenals

In a strategic deterrence situation, reliance on a single weapon-system is considered dangerous; a potential aggressor could concentrate on the best ways of attacking and destroying that system. Because it is a single system, it would be relatively easy for an aggressor to determine its mode of operation, thereby making it vulnerable and liable to destruction to an extent that would put the assured destruction capability of this weapon system in doubt. Similarly, the possession of only a single system would naturally diminish the range of options available for FLR deterrence. Again, in times of crisis, a deterrent based on a single weapon-system would be extremely vulnerable, especially to a surprise attack.

Despite these weaknesses, however, there are a number of measures that a state could take in order to maximize its possibilities of defence; these would involve giving attention to the survivability or invulnerability of the weapon-systems in question. A well-developed early-warning and air-defence system, fast take-off, proper dispersion and protection, and a high state of alertness would permit reliance on strategic bombers. High overpressure resistance, distant early warning and fast shoot-off, as well as liquid propelled missiles would allow a large number of ICBMs to escape destruction. Quietness, high speed, stationing close to the home waters and long range of submarine launched strategic missiles (SLBMs) would make nuclear submarines a powerful, invulnerable strategic force giving a high level of confidence to a state relying solely on them.

Among the different possibilities open to a state planning to base its deterrent on a single strategic weapons system, the most reliable alternative is the sea-based deterrent, especially if MAD deterrence is the underlying doctrine. However, as SLBMs are less accurate than other types of weapons, the sea-based deterrent is less suitable for FLR deterrence, so long as the accuracy of SLBMs is not improved.

US military doctrine strongly reflects the belief that reliance on a single-system deterrent is dangerous, and that the best solution for the stability of deterrence, in so far as the structure of its arsenals is concerned, is to base it on all three kinds of strategic weapons, the so-called Triad of ICBMs, SLBMs and bombers.[11] In addition it is always open to consider the possibility of new strategic weapons, as indicated by the case of cruise missiles. However, the more strategic systems there are the more difficult it is for the opponent to assess their weight and to control them: hence the arms race and an accompanying high degree of uncertainty, both of which are important destabilizing factors *per se*.

Proportions in numbers of weapons

Snyder's 'attacker-to-target ratio' applies in general to all reasoning about the rôle of numbers of weapons in the stability of deterrence. Basically this formula refers to 'the amount of attacking force required in order to eliminate a given amount of the attacked force'.[12] Relating this ratio to the potential of the second strike, Synder assumes that when both are high, then complete stability is preserved.

The impact of numbers on the stability of deterrence cannot be assessed at all without linking these numbers with their operational efficiency. If one assumes that the weapons on both sides are comparatively crude, then it is clear that large numbers on both sides do contribute to stability, notwithstanding the political issues connected with the question. Stability arises from the fact that the side which is attacked will automatically be in a better position, because by definition the attacker would have to use and therefore lose more weapons than could be destroyed on the other side. Thus there is no incentive to attack.

However, with gradual advances in the efficiency of weaponry, the attacker-to-target ratio diminishes rapidly. Now any increase or decrease in the number of weapons may undermine the stability of deterrence. However, the larger and more balanced the number of weapons of both sides the more stability is strengthened, because a larger number allows for a greater survivability of the attacked targets. This is clearly shown in the diagrams of Afheldt and Sonntag, where 'stable case 1' always covers the largest areas when the numbers of SLBMs and ICBMs are high.[13]

A disproportion in the numbers of weapons on both sides characterizes the reality of current deterrence. This is quite permissible given the variations in the counterforce capabilities of those numbers (in the case of ICBMs)[14] and in the degree of invulnerability that they enjoy (in the case of strategic weapon-systems). Even if the fluctuations in numbers continue, the stability of deterrence will not be endangered so long as the potential effects of the new weapons are not believed to be undermining the retaliatory assured destruction capacity of the other side.

One of the specific problems concerning numbers of weapons and their influence on the stability of deterrence is the multiplication of warheads carried to a target by a single missile (MRVing and subsequently MIRVing). However, the implications of MIRVing ICBMs are not limited by the fact that the attacker-to-target ratio is proportionally decreased. Equally important is the fact that, through MIRVing, a psychological situation is created in which it becomes tempting to attack first in order to make the most gains. Especially if the attack is preemptive will it destroy much more offensive force than the mere number of the attacking ICBMs indicates. This is clearly shown on the diagrams of Afheldt and Sonntag where the influence of MIRVs with a high destruction probability (60 per cent) causes an extremely unstable situation (case 2, the reciprocal first strike). The danger of MIRVs to the stability of deterrence thus lies not only in their growing numbers, but also in their increasing accuracy, a process which is apparently closely linked technologically.[15]

Deliverable megatonnage and throw weight/payload

Although the two terms are completely different measures of the capacity of strategic weapons, they are very much related. Both have been used for a rough comparison of nuclear military potentials, especially when the accuracy of weapons is small and the effectiveness of arsenals is measured in equivalent megatonnage rather than in hard-target destruction power. Measuring the stability of deterrence by either of these two yardsticks is typical of a number of methods using aggregates, all of them illustrative but nonetheless rather inaccurate. Deliverable megatonnage, that is, the explosive nuclear power which can be carried on to the target does not say much about the probable efficiency of that power over a range of specific targets: and to measure an expansion (or decrease) in strategic potential using either of the two criteria without measuring other factors cannot be used successfully to analyse the impact of that change on the stability of deterrence. For example, quite different results will be obtained for the nuclear exchange scenario if one state expands its total deliverable yield, and the other diminishes the total yield of its warheads but expands their accuracy. The difference between the military values of the two increments of power would produce an imbalance highly in favour of the country with fewer but more accurate weapons. Similarly, the throw weight of missiles may serve as an indication of the size of warheads, and hence enable an estimate to be made of the number that a given type of missile could carry on a ballistic trajectory. It does not indicate, however, how advanced these warheads are technologically, nor their level of reliability; furthermore, we still have no idea as to the actual number of warheads that this throw weight capacity can actually carry.

The increase in deliverable megatonnage or the installation of more powerfully thrusting missiles may be considered as destabilizing the balance of deterrence only when the other offensive characteristics of the weapons are expanded as well. Conversely, an expansion in these two values of an arsenal may not undermine the strategic balance so long as they are only directed at improving weapons which constitute the invulnerable second strike, for example the sea-based deterrent. However, although an expansion in these two values may not seem very useful in the analysis of strategic situations, it is often the subject of political debate; so it cannot be ignored.

Accuracy and reliability of weapons

Refinements in weapons resulting in their greater accuracy and reliability have a very strong impact on the stability of MAD and FLR deterrence, though in each case their effect is different.

The stability of MAD deterrence is highly sensitive to improvements in the efficiency of weapons. Greater accuracy and reliability give the state initiating a nuclear strike against hard targets an enormous advantage over the retaliating state, *per se* a highly destabilizing effect. In short, the effect of accuracy on the destructive power of a warhead can be exemplified by the fact that 'a factor of 100 in weapon yield can be compensated by a factor of $4\frac{1}{2}$ in accuracy'.[16]

In deterrence based on the doctrine of flexible limited response, the effect of developments in the accuracy and reliability of weapons is less drastic, except that they would obviously enhance the capacities of those weapons to be both flexible and limited, and so allow the possibility of a more accurate retaliatory attack. Because, as we mentioned before, FLR deterrence contains strong elements of MAD as its ultimate stage on the ladder of escalation, the same factors which strengthen the stability of deterrence at a low level of nuclear conflict will be highly destabilizing during the interim stages of a nuclear war, giving a great advantage to the side making the first move in a massive counterforce attack.

The accuracy and reliability of weapons are among those factors which fundamentally influence the military qualities of strategic arsenals, but which are completely hidden from the opponents. Examples of other such factors are command, control and communication (C^3), and improvements in anti-submarine warfare (ASW) capabilities. All of them depend on a wide range of scientific and engineering activity and their improvements are difficult to follow. Nor is their influence on the military environment immediately and easily well understood. It is these technological fields of the arms race that are at the core of all the dynamism and uncertainty in the field of deterrence.

Vulnerability of strategic weapons

Even the most powerful of offensive arsenals will not be an adequate deterrent if it is vulnerable to attack. Such was the case with the strategic bomber forces of the 1950s, when a swift surprise attack by the bombers of the other side could render them powerless. Then 'it appeared most unlikely that the crime would be followed by a suitable punishment'.[17] A similar situation existed when the first liquid-propelled ICBMs, unprotected and slow to launch, were introduced.

Invulnerability may be achieved through a variety of means, both technical and organizational. These may consist of dispersion; sheltering and hardening; air alerts; distant observation and warning; shorter take-off and shoot-off times; changes in fuels and engines; developments in quietness, speed of escape, and so on. All these developments would in principle have a positive effect on the stability of strategic deterrence, whether based on MAD or FLR, because they simply enhance the survivability of the retaliatory force. However, it is important to remember that because retaliation is closely related to the offensive element of deterrence, even such developments in the invulnerability of arsenals have a bearing on the strategic balance. This is so because an arsenal which is well advanced offensively, which is able to knock out a great deal of the opponent's forces in the first strike, and which has the rest of its unused forces invulnerable to a retaliatory counterforce strike, may deter the attacked side from actually making retaliation at all. The outcome of such a nuclear exchange, measured solely in the left-over strategic potential, would leave the retaliating side in a far worse position, because of those weapons left after an attack some more would have been used up in a fruitless retaliatory mission.

The rôle of changes in the invulnerability of strategic weapon-systems on the balance of strategic deterrence has been well demonstrated in Afheldt and Sonntag's study, where survivability is provided by the sea-based missiles, ABMs or mobile systems. In each case the stable area of mutually assured destruction is enlarged the more invulnerability is assumed for both sides. The impact of invulnerability depends, however, on the way in which the survivability of a given arsenal was built up *vis-à-vis* that of the enemy. One can envisage a specific case where the expansion of the survivability of a weapon-system may diminish the area of stability.

The variables discussed above, either quantitative or qualitative, do not exhaust all the possible changes in strategic arsenals which may undermine or shore up deterrence, and hence endanger (or improve) strategic security of one of the states. However, this description of the most important of them, based on historical experience and studies of deterrence and the arms race, should provide an indication of the way in which violations of a strategic disarmament agreement, motivated by hopes of gaining a unilateral strategic advantage, might affect the strategic balance.

IV. The stability of deterrence in disarmament

So far we have discussed only the stability of deterrence where the respective arsenals of the two sides are in the process of expansion, quantitatively and qualitatively. We now come to the main point of this study, which is to analyse deterrence in relation to disarmament, and to find the destabilizing factors at different stages of a disarmament process. Initially we shall confine our analysis to the destabilizing effects of violations of a disarmament treaty, subsequently going on to other factors which may upset the strategic balance, but which are outside the scope of the treaty itself. Underlying our analysis is the assumption that the changes in arsenals that take place in pursuance of a treaty have been well planned and agreed upon in advance by the contracting states as not jeopardizing their security, even though they may bring about substantial alterations in their military potentials.

The first question raised here is: What kind of violation and how much would undermine deterrence between two states engaged in disarming, so that both of them lose, or feel that they are losing their sense of security? Secondly: Does verification help to preserve that security? To answer the first question it would seem logical to draw from our experience of stability in connection with an arms race, and to apply that knowledge to strategic disarmament because the same numerical and qualitative factors play a similar rôle in both processes. One could, for example, use Afheldt and Sonntag's study as a basis, starting from the point of large numbers and high destructive probabilities, and continuing down to small numbers and decreased destructive probabilities. Such an approach would, however, clearly be wrong, as is illustrated by some of the conclusions of those authors themselves. Afheldt and Sonntag often found that stability may in certain cases be greater the higher the number of ICBM's, although they believe that, at low levels of destructive capabilities of offensive missiles, within the assured destruction strategy 'the risk of reducing the numbers of missiles is . . . the least serious' up to the point where the number of missiles becomes extremely small. However, they point out that 'the real problem is the increase of the counterforce destruction probabilities, (the introduction of ABM systems), and the introduction of MIRVs. With the introduction of these weapons systems, the balance becomes so precarious that the prospective consequence is anything but disarmament'.[18] Further on they conclude that 'reduction of the numbers of missiles on both sides could most probably lead into unstable areas'.[19]

At this point it should be pointed out that the disarmament scenarios considered in this study operate with destruction probabilities which are often considered to be higher than those used by Afheldt and Sonntag. Logically, therefore, our disarmament scenarios could be criticized as being even more unrealistic and dangerous for the security of states. However, we maintain that they are plausible. Seeing that the stability of deterrence in relation to an arms race is exposed to a number of dangers stemming from changing elements that are uncertain as to their consequences, it is logical to take the worst case for analysis. In the case of strategic disarmament one has on the other hand to assume that at the start of implementation of a treaty, a state of stability exists, and that the changes brought about by the treaty are the result of careful planning on both sides. What may be dangerous for the security of states, therefore, are only the clandestine activities of states – matters which are supposed to be taken care of by the verification system.

References and Notes to Chapter 5

1. Snyder, G. H., *Deterrence and Defense* (Princeton, Princeton University Press 1961), p. 3.
2. Raser, J. R., Deterrence Research: Past Progress and Future Needs, *Journal of Peace Research*, No. 4, 1966, p. 311.
3. On MAD deterrence see amongst other sources: Aron, R., *The Great Debate: Theories of Nuclear Strategy* (Garden City, New York, Doubleday 1965); Boyland, E. S. et al., *An analysis of 'Assured Destruction'*, Hudson Institute Research Report, HJ-1602-RR, 20 March, 1972; Brennan, D. G., Some Fundamental Problems of Arms Control and National Security, *Orbis*, Vol. XV, No. 1, Spring 1971; Elliot, J. D., Deterrence and the Art of War, *Military Review*, Vol. 51; No. 10, pp. 48–51; Holst, J. J., *Comparative US and Soviet Deployments, Doctrines, and Arms Limitation*, An Occasional Paper of the Center for Policy Study, The University of Chicago, 1971; Hunt, K., Deterrence, *NATO Review*, Vol. 22, No. 1, 1974; Ikle, F. C., Can Nuclear Deterrence Last Out the Century, *Foreign Affairs*, January 1973; Kahan, J. H., Stable Deterrence: a Strategic Policy for the 1970's, *Orbis*, Summer 1971, Vol. XV, No. 2, pp. 528–543; McNamara, R., Mutual Deterrence in: C. P. Beitz and T. Herman, eds., *Peace and War* (San Francisco, 1973); Snyder, G. H., *Deterrence and Defense, op. cit.*,; Stein, A., *Strategic Doctrine for a Post-SALT World*, Cornell University, Peace Studies Program, Occasional Papers No. 4.

4. Afheldt, H. and Sonntag, P., *Stability and Strategic Nuclear Arms*, World Law Fund, Occasional Papers, New York, 1971.
5. On the point of unacceptable damage and the minimum deterrent see: Legault, A. and Lindsey, G., *The Dymanics of the Nuclear Balance* (Ithaca and London, Cornell University Press, 1974), pp. 169–70.
6. On flexible limited response see amongst other sources: Ball, D. J., Deja Vu: The Return to Counterforce in the Nixon Administration: (Or, The Politics of Potential Nuclear Castration), Appendix in: R. O'Neil, ed., *The Strategic Nuclear Balance, An Australian Perspective*, (Canberra, Strategic and Defence Studies Centre, Australian National University, 1975); Carter, B., Flexible Strategic Options No Need for New Strategy, *Survival*, Vol. XVII, No. 1, January–February 1975; Davis, L. E., *Limited Nuclear Options, Deterrence and the New American Doctrine*, Adelphi Paper No. 121, (London, International Institute for Strategic Studies, 1976); Frisbee, J. L., Counterforce Revisited, *Air Force Magazine*, Vol. 55, No. 2, 1974; Gray, C. S., Rethinking Nuclear Strategy, *Orbis*, Vol. XVIII, No. 4, Winter 1974; Greenwood, T. and Nacht, M. L., The New Nuclear Debate: Sense or Nonsense? *Foreign Affairs*, Vol. 52, No. 4, July 1974; Intrilligator, M. D., The Debate Over Missile Strategy: Targets and Rates of Fire, *Orbis*, Vol. 11, No. 4, 1968; Kadane, J. B., *The Controversy Over Counterforce*, Interim Research Memorandum, IRM-44, Operations Evaluation Group, 12 August 1963; Martin, L., Changes in American Strategic Doctrine – an Initial Interpretation, *Survival*, Vol. XVI, No. 4, July–August 1974; May, M. M., Some Advantages of a Counterforce Deterrence, *Orbis*, Vol. XIV, No. 2, Summer 1970; Russet, B. M., Counter-Combatant Deterrence: a Proposal, *Survival*, Vol. XVI, No. 3, May–June 1974; Targetting Flexibility Emphasized by SAC, *Aviation Week and Space Technology*, Vol. 104, No. 19, 10 May 1976; Wagstaff, P. C., An Analysis of the Cities – Avoidance Theory, *Stanford Journal of International Studies*, Vol. 7, 1972; and a number of the US Congress Hearings, amongst others: Department of Defense Appropriations for FY 1975; Hearings before a Subcommittee of the Committee on Appropriations, US Senate, 93rd Congress, 2nd session, Part 1. Department of Defense, Defense Agencies, Public Witnesses, pp. 42–45 and 92–97.
7. In this study only strategic (or so-called central) deterrence, whether MAD or FLR, is considered. In the case of flexible limited deterrence we are not, therefore, considering the regional (theatre) modifications of this type of deterrence, such as those approved in the NATO doctrine. According to NATO's doctrine of flexible response, adopted officially in 1967 and subsequently developed in the documents prepared by NATO's Nuclear Planning Group since 1969, deterrence should prevent any kind of aggression, including conventional aggression. However, this concept of nuclear retaliation to any, even a conventional, attack seems ambiguous so far as the timing and the extent of use of nuclear weapons are concerned. For a further discussion of NATO's doctrine on flexible response see Karber, P. A., Nuclear Weapons and Flexible Response, *Orbis*, Summer 1970, Vol. XIV, No. 2, pp. 284–97; Bennet, W. S. *et al.*, A Credible Nuclear-Emphasis Defense for NATO, *Orbis*, Summer 1973, Vol. XVII, No. 2, pp. 463–79; Joshua, W., A Strategic Concept for the Defense of Europe *Orbis*, *Ibid.*, pp. 448–62; Polk, J. H., The Realities of Tactical Nuclear Warfare, *Orbis*, *Ibid.*, pp. 439–47; Richardson, R. C., Can NATO Fashion a New Strategy?, *Orbis*, *Ibid.*, pp. 415–38; Report of Secretary of Defense James R. Schlesinger on the FY 1976 and Transition Budgets, FY 1977 Authorization Request and FY 1976–1980 Defense Programs, 5 February 1975, pp. III-12; and Heisenberg, W., *The Alliance and Europe: Part I: Crisis Stability in*

Europe and Theatre Nuclear Weapons, Adelphi Papers No. 96, (London, 1973, IISS), p. 3.
8. See for example: Burns, A. L., A Graphical Approach to Some Problems of the Arms Race, *Conflict Resolution*, Vol. III, No. 4, December 1959; Hoag, M., On Stability in Deterrence Races, *World Politics*, Vol. XIII, No. 4, July 1961; Midgaard, K., Arms Races, Arms Control, and Disarmament, *Cooperation and Conflict* No. 1, 1970; Snyder, G. H., 'Prisoner's Dilemma' and 'Chicken' Models in International Politics, *International Studies Quarterly*, Vol. 15, No. 1, March 1971; Triska, J. F. and Finley, D. D., Soviet and American Relations: a Multiple Symmetry Model, *The Journal of Conflict Resolution*, Vol. IX, No. 1, March 1965.
9. See for example: Afheldt, H. and Sonntag, P., *Stability and Strategic Nuclear Arms, op. cit.*; Kent, G. A., *On the Interaction of Opposing Forces Under Possible Arms Control Agreements*, Occasional Papers in International Affairs, No. 5, (Cambridge, Mass., Center for International Affairs, Harvard University, 1963); Legault, A. and Lindsey, G., *The Dynamics of the Nuclear Balance, op. cit.*, pp. 166–99 and Appendix A; Pitman, G. R. Jr., A Calculus of Military Stability, *Journal of Peace Research*, No. 4, 1966.
10. Afheldt and Sonntag's paper develops a mathematical model elucidating the intricate relationships connecting the number of offensive missiles and their vulnerability with the number of defensive missiles and their accuracy, along with other defensive and offensive weapons such as MIRVs and land-mobile systems. The focus of the analysis is the stability of any given strategic situation between two adversaries X and Y. Three basic strategic situations are possible between the two states: I – second-strike capability (assured destruction), II – first-strike destruction but no second strike capability, III – incapability of first-strike destruction (invulnerability of the opponent). From these three positions the following combinations called 'cases' are derived, 1 to 7:
    1. reciprocal second-strike capability (stable deterrence through reciprocally assured destruction),
    2. both states capable of firsts-trike destruction but lack a second-strike capability (instability, coercion to disarm the opponent by striking first),
    3. both opponents are incapable of first-strike destruction (stability through reciprocal invulnerability),
    4. country X has a second-strike destruction, but Y is capable only of first-strike destruction (instability, pressure on X to disarm Y),
    5. same as 4, with X and Y interchanged,
    6. X has second-strike capability, but Y has no striking ability (X's superiority),
    7. same as 6, with X and Y interchanged.

    The variations in numbers of land-based, sea-based and MIRVed missiles as well as ABMs, together with different 'destruction probabilities' are shown in the form of diagrams. The individual cases 1–7 appear as 'areas' in the graphic representations. Large areas appear if the case remains unchanged even in the event of considerable variation in the data. Small areas appear if only minor variations of those data result in another case or another strategic situation.
11. See, for example: J. R. Schlesinger's statement in Hearing before the Committee on Armed Services, US Senate, 94th Congress, 1st Session on S. 920, Part 4. R&D. February 25 and 27. March 4 and 5, 1975, pp. 2153–54
12. Snyder, G. H., *Deterrence and Defense, op. cit.*, p. 98.
13. Afheldt, H. and Sonntag, P., *Stability and Strategic Nuclear Arms, op. cit.*, p. 24, figures 3.1.1 – 1/4; p. 35, figures 3.1.3.2 – 15/16; p. 37, figures 3.1.3.3 – 1/4.

14. *Ibid.*, p. 24.
15. *Ibid.*, p. 30, figures 3.1.3.1/4; see also Kaysen, C., Keeping the Strategic Balance, *Foreign Affairs*, Vol. 46, No. 4, 1968. 'The more successful the developments of MIRVs in terms of both numbers of re-entry vehicles ... and the accuracy ... the more difficult it becomes to be confident about the security of a deterrent force'.
16. Legault, A. and Lindsey, G., *The Dynamics of the Nuclear Balance, op. cit.*, p. 50.
17. *Ibid.*, pp. 148–49; see also Raser, J. R., *Deterrence Research: Past Progress and Future Needs, op. cit.*, p. 310.
18. Afheldt, H. and Sonntag, P., *Stability and Strategic Nuclear Arms, op. cit.*, p. 68.
19. *Ibid.*, p. 69.

6. Security and verification in strategic arms limitation—a case study

I. Introduction

Verification as a means of enforcing the provisions embodied in a disarmament treaty is widely considered the best guarantee of the security of states complying with the treaty provisions.[1] It is held that the would-be violator is deterred from deviating from the norms of the agreement by the fear of his being discovered and exposed by an efficient verification system.

This view of the rôle of verification has to be understood against the background of the political climate of post-war discussions on disarmament, in which each side, especially those of different socio-economic systems, was highly mistrustful of the other. In an atmosphere such as this, disarmament measures could not be based on mutual confidence of states in each other, but rather on a high degree of suspicion. Verification thus became a kind of substitute for trust, and as such assumed a vital rôle in all considerations of disarmament.

It is commonly assumed that before the start of disarmament a country's security is assured by its military forces, the size and quality of which are determined by a state's subjective view of its own defence needs, and by the extent of a possible threat. According to this assumption it follows that when armaments are replaced by disarmament – even partially – there is a danger of a corresponding loss of security through the possibility that the obligations of states, though evenly balanced, and being parties to a treaty might change the general balance of power in an unpredictable way. Moreover, if the opponent does not comply with the terms of the disarmament treaty, it may gain a useful strategic or political advantage that will upset the balance which formerly existed and so put the whole security of the complying state at risk. To avoid such a possibility an efficient system of verification is required to be able to check and inform the other parties whether or not all the provisions of a treaty are being observed.

It was this understanding of the crucial importance of verification in periods of disarmament that gave rise to a number of questions such as how much verification is necessary; how closely is the degree of disarmament attainable tied up with the efficacy of the verification system; does verification guarantee an adequate level of security in all disarmament situations, and so on. Questions of this nature are intimately bound up with 'a theory of inspection' or 'a verification theory'.

One of the problems connected with this theory, which became an issue of great political controversy, was the question as to which should come first, disarmament or verification. In general two positions developed. According to that adopted by the United States and its allies the verification system should be set up before disarmament so that it would be able to function efficiently as soon as the agreement took effect.² The Soviet Union and the other socialist states, on the other hand, adopted the view that actual disarmament should precede measures to ensure that an agreement was being observed.³ This issue was finally solved by the Zorin-McCloy agreement of 1961 in which it was decided to apply the verification system simultaneously with, not before or after, a disarmament agreement.⁴

Subsequently the theory of verification has progressed from such political questions, and has turned to issues of perhaps a more fundamental nature, such as what is the real meaning of security, and how are disarmament, verification and the security of states interrelated. This latter problem is not as theoretical as it might at first appear. If one accepts the basic assumption of conventional armament theory, namely, that a state's security is guaranteed by its armed forces, and that disarmament, if not exactly balanced in content and effect and even if not carried out identically by all parties, will cause a corresponding decline in that security, then the rôle of verification in relation to disarmament and security must be established more specifically. It is believed that, in order to avoid creating a hazardous military situation for any of the parties to a treaty during the transition period, there must be some kind of phasing scheme which relates the degree of inspection at any one time to the amount of disarmament achieved.⁵ To do this one must have more than a vague idea of the kind of relationship that exists between disarmament, verification and security.

II. *The simplified concept of the relation between disarmament, security and verification*

An inductive approach to the problem was made by J. Wiesner, who wrote:

> The level of intensity of inspection required to monitor a disarmament agreement is in some way proportional to the degree of disarmament. In other words, the more completely weapons of all kinds are eliminated the greater will be the necessity for an inspection system sufficiently sensitive to discover small discrepancies in the size of remaining forces.⁶

Later in the same essay Wiesner draws the graph (see graph 6.1) in which the curve showing the numbers of weapons legally possessed and reduced during arms limitations is inversely proportional to the increase in the amount of inspection required.⁷ In other words it can be inferred from the way the Wiesner graph is drawn that the amount of inspection needed is exactly proportional to the numbers of weapons being phased out according to the stipulations of an agreement on disarmament. In addition the graph shows that as the numbers of weapons legally possessed decline, then the uncertainty of estimates about the numbers of weapons actually existing also diminishes. This reduced uncertainty provides the states concerned with an appropriate measure of security. After

Graph 6.1. The Wiesner curve. Source: Wiesner, J., Inspection for disarmament in Henkin, Louis (Ed.), *Arms Control: Issues for the Public* (Columbia University, 1961) p. 137.

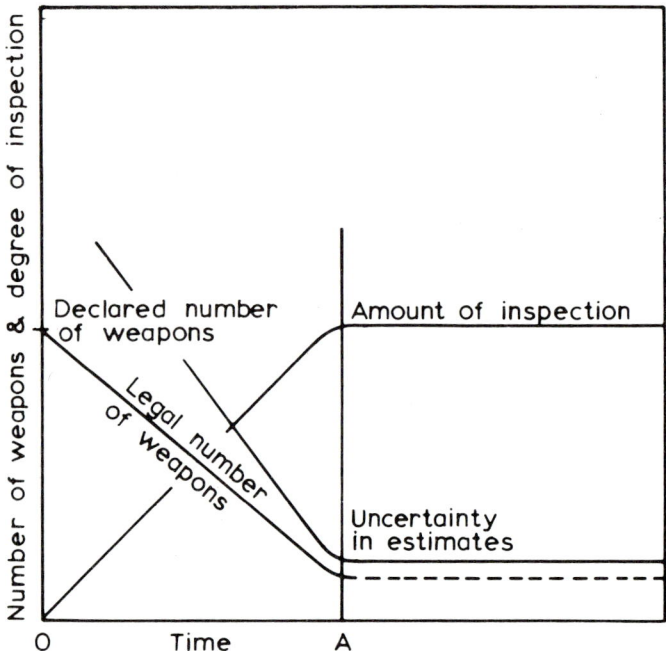

reaching point A on the time axis the very low level of arms legally possessed will remain intact and the amount of inspection is constant.

In a review of Wiesner's graph R. Falk[8] makes a number of comments which can be summarized as follows:

1. Wiesner's assumptions are too broad. He lumps together all kinds of disarmament measures without making a distinction between the different kinds of verification technique necessary for different disarmament measures. Some measures such as those in the areas of military R&D and CBW are non-verifiable, yet these he ignores. Moreover, he fails to consider such questions as the 'necessity' or 'feasibility' of verification. In general, Falk argues in favour of more specificity in the design of such a model verification system.

2. Wiesner assumes a proportional relationship between inspection and disarmament without giving any evidence for it.

3. The slope of inspection on the graph rises without any explanation in military-strategic terms. In other words, Wiesner assumes that at the start of disarmament the amount of inspection is low, and that as disarmament progresses so the amount of inspection increases. Falk argues that the converse is possible, that is to say that at the start of disarmament suspicion is high, and therefore the amount of verification is also high: whereas as the agreement

progresses, so does the amount of mutual confidence between the parties; therefore the level of inspection can decline.

4. According to Wiesner the quality of security increases with the level of inspection. This assumption is not proved, especially in respect of certain specific disarmament measures.

5. The whole concept of security is too simplified in Wiesner's model. He makes no distinction between perceived security on the one hand (that is, subjective requirements of domestic political acceptability) and actual security (objective requirements of national security) on the other.

Some further points can be added to Falk's objections:

1. The indicators used by Wiesner, such as 'amount of inspection', 'uncertainty in estimates', and 'legal number of weapons', may in theory be acceptable, but in practice they demonstrate the difficulties that can be encountered when considering correlations between disarmament, inspection (verification), security and trust among nations. The following queries arise: (*a*) at what quantitative level is disarmament proceeding; (*b*) what objects are being measured by the inspection; (*c*) of what quality is the inspection and (*d*) by what yardsticks are 'security' and 'trust' measured?

2. The level of uncertainty in the estimates of Wiesner's curve diminishes according to the simple statistical observation that when the estimated numbers are small, then the margin of error diminishes accordingly. However, in his discussion of this, Wiesner attributes the decrease in the probable error of the inspection system to the fact that the inspection system is continually being developed.

Falk makes various specific follow-on suggestions concerning the 'verification theory':

> We need a series of specific studies about the relevance of inspection to security during disarmament ... The objective would be to produce a series of specific correlations between the need for inspection and the type of disarmament measure ... if we are concerned with actual security, then we should conduct specific studies of the relationship between different kinds of violations and the maintenance of military stability.[9]

The following elaboration has been stimulated to a large degree by Falk's proposals.

III. The purpose and scope of the study

The problem of the relation between disarmament, security and verification has been hampered by a lack of comprehensive study and by the fact that, because it is a politically sensitive issue, substantial differences of opinion exist. The purpose of our work is to throw further light on the question by determining and possibly extracting a theoretical correlation between strategic disarmament, its verification and the security of states pursuing the process of disarmament. In other words, and more specifically, the purpose is to measure, even quantitatively in part, the 'need for security' through verification in strategic arms limitations.

The belief is widely held that when there are many military forces which are much diversified, then the military stability and security relationship between states undertaking disarmament is not sensitive to small numerical or qualitative changes in the weapons structure.[10] This situation is believed to exist particularly in the relationship characterized by so-called nuclear overkill capabilities and where equivalence of military potentials on account of their different structures must be 'essential' rather than exact.[11]

Hardly any theoretical studies have been devoted to this problem, and the evidence drawn by practical experience from existing disarmament treaties is negligible, because the weapons disarmed are usually of minor significance, being peripheral to the main stream of armaments and military potential, and therefore have little bearing on security as a whole. Thus the belief mentioned above is based more on intuition and common-sense than on the grounds of any evidence.

Moreover, even if observations on the insensitivity of the security of states to violations in the early stages of disarmament were accepted as self-evident, the following questions cannot be answered so easily:

1. Up to what size of a violation is the given security-relationship insensitive at a given stage of disarmament?

2. Does this insensitivity continue for long, or for only a short period of disarmament?

3. When, and at what stage of disarmament does the security-relationship become sensitive and even highly sensitive to violations?

All these questions are fundamental for an analysis of the rôle of verification in the preservation of the security of states at the different stages of disarmament. Henceforth, these questions will be treated here in Chapter 6 and, in more a specific and restricted way, in the Appendix.

IV. Terminology

Many terms are used here in a specific connotation. They therefore require careful definition and explanation.

First of all, the term 'strategic disarmament' will be used in connection with the disarmament of two rival states. It is assumed that these states have already agreed to limitations of strategic delivery systems for highly sophisticated nuclear weapons. The two states find themselves in a situation of mutual strategic deterrence as explained above (Chapter 5, pages 61–62).

Naturally, by restricting our consideration of 'strategic disarmament' to two states only, any conclusions to be drawn from the study will have only limited application in practical political terms. However, this limitation is justified by the fact that in the real world, too, essential strategic deterrence exists above all only between the two great nuclear powers, the Soviet Union and the United States.

Weapons are said to be strategic when they constitute the material basis for deterrence, namely, nuclear weapon delivery systems such as intercontinental land-based and sea-based ballistic missiles, nuclear-powered submarines and long-range bombers. Long-range cruise missiles should be included in the strategic category when they become operational, together with any other weapons and forces which have a substantial influence on the deterrent effect between states. Not all the above-mentioned weapons will, however, be considered here in the same detail.

Strategic bombers and cruise missiles were excluded completely from the calculations made in the Appendix. The considerations concerning them in this chapter are therefore not based on any quantified analysis by the author. These weapon systems were omitted from the calculations because of the difficulty in quantifying their operational features.

Many of the problems analysed here, as well as many terms and concepts, resemble real world problems, doctrines and discussions. It will also be noted that the figures used in the Appendix supporting many of the observations in this chapter concerning the number and quality of strategic weapons are taken entirely from data relating to actual arsenals of the Soviet Union and the United States. It should not be assumed, however, that this study is directly concerned with problems discussed by these states at the SALT negotiations or elsewhere. The real figures have been used simply because they represent the situation in all its complexity: complexities of this nature could never have been invented for the purpose of the study. The arsenals of the Soviet Union and the United States are taken as a model, and only as a model, suitable for research purposes: the conclusions of the study are not intended as a comment on the actual disarmament negotiations. For this reason these countries' names will not be used, but are replaced by the symbols A and B.

The notion of calculable security

The security of a state has a double connotation: it can be defined as (*a*) the actual probability of survival for a state in its international environment; or (*b*) the perceived probability of survival and the satisfaction of national vital interests. The latter definition is a subjective assessment which depends on the observer's knowledge, attitudes and political inclinations. Neither the actual nor the perceived probability can be measured with confidence. The final assessment will be the result of the interaction of a large number and variety of factors such as the time when it is made; the external and internal military, economic and social situation in which a nation-state finds itself; and in the case of subjective security the whole complex of unique conditions which form a human being's mind and judgement.

However, measurable factors which play a crucial rôle in both objective and subjective assessments of a state's security do exist. These factors include numerical military strength, qualitative factors within military forces (where calculable), economic wealth and potential, demographic and geographical factors. Among them the military factors are conventionally believed to play a very, if not the most, important rôle. This 'calculable security' – and it should be understood that this security is calculable only in the military sector – is the matter under consideration here. Clearly it is a much narrower sense of 'security' than could be wished for scientific use, but still it seems to form a sufficiently significant basis for measuring security. Therefore security as discussed here will always be taken to be the calculable security of a nation-state determined by quantitative and qualitative military factors. It is from these factors that the security verification requirements will be drawn.

In the case considered further on in this study, strategic military security between two states, called states A and B, is defined as their mutual ability to deter each other from a nuclear attack on their respective territories. During the process of strategic disarmament undertaken by the two states this ability for deterrence will be exposed to serious changes corresponding with the reductions and restrictions imposed by a mutual disarmament agreement upon their strategic arsenals. Seeing that the composition and technical characteristics of the weapons that are reduced are very different in countries A and B, the changes in their deterrence capabilities cannot be balanced exactly. Their capabilities fluctuate, but they must, however, fluctuate in a manner acceptable to the belief held by those states that the disarmament measures carried out by them are not undermining the basic deterrence ability which preserves what has been called 'essential equivalence', 'rough parity' or 'symmetry of residual second strikes'. The advantages retained by the two sides would vary from stage to stage during the reductions; but it would be essential for neither side to achieve a unilateral advantage of such magnitude that it could endanger the strategic security of the other, that is, its ability to retaliate upon an attack.

V. Verification and the preservation of security during strategic disarmament

Although a state's strategic security is not fundamentally changed by entering into a disarmament agreement, the character of the strategic balance, and in fact the relations between the sides to the agreement, are bound to be somewhat altered, and even softened. This is inevitable, because, in order even to conclude a disarmament agreement, states are forced to cooperate and to display some degree of mutual trust.

However, this does not mean that states feel more secure. In fact, the balance of deterrence during the process of disarmament may theoretically be sensitive to two sets of factors:

1. Those outside the scope of the treaty régime, such as developments by third parties; internal political developments inside the territories of the other signatories; and developments in military technology which change the whole strategic military context in which the treaty is operating;

2. Those under the treaty régime. Here the most important seem to be those potential disparities between the obligations undertaken by the parties to the treaty, and their actual implementation. To check whether such a disparity exists or not the verification system is established.

To analyse the relation between verification and security during strategic disarmament, two scenarios will be considered separately: first, the simpler case, when all external factors are eliminated; and second, the situation in which factors being controlled by the treaty régime, and those outside the régime are taken into account. In order to make this possible, Scenario I presupposes that the strategic disarmament treaty covers the totality of technological improvements that could be made in the arsenals of the two sides; and Scenario II assumes the free interaction of all factors, that is, uncontrolled military technology together with all possible evasions of the agreement.

Scenario I: disarmament with frozen military technology

According to this scenario the numbers of strategic weapons would be reduced gradually, and throughout the entire process of the disarmament agreement (15 years, or stages) the qualities of the weapons remaining in the arsenals stay at the same level as they were when the treaty began to operate. Realistically speaking this is of course a rather dubious assumption, because strategic weapons tend to grow obsolete rather quickly when overhauls, improvements and tests are not carried out. Nevertheless, for the purpose of this study these problems can be left aside. Nor will the specific procedures for implementing the disarmament agreement be discussed here. We need only to establish some rules in order to underline the importance of preserving the balance of military capabilities, measured with the yardstick of the strategic residual second strike.

Strategic security and numerical violations

Given the enormous overkill and great numbers of weapons of the two arsenals it is logical to assume that the overall strategic balance between A and B, at least at the beginning of disarmament, is not sensitive to deviations from the prescribed numerical reductions. This is well corroborated by the values of the security verification requirement calculated for ICBM reductions in the Appendix. These values, shown in Table 1A.10, page 131, are very high throughout the entire process of the ICBM reductions until the very last stages of disarmament. This means that, in order to gain any substantial military advantage from a numerical violation of the treaty, very large numbers of the large-size weapons would have to be deployed clandestinely, an operation which does not seem to be technically feasible.

So far as preserving strategic security is concerned the requirement for verification in ICBM disarmament is actually very small. Only during the last two stages of reductions does the requirement for more stringent verification grow (see Graphs 1A.3 and 1A.4, where points β_A and β_B are indicated, that is, the levels at which the value of the security verification requirement is less than 100).

The importance of verification for the strategic security of states A and B is further diminished when other weapon systems such as SLBMs and bombers are included in the analysis. Their addition enlarges the residual second strike of both states, and thus increases the value of the security verification requirement in MAD deterrence (although it cannot be quantified for SLBMs). We can, therefore, make the broad conclusion that when invulnerable sea-based weapons exist during strategic disarmament, numerical violations cannot endanger the calculable strategic security based on mutually assured destruction.

For FLR deterrence the influence of violations on the balance can only be hypothetical, because in this case no calculation of the security verification requirement can be made. However, in this study we have assumed that logically the most efficient weapons would be the last to be reduced under the scheme of reductions in the agreement. Furthermore, the numbers of weapons available are large enough to enable a 'limited retaliation'. We may conclude, therefore, that in FLR deterrence as well the requirement for verification is limited, and certainly not greater than that in MAD.

Strategic security and qualitative violations

Consequent upon a disarmament treaty to freeze the quality of weapons states A and B would have to take a number of measures, such as stopping military R&D in the areas covered by the treaty, halting weapons testing and conversion, as well as ceasing to upgrade ICBM and bomber defences. No improvements in the offensive or defensive capabilities of the two arsenals would be permitted at all. Most of these restrictions could be quite easily monitored by contemporary observational systems. As is known from public reports, the great powers have accurate information on each other's missile tests, and are able to discover and to evaluate correctly all construction works where strategic weapons are located on the territory of the other side. Even the conversion of weapons (such as MIRVing) probably could not escape verification if carried out on a large scale.

The most serious difficulty with verification of a qualitative freeze would be monitoring military R&D. None of the technical and non-technical means of observation would be able to provide very accurate or reliable information as to what goes on in scientific laboratories, especially if these R&D activities were highly secret. There are various ways of gaining a rough idea about R&D trends, such as following the scientific literature, examining financing procedures, records from conferences, licences and so on; but the information gained in this way is necessarily secondary, delayed and incomplete.

However, even the difficulty of verifying military R&D is not of decisive importance. There are three main reasons for this:

1. All militarily important technological improvements in strategic weapons have long lead-times from their inception to production and operational deployment. This would permit prolonged observation of the other side's activities.

2. All new strategic weapons must be tested at every stage of their development. It would be unlikely that these tests could be evaded by the sensing devices of the other side.

3. Any disarmament agreement assumes a certain amount of cooperation between the parties, which would tend to work in favour of increasing scientific collaboration, and hence in more information regarding R&D efforts.

To conclude then, verification of a technological freeze, especially at the post-R&D stage, would not be difficult. In the case of MAD deterrence the specific impact of violations of a ban on technological improvements will be analysed and quantified in the discussion of Scenario II, on page 89. In the case of FLR deterrence a proposed freeze on the technological characteristics of weapons could be regarded as diminishing their chances of being able to be either flexible or limited, and so may cause the FLR doctrine to lose its credibility. The natural outcome of such a freeze would thus be a reversal from FLR deterrence to MAD, a doctrine which is much less sensitive to the technical efficiency of weapons.

The above discussion has so far been confined to a technological freeze on weapons and weapons development under the scope of a disarmament treaty. However, the strategic balance would obviously also be responsive to developments in areas not covered by the treaty (such as, for example, tactical weapons capable of strategic missions), and other fields which might affect the deterrent value of the arsenals. This is especially true of anti-submarine warfare.

Because of the character of present-day SLBM forces, enjoying as they do, a very high degree of invulnerability to a first strike against them, the very existence of the residual second strike represented by these sea-based missiles would not depend on any kind of open or clandestine numerical expansion or qualitative improvement made in the submarines themselves. This fact is symbolized by the impossibility of measuring the security verification requirement as we were able to do with ICBM reductions. Being undetectable, and thus invulnerable, strategic submarines have an infinitely large survival potential (KS); hence their residual second-strike value cannot be calculated.

There is an extremely theoretical possibility that a country would consider clandestine numerical expansion of its SLBM arsenal worthwhile, because this larger number would make the equally clandestine efforts in ASW technology by the opponent more difficult. Such production would, however, be quite easy to discover, even for existing monitoring systems the efficiency of which has already been demonstrated by press reports on actual submarine production.

So the only violation of a strategic SLBM disarmament treaty which could jeopardize the security of the states concerned would be the development of more efficient methods of anti-submarine warfare. Once a state was in possession of equipment able to detect and locate its opponent's submarines accurately, wherever they might be, it would be close to acquiring a capability of destroying them. And if the other components of the opponent's strategic arsenal were already endangered by a large number of accurate weapons, such an ASW capability would be tantamount to a position of strategic superiority. Thus all developments in submarine detection techniques would have to be incorporated in an agreement on a qualitative freeze of armaments. In the case of SLBM reductions the security verification requirement could therefore be defined as the need to discover such developments in ASW technology and would not be concerned with the numerical parameters of SLBM forces.

Current ASW activities are a serious obstacle to the present analysis and to any subsequent projections, because on the one hand they are kept highly secret, and on the other they concern an extremely sophisticated technology. For the same reasons it would also be difficult to formulate in detail an agreement concerning a freeze on ASW efforts as part of a general ban on the qualitative arms race. Ideally such an agreement should contain a general ban on both tactical and strategic anti-submarine warfare. At the same time such an agreement, by its very comprehensiveness, would perhaps be the most difficult to achieve and subsequently to verify. An agreement forbidding the production and operation of equipment used solely for anti-strategic submarine warfare would be closer in scope to a treaty on strategic disarmament, but the distinction between tactical and strategic ASW could be difficult to define.

Existing detection systems and movable detection platforms do not as yet present a serious threat to the survivability of nuclear submarines.[12] However, taking into account the vast R&D programmes currently being undertaken in ASW technology, the possibility of a rapid expansion in ASW capabilities cannot be excluded. Such a development would make the survivability of all or at least part of the SLBM force doubtful, thereby undermining the credibility of its rôle of deterrence, and hence its value as the guarantee of strategic security. Because of the secrecy surrounding the real capabilities of these existing detection systems, any freeze on their qualitative improvements in order to avoid surprise of this kind would probably be tantamount to dismantling them. In turn, such operations directed at the destruction, incapacitation or dismantling of the devices lying on the ocean floor, or suspended at great depth, would probably be extremely difficult to monitor, especially if the cooperation of the parties were not secured in advance.

An alternative solution to the problem of SLBM limitations would be to include hunter-killer submarines in the agreement because they are the greatest potential threat to missile-carrying submarines. Such a comprehensive limitation on the different types of nuclear-powered submarines would substantially reduce the danger.[13]

If hunter-killer submarines were abolished the greatest threat to the survivability of SLBM forces would be removed and thus the rôle of those forces as the guarantee of a state's security would be maintained. However, to include hunter-killers as part of an SLBM agreement would probably cause major difficulties in negotiations, especially in view of the fact that these submarines have not hitherto been regarded as strategic weapons in discussions of strategic deterrence or strategic disarmament.

The substance of the security requirement in SLBM limitations is thus the freeze on the qualitative arms race in ASW technology. Although the SLBM reductions considered here are quantitative ones, the security verification requirement during these reductions will be fulfilled completely only if the verification system is successful in monitoring the freeze on qualitative advances in ASW technology.

This freeze on the qualitative arms race could be understood simply as a preservation of ASW capabilities at the level prevailing at the time of concluding the treaty without any expansion or intensification. A more progressive interpretation would have to include some reduction of existing capabilities by dismantling some systems and prohibiting certain operations. Without such limitations on existing systems and activities the states taking part in SLBM reductions would never be assured that the old systems were not being improved and upgraded by the simple exchange of electronic components. Whatever the solution the system verifying such a freeze of ASW capabilities would have to be capable of registering:

1. The emplacement of any new fixed arrays of acoustic detectors. This requirement does not seem very difficult to meet. The emplacement of large and sophisticated sonars would take a long time and would involve large-scale operations.

2. The intensified operations of hunter-killer submarines (if these were not already banned) and their equipment operating in a trailing mode or otherwise. This would probably be a more stringent requirement. However, the trailed missile-carrying submarines themselves should be able to provide enough data about these operations.

3. The full-scale training of crews in ASW operations, especially in trailing modes both of surface and submerged vessels. As the mutual monitoring of all military activities is already a routine matter for the great sea-powers, the verification system could largely rely on this practice.

4. The emissions of the active part of any detection system. This would probably be extremely difficult for a verification system to cope with, because some detectors have direct links with control centres, and others relay data in irregular and cryptographic form.

5. ASW research activities. It would only be possible to register these activities when large-scale operations or tests were being made; otherwise it would be a very unreliable indication of the potential and capabilities of the opponent's ASW technology.

To sum up, the security verification requirement for SLBM reductions amounts to the ability to detect efforts directed at the improvement of the opponent's ASW capabilities. The problem of detection is complicated by the fact that it is difficult to distinguish between ASW against strategic nuclear submarines and ASW against surface traffic and conventional submarines. In accordance with the rule of making the worst plausible assumption when a state's security is at stake, any such expansion and effort would have to be treated as endangering the invulnerability of a state's own submarines.

It should be stressed that a so-called pre-emptive anti-submarine first strike to obtain immunity for the first strike on land-based targets demands that all, or at least the vast majority of the submarines must be destroyed simultaneously.

This demand is extremely difficult to meet; it is conceivable, but only if the number of missile-carrying submarines is very small. The pre-emptive anti-submarine first strike would therefore be theoretically possible at the later stages of SLBM reductions. Even then such a first strike would require a number of favourable conditions for the attacker. Moreover, such an eventuality seems highly improbable from a political point of view, when one considers the degree of the long-term cooperation between disarming states that would be needed in these late stages of SLBM reductions.

This discussion of the influence of ASW on the stability of MAD deterrence stresses the fact that in order to be resilient to changes in the strategic military environment an agreement on strategic disarmament must take into account all those areas relevant to the working of deterrence. Consequently, without provisions controlling strategic sea-based activities, sea-based strategic weapons will be in jeopardy: and because these are the cornerstone of a residual second strike, treaties on strategic arsenals that do not cover them also are bound to operate in much less stable conditions.

The relation between verification and security in Scenario I

So far as ICBM reductions are concerned, the relation between the amount of disarmament and the required level of verification may be summarized as follows (see Graphs 1A.11 and 1A.12, pages 139–140). The relationship is not inversely proportional as Wiesner's graph suggests, except at the very last stages of disarmament. Possible violations of the treaty's stipulations on weapon reductions need not affect the security of the disarming state throughout the length of the disarmament period. Verification solely concerned with security (and not with the actual quotas of weapons reduced) thus has an extremely low requirement of stringency. The requirement for a more stringent verification system increases only when substantial reductions at the final stages of the disarmament scheme diminish the residual second strike of a state to a level below its minimum deterrence threshold. Only at the very end of disarmament will verification require very strict detection capabilities. However, in effect, even this increase in the security verification requirement is only a theoretical concept, because the existing SLBM potential of a country which is disarming can be regarded as the guarantee of its strategic security.

Only during the last stages of comprehensive strategic disarmament, when ICBMs, bombers and SLBMs have been phased out, may the need for strict and intrusive verification methods arise; whether or not it does, will depend on the actual political situation at that stage of disarmament.

It seems then that verification of violations of a technical freeze is of much more relevance to the preservation of the security of states than verification of numerical violations. Whether or not verification can play such a rôle depends, however, on the extent of the freeze; if the agreement covers all the relevant military activities based on highly advanced technology, with nothing left out, then it could play a rôle. What can be ascertained at this stage is that verification which is limited to the numerical aspects of strategic security (numbers of disarmed weapons and numerical violations) has little to do with the preservation of security, and that in order to provide states with a real assurance that the treaty will not harm the balance, the verification system must also be directed to all the technological circumstances surrounding the treaty.

Scenario II: disarmament with unrestricted military technology

Logically, Scenario II would also appear to be an improbable situation. On the surface it would seem irrational for a country to proceed with a substantial and comprehensive strategic disarmament programme, and yet at the same time to engage in an unrestricted technological arms race, because the two processes appear to be diametrically opposed. The absurdity of such a situation is clearly illustrated in Tables 1A.12 and 1A.16, which show the process of synchronous reductions on the one hand and the introduction of hypermodern weapons on the other.

Inconceivable though it may seem, however, Scenario II is not as unrealistic as it might appear; and in certain aspects it closely resembles the real-life situation, where despite widespread disarmament efforts there is still no strong indication that the qualitative arms race is being halted. Thus, although the conclusions drawn from our analysis of Scenario II are inevitably highly theoretical and based on extremely simplified assumptions, they can in fact give some indication of the future impact of the current technological arms race on the issue of disarmament, verification and security. In more concrete terms, by using the analytical tools designed in Scenario I, where we were able to draw certain conclusions about the relationship between disarmament and security in a situation of frozen technology, we can now show what effect this new factor, that is, qualitative improvements in weapon systems, will have on the other two variables. Moreover, the analysis in Scenario II may allow us new, and perhaps more realistic insights into the problems of the relationship between disarmament, verification and the security of states undergoing strategic disarmament.

Throughout the discussion about the merits of the technological arms race between countries A and B the following reservation should be borne in mind as far as the Appendix is concerned: replacement and conversion of strategic weapons systems which, in the real world are extremely complex and politically controversial matters, cannot be predicted with accuracy even in the short term, and even less for a period lasting 15 years. The improvements in arsenals proposed in the Appendix therefore do not pretend to predict future developments accurately, either in numbers of new weapons produced, or in their qualities. The figures adopted there should not be criticized, therefore, on the grounds of inaccuracy, misinterpretation or bias: they merely serve as an indication of the possibilities. Even if we were to change the details of the weapons parameters used, it would have no effect on the method of calculation, nor on the basic logic of the argument.

The figures relating to the qualitative arms race between A and B in the

Appendix are as close as possible to real sources, where information was available. Projections of new weapon procurement plans and information about future weapon development were mainly based on documents from the US Department of Defense.

The calculations made in the Appendix for ICBMs by themselves, show that despite the reductions, and even at a very advanced stage of disarmament when the numbers are almost down to nil, the destructive potential of the two arsenals grows. This results from the technological refinements that have made up for the loss of numerical military capability. Our calculations shown in Table 1A.19 indicate that the offensive potential (measured in KN values) of A's arsenal expands despite the reductions, and falls only as late as the thirteenth stage of reductions below the 1974 level which was that at the beginning of the agreement. By then the number of its ICBMs had fallen from about 1 567 to approximately 150. Similarly, B's offensive potential grows also, and only falls at the eleventh stage to the level at which it started, when its ICBMs decreased from 1 054 to 50 MARVed missiles. This observation, though necessarily rather theoretical, corroborates the well known fact that the quality of strategic weapons is far more important than their quantity.

Even more striking are the fluctuations in the ICBM residual second strikes of countries A and B. It appears that if an inequality in the levels of technological capability is allowed to continue for a long period, then strategic stability may be totally destroyed, because according to the calculations in the Appendix, B acquires a first-strike capability over A's land-based missiles. In relation to ICBMs, therefore, MAD deterrence would then cease to function: country A may inflict substantial damage on B only if it strikes first. The disparity between the retaliatory potential of the two countries is such that before A loses its residual second strike, its security verification requirement is small; and after A is deprived of its retaliatory potential, only a massive production of missiles can re-establish it. Hence, seeing that B possesses an ICBM first strike against the land-based missiles of A, any clandestine ICBM production would have to be of such an order of magnitude that it would be quite easy to detect, and in any case would be so large that it would probably entail a complete breakdown of the limitation agreement. Country B does not therefore need to bother about a tight verification system; from the point of view of its own security such stringent verification would be superfluous.

One of the conclusions from Scenario II may thus be that in terms of ICBM reductions verification provides no security for a country which has lost its land-based second strike; nor is it important for the security of the other state which has acquired a first-strike capability.

This last observation is of great importance to any analysis of the relation between security and verification in bilateral strategic disarmament. It appears that the factor which permits this relationship to exist is the presence of the residual second strike, when both sides reduce their armaments.

In terms of ICBMs alone verification has no bearing on security so long as reductions concern the stock of missiles representing the over-kill capacity of each arsenal. When the reductions enter the phase at which the country's residual second strike is smaller than its minimum deterrence threshold, then verification tends to grow in importance. However, at this stage it must be reiterated that the real 'security' rôle of verification is not arbitrarily to check any action of the other state, but only those actions which have a direct bearing, that is, which directly threaten, one's own residual second strike. In Scenario II it is the critical factor of technology which provides the threat to the residual second strike. As this factor is omitted from the scope of the disarmament agreement, and is therefore uncontrolled, and because verification can only monitor the terms of the agreement, it has no rôle here.

At this point of the analysis we may refer back to Scenario I, where it was asserted that the security protection rôle of verification in monitoring possible numerical violations of the ICBM agreement was small indeed. It is now seen that what really mattered in Scenario I also was monitoring whether or not the basic premise of the scenario, that is, the qualitative freeze on weapons, was being adhered to. This point has been underlined in Scenario II, where we have seen how technological improvements in accuracy and reliability of weapons make a verification of only numerical reductions of strategic weapons redundant. Having made this observation we may now note that in Scenario I, as well as in Scenario II, the real substance of the security verification requirement is not the number of weapons which would need to be clandestinely produced, but the qualitative side of the agreement. In Scenario I we saw that if this could be successfully monitored, then both sides would be assured of security until the end of the ICBM reductions. In Scenario II we have seen the probable consequences of undetected violations of an agreement to a freeze on technological development of weapons. Technological developments were left out of the scope of the agreement, and therefore verification had no rôle to play in the preservation of each side's security.

This can be further exemplified by pointing to the fact that in Scenario I the gradual diminution of the value of the residual second strike was caused only by reductions in each side's arsenal. In Scenario II it is not so much the annual reductions that diminish the practical effect of this residual second strike as developments in the offensive force of the opponent. Thus the reason for the loss of A's residual second strike is not the rate of limitations to which A is subject, but the growing destruction capability of B's arsenal. This growth cannot be controlled by A under the agreement considered in Scenario II, and no verification system operated by A can provide guaranteed defence against the rapid disappearance of its land-based second strike. Given such a situation, in which one country finds that its residual second strike is completely lost, can a strategic disarmament agreement, such as that being discussed here, possibly survive? The answer to this question is positive. Our premise here is that the security of a state *vis-à-vis* its opponent is preserved when it continues to possess a reliable and credible strategic second strike. This second strike is based on a number of different components in each side's arsenal, such as ICBMs, SLBMs, bombers and other strategic weapons existing at the time of the disarmament agreement, and which are being gradually and proportionally reduced during the course of the agreement. Even if the proponents of the Triad in strategic forces were to argue against this, it is obvious that if the numbers of ICBMs are proportionally reduced on both sides, thereby reducing their rôle as the main component of deterrence, then the fact that these other components exist still means that deterrence is credible. Although in Scenario II country A theoretically lost its land-based residual second strike its position was worsened much more in political terms than in terms of real military disadvantage. The existence in its arsenal of an SLBM force allows it an ample residual second strike in the case of an all-out attack by B on its remaining ICBMs. So, despite the 'calculated' disappearance of its land-based residual second strike, it would be to A's advantage to continue reducing its ICBMs under the terms of the agreement, because only by carrying out the reductions to the end, and thus waiting for B to abolish its sophisticated MARVed MIIIs, can it hope to restore an equal strategic balance between itself and country B.

Slightly different reasoning applies to the situation in the Appendix, Scenario II, where FLR deterrence is concerned. Even after country A has lost its residual second strike, it still possesses a number of missiles which may carry out the rôle of deterrence, although below the MAD level, especially when its SLBM forces are still in existence. However, this situation arises simply from the fact that FLR does not permit all-out comparisons of forces, as we are able to make with MAD deterrence; but this does not imply any greater resistance on the part of FLR deterrence to the changes envisaged in Scenario II. On the contrary the more intensive developments in B's military technology would permit activities to which A would probably find it impossible to respond in kind. Consequently country A would have to surrender, because it had already lost its MAD capability as the last resort. Again, in this case too, it follows that any numerical violations would not have much effect on the situation, if of minor importance, and could not be clandestine, if of major importance. Even more than in Scenario I, the importance of the SLBM force cannot be over-emphasized, for here it is only the sea-based missiles that could give A any chance of deterring its opponent.

The assumptions made in the Appendix on the probable expansion of SLBM arsenals are similar to those made about ICBM expansion: B introduces its best missiles with MARV technology, which is not yet available to state A. This MARV technology could rapidly give B's SLBMs an enormous capability, because by expanding the accuracy of its warheads, the probability of kill of these warheads would be so high that re-targeting and repeating the attack on the same target would become unnecessary. Therefore this kill potential is much more real than that based on the aggregated figure of the individual kill potential of warheads, made up by their number rather than by their qualitative characteristics. Country B's SLBM potential after MARVing would therefore become the counter-silo, first-strike arsenal, whose capabilities would be restricted only by problems of command, control and communications (themselves presumably the object of technological developments during an unrestricted qualitative arms race).

Such technological developments in the field of SLBMs would have a destabilizing influence on the balance of security between A and B similar to that occurring in the field of ICBMs. It has already been stressed that the existence of an invulnerable fleet of SLBMs would permit country A to feel strategically secure and to continue its ICBM reductions despite the exposure of its land-based missiles to B's first strike. The abolition of A and B's ICBMs at the end of Scenario II would finally remove the strategic inferiority of A, and restore the strategic balance of the sea-based forces of both countries. Having learned the lesson of the impact of new technology on security relations between A and B during ICBM limitations, it is difficult to imagine that the next phase of strategic reductions would continue without including some provision to restrict the qualitative arms race. However, for the sake of argument, and to illustrate further the impact of unrestricted military technology on disarmament and security-orientated verification, this possibility has been discussed.

First of all, the improvements of weapon qualities greatly strengthen the counter-silo capability of B's SLBMs. If these improvements are made while B is still in possession of its ICBMs, then together these two elements of B's strategic arsenal may be treated by country A as being extremely dangerous for its ICBM residual second strike, assuming it still existed. This does not include the whole complex of political relations that would be disrupted by the disturbed balance of power. Despite all this, however, A's existing sea-based second-strike potential would still be strong enough to preserve a functioning strategic deterrence between itself and B. Even if A's residual land-based second strike were additionally discredited by the new counterforce potential of B's SLBMs, the ICBM disarmament agreement described here need not be affected, nor would security-orientated verification have a rôle to play in these reductions. There is no logical reason for B to strive for even greater counterforce capacity against A through the clandestine production of additional ICBMs. If we accept that a treaty could survive the dramatic change in the strategic situation between A and B, such a violation, which would be easy to discover, would be an extremely good excuse for A to denounce the treaty. There is therefore no need for A to demand a tightening up of the verification system.

Moreover, there is no logical incentive for A to try in a clandestine way to endanger the treaty by installing additional silos to re-establish its lost residual second strike. It would have to build hundreds of them in order to match the offensive potential of B, an effort futile as well as easily discovered by routine monitoring. Another escape for A would be to embark on a programme of building mobile launchers for its ICBMs.

To summarize, the technical improvements in nuclear submarines and SLBMs, though creating an additional imbalance between A and B's strategic forces, would not deprive country A of its strong sea-based residual second strike and would not, therefore, call for a strong, security-orientated verification system to monitor a possible clandestine expansion in numbers of SLBMs. It has already been established in Scenario I that whether or not a state verifies that its opponent has phased out its submarines according to the quotas prescribed by the treaty is immaterial to the preservation of its sea-based second strike and hence for its strategic security.

In the case of SLBM reductions in Scenario I, a prime interest of a security-concerned verification system would be to monitor developments in ASW technology that are part of the wider qualitative arms race prohibited by this scenario. Only by effectively monitoring this aspect of the qualitative arms race can a verification system be regarded as a guarantee of the security of states. Seeing that in Scenario II qualitative improvements in weapon systems are unrestricted and the agreement on SLBM reductions is limited only to quantitative measures, no research and development in ASW and other relevant military activites are prohibited. The outcome of ASW developments cannot be predicted as far ahead as 15 years or more; they are, however, known to be intensive and thoroughgoing. Eventually, and in the long term, such efforts may lead to the ability to locate and identify nuclear submarines, thereby endangering SLBMs to some degree. Once again the state which was more advanced in ASW technology would gain the advantage, causing the other to lose confidence in, or to doubt the invulnerability of, its SLBMs. Just how much damage would be done to the credibility of a country's strategic second strike by undermining its SLBMs' invulnerability is not clear. A country which could rely on other components of its strategic arsenal would perhaps be more reluctant to consider such a situation as a grave danger; but if the sea-based second strike were the sole or most important element remaining in a state's strategic deterrent the loss of its belief in its own invulnerability would mean a serious blow to its perceived security. Furthermore, because the treaty does not apply restrictions to technological advances, such as developments in ASW capabilities, a verification system can only monitor the quantitative terms of the treaty, a function which has no bearing on the maintenance of either state's security.

An additional ASW threat would be the lack of a clause restricting the numbers of hunter-killer submarines in any SLBM reduction agreement. At first glance this may seem an easy problem to solve, because restrictions in the number of these submarines could be just one more quantitative measure linked to SLBM reductions. However, in view of the strategic importance of hunter-killer submarines as the most efficient platform for ASW systems, and thus the core of any serious strategic ASW potential, it would be difficult to make numerical reductions in their number without incorporating ASW developments as a whole. At the same time to leave these weapons outside the control of an agreement would expose the missile-carrying submarines to an ever-increasing danger. Hence, a verification system, if not monitoring reductions in hunter-killer submarines, would not have a protective rôle *vis-à-vis* the SLBM second strike and consequently a state's strategic security. If these submarines were being monitored, a state of affairs which would present much higher demands on the efficiency of verification system, then a relation between verification and disarmament would exist, though it might be difficult to quantify.

In drawing conclusions about the place of hunter-killer submarines in SLBM disarmament, it may be reiterated that, in order to find a relation between verification and the security of a state undertaking a strategic disarmament agreement, this disarmament agreement cannot be restricted only to the narrow core of strategic arsenals, but must cover those areas of military developments in which a threat to the residual second strikes of the disarming states could appear. Otherwise, verification cannot play any substantial rôle in the preservation of the security of states.

When assessing the degree of verification required in an SLBM limitation agreement the important variable is the extent to which developments in ASW might degrade the invulnerability of the SLBM force, and similarly the extent to which the SLBM force can be built to withstand the threat from ASW. On the one hand, ASW is permanently expanding; on the other hand, submarines themselves undergo constant refinements enabling them to operate at greater depths and more quietly, thus making it difficult to locate them accurately. The threat posed by the opponent's ASW can be eliminated to some degree by stationing the SLBM-carrying submarines near one's own coastline. No firm conclusions can be drawn from these variables. Broadly speaking, the smaller the possibility of ASW to locate, identify and thus threaten the invulnerability of SLBMs, the smaller the need for verification because the second strike represented by these SLBMs is not endangered, and so security is kept intact. Conversely, if future developments in ASW technology make possible the accurate detection, identification and localization of these submerged submarines, then the SLBM second strike will be jeopardized, and there will be a need for substantial and efficient verification. Thus in Scenario II where no restrictions on ASW developments were imposed, verification of the quantitative aspects of SLBM reductions would have no relevance to the stragetic security of states carrying them out.

At this point mention may be made of the fact that even without specific agreements on ASW verification some countries possess and utilize their capabilities to monitor the ASW activities of all other states as a matter of course. Information about extensive ASW operations would, therefore, be available to these countries in any case. A specific verification agreement would then be very helpful, but not indispensible, for the protection of the sea-based second strike of the disarming states.

If the reductions of SLBMs were continued until the very end of the agreement, when only few submarines were left in stock, then the real issue of verification as a protector of the security of states pursuing SLBM reductions would arise. This would be particularly difficult where ASW capabilities were not subject also to restrictions and control. A small number of submarines would be easier to locate, and by virtue of this, easier to destroy. Even one submarine, existing illegitimately, would undermine the delicate balance of strategic forces and pose a serious threat to a number of targets through the multitude of its accurate warheads. However, such an eventuality must be treated as an extremely theoretical and doubtful possibility because it would become apparent only after many years of disarmament, when cooperation and goodwill between the disarming states had become established, and when creation of a comprehensive mutual and stringent verification system would not be the same difficult political issue that it is today.

The question of strategic bombers undergoing reductions in Scenario II will be touched on only briefly here. Suffice it to say that air bases would be even more exposed than other weapons to a large number of very accurate ICBM warheads. In addition the advanced SLBMs now able to undertake hard-target attacks and to destroy any shelter would cause a very high rate of attrition, especially if they were fired from platforms close to their targets. Thus, in the case of country A the existence of strategic bombers would not be able to be a substitute for a non-existent ICBM second strike, particularly because the more technologically advanced state B would probably be able to develop appropriate countermeasures against the retaliating bombers of state A (that is, those left over after, or in the air during, the attack). However much state A in turn expanded the offensive capabilities of its bombers, especially by enhancing their ability for penetration and firepower, B would still be in the stronger position.

To summarize, it seems clear that the strategic situation between states A and B would not be sensitive to clandestine violations of an agreement to reduce bombers, neither in MAD or in FLR deterrence. This is because these weapons are so much easier to monitor than others, and the deployment of large numbers would be easy to discover, whilst small numbers would not matter decisively. Moreover, a verification system checking the numbers of bombers reduced could not prevent their higher rate of probable destruction, represented by technologically more advanced weapons such as SLBMs. Similarly the numbers of weapons being reduced matter less than the technological state of the art in the weapons system which is able to threaten the reduced armaments.

New strategic weapon systems

It seems obvious that in a situation such as that evolving in Scenario II, where state A lost its residual second strike, it would be forced to take appropriate countermeasures. As, by definition, A is inferior to country B, it cannot hope to catch up by directly competing in the field of military technology. What it can do, however, is to strive for improvements in the invulnerability of its strategic forces, either by making its missile force mobile; by designing anti-ASW systems to protect its missile-carrying submarines; or by establishing ABM systems able to defend to some degree its ICBM sites. Though these measures by themselves may not be regarded by country A as threatening the mutual military stability between itself and B, the final effects of such action would be bound to undermine this balance, especially so far as country B were concerned. This would be particularly the case if ABMs were introduced into the deterrence picture, as shown in Afheldt and Sonntag's study, and by the actual ABM debate in the USA. What one side may regard as purely defensive and security-orientated is seen by the other as a dangerous encroachment on the efficacy of its second strike.

So, even apart from the negative consequences of unrestricted military technology on the security relationship between countries A and B, merely defensive efforts on the part of one state would undermine the entire logic of an agreement. Moreover, if the arms limitation agreement did incorporate some provisions for controlling new areas of weapons development, such provisions would create exceptionally great demands on the efficiency of a verification system, especially so far as mobile systems and anti-ASW developments are concerned.

The relation between verification and security in Scenario II

Despite the different conditions underlying Scenarios I and II our conclusions are largely the same for both: namely, that verification is not directly related to the strategic situation of states undertaking numerical reductions of their arsenals, either when taking place against a background of a freeze on the qualitative arms race, or when such a qualitative arms race is allowed (see Graphs 1A.19 and 1A.21).

The strategic balance between states A and B, and their security based on this balance, can in principle be undermined only by technological military developments, not by quantitative changes in their arsenals, whether legal or illegal. Because of this destabilizing effect of technological developments, both in ICBM and SLBM reductions, the process of disarmamant considered here has been seriously disturbed, if not completely disrupted. In the case of ICBMs, unrestricted technology brought about a situation in which one state acquired a first strike against the other. Similarly, in the case of SLBMs, uncontrolled refinements in ASW technology undermined the fundamental feature of the sea-based deterrent, that is, its invulnerability. If verification were not involved in monitoring these technological developments, it would have no rôle whatsoever in the preservation of the strategic security of states.

Thus two observations of a general character can be made: first, that the only function for verification so far as the strategic security of disarming states is concerned is to preserve the existence of their residual second strikes; to check that they are not imbalanced by the clandestine actions of states; and in the case of SLBMs, to insure that they remain invulnerable. If verification cannot play this rôle, or if these residual second strikes cease to exist for whatever cause, the verification of strategic disarmament has no influence on the preservation of a state's security. Secondly, the main object of verification in strategic disarmament, if it is to fulfil the aforementioned function, is the development of military technology, or rather to see if that technology is being kept at the mutually agreed level. To what extent military technology is verifiable, if at all, will not be discussed here, although it is obviously a crucial and consequential issue.

To conclude, it may be said that to be able to protect a state's security the verification system need not be linked with the objects of strategic disarmament. It should rather direct itself to those military areas where a threat to the residual second strike may emerge. Alerting the parties of an agreement to the dangers to their deterrent capabilities is thus another facet of the security-linked function of verification. However, the implications of this are that all strategic agreements must be wider in scope than merely covering the strategic weapons themselves. Hunter-killer submarines are a case in point. Whereas they would not normally be classified as classical strategic weapons, any treaty to reduce SLBMs which did not also include limitations on hunter-killers as well as provisions for monitoring their numbers and technological improvements would be irrelevant, because the SLBM residual strike would remain exposed and thus jeopardize a state's security.

References and Notes to Chapter 6

1. Verification was understood from the very beginning as a protection for states which comply with treaty provisions 'against the hazards of violations and evasions' according to the Joint Declaration of the Heads of Government of the United States, the United Kingdom, and Canada, 15 November 1945, or to the Moscow Communiqué by the Foreign Ministers of the United States, the United Kingdom and the Soviet Union, 27 December 1945, and several other documents.
2. See, for example, the stipulation in the Baruch Plan: 'When an adequate system for control of atomic energy, including the renunciation of the bomb as a weapon, has been agreed upon and put into effective operation . . . we propose that:
    1. Manufacture of atomic bombs shall stop;
    2. Existing bombs shall be disposed of pursuant to the terms of the treaty . . .';
    and also US Representative H. Stassen's proposal on the reduction of conventional forces: 'if the inspection and control methods were installed and operating reasonably and satisfactorily, the United States would be willing under the circumstances to make definite reductions in the first stage in the levels of its armaments . . .'
    T. N. Dupuy and G. M. Hammerman, eds., *A Documentary History of Arms Control and Disarmament* (New York 1973), pp. 305 and 383.
3. Statement of the Soviet Representative, A. Gromyko, of 19 June 1945, and the other documents in *A Documentary History of Arms Control and Disarmament, op. cit.*, pp. 310 ff.
4. Point 6 of the Joint Statement on Principles for Disarmament Negotiations, 22 September 1961, UN Doc. A/4879; see also Exchange of letters of McCloy and Zorin in *Documents on Disarmament*, (Arms Control and Disarmament Agency, 1961), pp. 442–44.
5. Rodberg, L. S., in S. Melman, ed. *Rationale of Inspection in Disarmament: Its Politics and Economics* (Boston, 1962), p. 68.
6. Wiesner, J. B., Inspection for Disarmament, in L. Henkin, ed., *Arms Control, Issues for the Public* (Columbia University, 1961), p. 113.
7. Wiesner, J. B., Inspection for Disarmament, *ibid.*, p. 137.
8. Falk, R. A., Inspection, Trust and Security During Disarmament, in: R. A. Falk and R. J. Barnett, eds., *Security in Disarmament* (Princeton, 1965).
9. *Ibid.*, pp. 41 and 48.
10. Davis, J. K. *et al.*, *The SALT II and the Search for Strategic Equivalence*, Foreign Policy Research Institute Monograph Series, Number Nineteen, 1975, Philadelphia, in association with Lexington Books (Lexington, Mass., D.C. Heath and Co., p. 46); Rathjens, G. W. *et al.*, *Nuclear Arms Control Agreements: Process and Impact* (Washington, Carnegie Endowment for Peace, 1974), p. 4; Kahan, J. H., Stable Deterrence: a Strategic Policy for the 1970's, *Orbis*, Vol. XV, No. 2, Summer 1971, p. 532; Lambeth, B. S., Deterrence in the MIRV Era, *World Politics*, Vol. XXIV, No. 2, January 1972, p. 224; Moulton, H. B., *From Superiority to Parity, The United States and the Strategic Arms Race, 1961–1971* (Greenwood Press, Inc., 1973), p. 280.
11. Neither the numbers nor the technical characteristics of weapons existing in the US and Soviet arsenals are equal – quite the contrary. However, these two qualitatively and quantitatively different stragetic arsenals match each other in a peculiar way described in various terms, such as 'nuclear parity', 'essential equality' (President Nixon's Report to the US Congress, 1973, p. 202); 'rough comparability' (Kahan, J. H., Stable Deterrence: a Strategic Policy for the 1970's, *op. cit.*, p. 528);

'dynamic equilibrium' (Hahn, W. F., The Nixon Doctrine: Design and Dilemmas, *Strategic Digest*, Vol. II, No. 12, December 1972, p. 24); and 'equality of deterring power' (Moulton, H. B., *From Superiority to Parity, op. cit.*, p. 27, quoting Arnold Wolfers), to give a few examples.

J. K. Davis *et al.* cite three basic criteria for essential equivalence between strategic forces:

1. both sides should maintain survivable second-strike reserves,

2. there should be symmetry in the ability of each side to threaten the other, including counterforce options,

3. there should be a perceived equality between offensive forces of both sides. (*The SALT II and the Search for Strategic Equivalence, op. cit.*, p. 47).

For the definition of 'essential equivalence' see also 'US–USSR Strategic Policies'. Hearing before the Subcommittee on Arms Control, International Law and Organization of the Committee on Foreign Relations, US Senate, 93rd Congress, 2nd session on US and Soviet Strategic Doctrine and Military Policies, 4 March 1974.

12. *Tactical and Strategic Antisubmarine Warfare*, SIPRI Monograph (Stockholm, Almqvist & Wiksell, Cambridge, Mass., MIT, Stockholm International Peace Research Institute, 1974); Tsipis, K. *et al.*, eds., *The Future of the Sea-based Deterrent* (Boston 1973); and Garwin, R. L., Antisubmarine Warfare and National Security, *Scientific American*, Vol. 227, No. 1, July 1972.

13. Davis, J. K. *et al.*, *The SALT II and the Search for Strategic Equivalence, op. cit.*, p. 59.

Conclusions

The difficulties connected with the verification of disarmament have, for a rather too long period, been seen as a function of the technological inadequacies of the means and methods used for gaining the information necessary to check whether or not treaties were being fully implemented. The present study has tried to avoid these specific technical problems of verification, maintaining that, although they still represent a problem to be dealt with by disarmament negotiators, they no longer play a crucial rôle in hindering disarmament progress. Instead we have found that political will and confluence of a number of other political factors are the main conditions necessary for an initial agreement on disarmament and for ensuring that the provisions of that agreement are carried out. Without this political will, and no matter how much verification there is, disarmament treaties are unlikely to be successful.

In view of this we see the rôle of verification more in terms of preserving general political stability than in its purely legal and technical function as a monitor of the mere terms of a treaty. We imply that the basic function of verification is a mechanism for building confidence; that its rôle is to help preserve the political context on which states based their expectations when they constructed, and became participants in, a disarmament agreement. More specifically, this function consists in providing not only the basic information necessary for demonstrating the proper implementation of the provisions of a treaty, but also in providing a channel for querying and explaining ambiguities in the conduct of the parties and in the treaty itself. More indirectly, verification would tend to enlarge the sphere of international cooperation in the sensitive field of disarmament.

In short, therefore, verification is seen as having a 'pacifying' rôle, ensuring that the implementation of a disarmament agreement actually lives up to the expectations of the parties and does not undermine their security. Such a rôle would have to be considered as being quite different from the 'watchdog' function attributed so strongly to verification in the past.

This shift in our understanding of the tasks that verification may and should fulfil in disarmament is corroborated by our analysis of all the factors other than verification that condition the implementation of disarmament agreements. It appears that, although these factors are not incorporated in any formal way into agreements, they nevertheless play a decisive rôle in shaping policy of states towards disarmament – both before such agreements are concluded, during their implementation, and in the case of breaches or withdrawals. Verification may provide the factual evidence on which certain actions of states may be based, or which may *ex post* justify their behaviour; there are, however, certain conditions on which verification, and the data provided by it, have no influence at all, such as the factor of military technology in the fields not covered by a disarmament treaty, or the factor of developments in a third party, not a member of the treaty.

Our analysis of these factors indicates that the balance between them generally supports the drive of parties to an agreement to carry out their disarmament obligations once they undertake them. Only a drastic change in the international situation introducing new, critical factors which might influence the security of the parties to an agreement would be likely to force them to reconsider their position *vis-à-vis* the agreement, and ultimately possibly to renounce their obligations. There again, verification would hardly have a rôle to play, because the renunciation of a treaty is more likely to be an open, rationally taken political action than a covert and time-consuming violation.

Thus it may be assumed that the verification of disarmament plays a rôle primarily as one of those factors helping to create a positive international atmosphere in which disarmament can function. Together with all the other factors it can help to provide an environment in which disarmament not only does not undermine the security of states, but also benefits the positions of the participating states.

National interests are commonly cited by governments and politicians as a fundamental basis for their actions, and for this reason they must be regarded as an important factor in determining the domestic and foreign policy of states. At the same time, as our analysis indicates, the scope and meaning of the term is extremely vague and undefined, depending on the subject, social group or class using it, and the point in time at which it is used. The same applies to the concept of national security, which is rarely, if at all, objectively defined; and rather depends on what is subjectively conceived to be security or insecurity at a particular point in time. Both these terms have been extensively used in connection with disarmament. How pertinent they are to the subject, and whether or not their usage has been ambiguous, may well be exemplified by the fact that the same concepts might be used both as a justification for the conclusion of a disarmament measure and as an excuse for the renunciation of exactly the same disarmament measure.

What must be taken into consideration, however, is the fact that the condition of security is a constant requirement for all states. All countries desire to be permanently secure. It is the external and internal conditions for maintaining that security which vary and which are so difficult to assess properly. It is this that makes the application of the concept so controversial.

One of the most dynamic factors which may drastically influence these conditions is disarmament; hence a great amount of concern about security in disarmament. A classical approach to the problem is one which assumes a direct link between disarmament and the security of states, so that any progress in disarmament (that is, a reduction in the numbers of weapons in a state's arsenal) is tied up with a corresponding decline in that state's security. In such a situation it is believed that the only substitute for the decline in security is the mechanism of verification which monitors the agreed levels of arms limitations. The present study has analysed the validity of this assumption so far as strategic disarmament is concerned.

We acknowledge that the analysis was much simplified. It considers only the case of strategic nuclear disarmament between two states; it concentrates only on one element of a state's security, the military one, because it seems to be the most important, and most easily quantified one. (It also has the advantage of being the element most easily discerned and the one that is the most stable.) Moreover, the present study lacks any political and economic analysis, and the calculations on which it is based are loaded with a number of shortcomings and oversimplifications. However, given the purpose of the study, it is believed that these limitations do not undermine its main conclusions.

The military security of the states analysed here is a special case (which adds to the unique character of the situation under consideration). It is strategic military security based on the existence of stable nuclear deterrence between two countries undertaking strategic disarmament, both of which countries have a vast overkill capability provided by a great number and variety of weapons. The preservation of this stability of deterrence during the process of strategic disarmament has been assumed to be the main rôle of verification if it is to be regarded as a substitute for security in disarmament.

However, the results of the analysis at least undermine, and seem in fact to contradict the assumption of a direct relationship between the verification of disarmament and security, at least in the context of nuclear deterrence. This is illustrated by the graphs in the Appendix, which give rise to our conclusion that the relationship is not a direct one: the numerical reductions in strategic weapons do not cause a corresponding decline in security until the very last stages of the disarmament process, and thus verification does not need to be increased as weapons are reduced. When measured as the value of the security verification requirements, the 'real' demand for verification from the military security point of view is strikingly small. This situation lasts until the very advanced stages of strategic disarmament, and even more so when the disarmament scheme is designed in such a way that the sea-based deterrent forces are maintained for as long as possible. In short, therefore, only when the arsenals have been substantially reduced, and are therefore vulnerable to a rationally planned and successful rate of concealed development and deployment of strategic weapons, does verification become a critical factor in maintaining the security of disarming states. On the other hand, it can be said that so long as the states concerned continue to possess their residual second strikes, the rôle of verification in preserving security, though extremely limited, undoubtedly exists; moreover, this rôle grows with the advances in disarmament. In such a context the basic rule saying that: 'disarmament is attainable only as a controllable process' is still valid.[1]

This observation is, however, seriously undermined when the same disarmament schedule takes place against a background of uncontrolled technological improvements in strategic weapons (assuming at the same time that the technological capabilities of the disarming state are unequal). The situation evolving from such a new setting is bound, obviously, to be regarded as exaggerated and lacking in precision, especially in that it assumes the possibility of the acquisition of a first-strike capability. This assumption is, of course, fallacious in real terms; however, theoretically, a scenario which allows uncontrolled advances in military technology, both in qualities of missile systems and ASW technologies, may logically result in something close to an overall strategic preponderance of one side over the other, which would resemble a strategic first-strike situation.

In the context of disarmament carried out alongside an unrestricted technological arms race, the relation between verification and strategic security appears at first to be completely irrelevant, and later on ceases to exist at all. It appears, moreover, that the real security requirement in strategic disarmament is not verification, but the control of technology. It is in this field that the means of destroying the other side's residual second strike are created and developed, thereby jeopardizing the scheme of disarmament, and even ultimately halting it.

The direct relation between disarmament, verification and strategic security as outlined by Wiesner seems therefore to need to be strongly qualified by the strategic context in which disarmament takes place. We argue that it is not disarmament, but unrestricted and hence unverified technology which deprives one country of its security *vis-à-vis* the other, and that it is not verification of numbers of weapons being potentially concealed, but the verification of the technology itself, which may provide disarming states with security, understood as the maintenance of their residual second strikes. The existence of the residual second strike, as was seen in Scenario II, depends not so much on the maintenance of numerical balances – which is the classical understanding of the rôle of verification – as on the preservation of a balance between military technological developments in both disarming countries. Thus, if verification is to play a rôle in preserving a state's security, it follows that it must guarantee the existence of the residual second strike, and by the same token must be technologically able and legally entitled to monitor military technological progress, which is the only real threat to this second strike. To be able to do this, an agreement on strategic disarmament must cover the relevant military technological areas, in addition to numbers and types of weapons.

Two observations can be drawn from the above statement. The first is that verification has only a small rôle to play so far as numbers are concerned. The second is that its rôle in safeguarding the implementation of constraints in technological arms developments is vital.

The function of verification in disarmament thus finds a new emphasis as the crucial means of maintaining security during disarmament. At the same time it must be noted that the technical difficulties in verifying technological activities will be even greater than those associated with the verification of mere numbers, thereby putting additional demands of stringency and flexibility on the verification system, and such difficulties may even be insurmountable without special political effort.

Given the complexity and size of the present strategic arsenals, it is believed that, even in a situation of constant developments in military technology, little possibility exists of a breakthrough able to threaten the existing strategic equilibrium. H. Brooks, for example, writes: 'In the forseeable future, the qualitative arms race is not likely to lead to major strategic instabilities, provided the ABM treaty remains in force.'[2]

This opinion seems correct only in so far as the arms race is concerned.

In the case of disarmament, which gradually limits the numbers as well as the room for free expansion in the qualities of weapons, qualitative violations of a disarmament agreement could lead to great instability and hence insecurity. The rôle of verification then seems to be vital.

In stressing the importance of controlling and verifying military technology during a disarmament agreement, it must be noted that the issue is inherently contradictory: the stress on control and verification of technology as a vital necessity means that technology becomes the main object of verification, which is at the same time technically the most difficult object for verification.

That progress in military technology makes verification a more urgent matter may be seen from Graph 1A.22. There the lines illustrating the level of required verification in Scenarios I and II for countries A and B are shown. It is clear that the lines of the required level of verification for both A and B ascend earlier in Scenario II than in Scenario I. This is particularly clear in the case of country A.

Similar evidence is given in Graph 1A.20. Here we consider points α of these two countries and their values in Scenario II. The level of completely satisfied security is tantamount to the value of verification required, and in both cases equals unity. The lines of the verification required in Scenario II miss these points and ascend much earlier. It may be seen that what has been one unit required in Scenario I is equal to 37.64 in Scenario II for country A and what has been unity in Scenario I is equal to 4.32 for country B in Scenario II. This illustrates an expansion in the requirement for verification at the level of fully satisfied security due to the technological changes as envisaged in Scenario II.

A more visible impact of military technology on verification is that of the introduction of new weapon systems which complicates the verifiability of the existing and improved weapon systems. This point can be illustrated by the following table, which is obviously far from complete and serves only as a simple illustration:

Unit of reduction	*Unit of verification*
ICBM	ICBM
Bomber	Bomber
SLBM	Submarine
MIRVs (on ICBMs)	ICBM
MIRVs (on SLBMs)	Submarine
ALCMs	Bomber
SLCMs	Submarine
Military R&D	? (expenditure?)

This table shows the growing discrepancy between the terms in which a disarmament agreement is bound to be worded and the actual 'unit of verification', namely, the object which can in fact be monitored. This tendency may pose serious problems, because it may cause any verification system to be very inaccurate – inaccurate beyond the acceptable limits – thus restraining negotiators from accepting both the verification and the legal norm which was to cover the weapon system in question.

The aforementioned difficulties with the expansion of weapons technology appeared already during the SALT negotiations in connection with MIRVs. A new problem of the same nature emerges as a result of the appearance of strategic cruise missiles – objects which are rather small and which can be stored in large numbers on aircraft, submarines, surface ships and any other means of transport. These weapons, when finally introduced into the strategic arsenals, would be virtually unverifiable by national means of verification, and hardly verifiable even by very intrusive systems of inspection.

Thus military technology has four negative implications for strategic disarmament:

1. It makes the negotiation of an agreement more difficult and in the extreme case may even foreclose the possibilities of concluding it.

2. It may jeopardize agreements that have already been concluded. The disarmament scheme may then be halted and subsequently reversed.

3. It makes the verification of disarmament less efficient, and may in specific instances completely inhibit the capabilities of verification, even when the verification system is highly costly and intrusive.

4. It undermines the security of states undertaking disarmament, regardless of whether verification is operating or not.

Furthermore, in connection with the third point it would be improper to omit yet another contradiction in the rôle of new technology in disarmament and verification. It has been argued so far that the military technological drive is extremely dangerous when states undertake disarmament simultaneously. However, it must be realized that technology is also responsible for making possible the existence of technically advanced means of monitoring. The rôle of the national means of verification is already well known. There is also the growing possibilitity of the international application of many different technical devices able to check, monitor, analyse and store various data useful in the verification of disarmament, whether in seismology, chemical production or nuclear energy. Having accepted the positive influence of technology on the capacity for verification, it is important to stress the well known fact that verification lags permanently behind the requirements posed by developments in military technology, and moreover that there are areas, such as military R&D, in which no technological breakthroughs are possible to make it more verifiable. The only cure in this case may be rational political effort.

The last observation made on the basis of our study concerns a more general disarmament question, that of the general principles of disarmament settled in the Zorin–McCloy agreement of 1961 and applied during subsequent disarmament negotiations. Two points of the agreed principles concerning the equality of security in disarmament and the requirements for verification, namely, points 5 and 6, are most relevant to our study. They read:

> 5. All measures of general and complete disarmament should be balanced so that at no stage of the implementation of a treaty could any State or group of States gain a military advantage and that security is ensured equally for all.
> 6. All disarmament measures should be implemented from the begin-

ning to end under such strict and effective international control as would provide firm assurance that all parties are honouring their obligations . . .²

Undoubtedly, these principles have proved to be generally adequate in the context of theoretical and comprehensive disarmament measures. However, seeing that they were intended to be guidelines for general and complete disarmament, comprising problems of enormous variety and complexity, they were of necessity imprecise. It seems, therefore, that any single disarmament measure, though in broad agreement with the Zorin–McCloy principles, would require much more precise definitions so as to respond adequately to the demands of the specific acts of disarmament covered by the agreement.

With reference to point 5 of the agreed principles it appears from our study that the only way of ensuring a true balance during strategic disarmament is to incorporate measures which would control technological military developments. Without them there is no way of fulfilling this principle, at least, not in the long run. Sooner or later the technologically more advanced state will overrun – by a margin, or decisively – the other state in fields that are not governed by the treaty régime, and though states may keep to the letter of the agreement, their security would not be equally ensured. Either in actual fact, or only subjectively, the result would be the same: eventual renunciation of the treaty, or a breach. This observation seems to apply not only to pure strategic disarmament but also to a large extent to general and complete disarmament, because GCD will also have to begin with, or contain, elements of the field of strategic disarmament, and it is here that the impact of highly developed technology is at its greatest.

Secondly, in the light of the case-study considered in this book point 6 of the agreed principles might be revised even more drastically. Though the models considered here are largely oversimplified and deficient, we maintain that in a situation of deterrence based on roughly equal or comparable strategic forces composed of a variety of numerous weapon systems, both on land, sea and in the air, any 'strict and effective international control' would not be necessary from the point of view of military security. This is not to say that there may not be a political demand from either side for such control, which would be easily justifiable on the grounds of strict legality. In fact the value of a verification system in strategic disarmament must be seen rather in terms of its function as a 'conducive' or 'pacifying' element in disarmament.

References to conclusions

1. Kurs Miezhdunazodnogo Prava. Vol. V, Izdatielstvo 'Nauka', Moskva 1969, p. 225.
2. Brooks, H., Military Innovation System in, *Arms, Defense Policy and Arms Control* (Daedalus, 1975), p. 81.
3. *Documents on Disarmament*, (Arms Control and Disarmament Agency, 1961), p. 440.

Appendix

This appendix is a specific case-study of strategic disarmament between two countries, A and B. Its aim is to illustrate fully the questions discussed at length in Chapter 6. Because it is so specific and full of figures, formulae and quantified data, it seems appropriate to separate it from the rest of the book. In this Appendix mathematical methods are used to calculate the specific quantified expressions of such notions as 'strategic security' and 'military security verification requirement'. The purpose of these calculations is in line with the underlying idea of the whole book; namely, to make precise, in an objective (quantified) way, the relationship between security and verification during the process of strategic disarmament. The material obtained from these calculations was used extensively to support the conclusions of Chapter 6.

In order to indicate the rôle of military technology, which is a factor of special significance during strategic disarmament, two scenarios were designed: one, where technology is kept frozen during the process of disarmament; and the other, where technology is allowed to develop unhindered. A comparison of the results from the two scenarios should point to the effects of technology on disarmament in general, and on the relationship between verification and security during disarmament in particular.

The arms reductions discussed in Scenarios I and II began in 1974. This process of reduction is planned to take 15 years, after which period the strategic arsenals of both participants will be completely abolished. The structure of the arsenals is initially identical for both Scenario I and Scenario II. During subsequent years the weapons structures of the two scenarios diverge on account of the qualitative technological changes envisaged in Scenario II. In each scenario, reductions of land-based ICBMs will be considered first, followed by a discussion of reductions in sea-based missiles.

At the outset of ICBM reductions, the numbers of strategic weapons are 'frozen' at the 1974 levels, and a complete freeze on the qualitative features of strategic weapons is simultaneously agreed upon. This freeze means that no improvement which augments the offensive or defensive capability of the reduced arsenals may be made. No new weapon may be introduced during the period of reductions, no silos may be reinforced and no underground nuclear tests may be carried out. Finally, no work aimed at improving the accuracy of weapons is allowed, that is, no tests with ICBMs are permitted at all.

In fact a freeze on performance parameters such as that proposed here has never been made. Here it is only a theoretical concept. The intention is not to describe real procedures of disarmament but to illustrate the impact of qualitative factors on security and verification during strategic disarmament.

Table 1A.1. ICBM forces of countries A and B at 1974, and their characteristics

Type of missile	Number of missiles and silos	Yield of warhead (Y) Mt	Accuracy[a] (CEP) nmile	Reliability[a] (OAR) per cent	Silo hardness[a] (H) lb/in²	Category silo
Country A						
SS7	139	5	(1)	75	100	Soft
SS8	70	5	(1)	75	100	Soft
SS11 model 1	500	1	1	75	100	Soft
SS11 model 1	470	1	1	75	300	Hard
SS11 model 3	40	1	1	75	300	Hard
SS13	60	1	1	75	300	Hard
SS9	188	20	1	75	100	Soft
SS9	100	20	1	75	300	Hard
Total	*1 567*					
Country B						
TII	54	5	0.5	80	300	Hard
MI	100	1	0.5	80	300	Hard
MII	500	1	0.3	80	300	Hard
MIII	400	3×0.16	0.2	80	1 000	Super
Total	*1 054*					

[a] The figures are estimates and rounded.

I. The structure and characteristics of A and B's ICBM arsenals, 1974

The structure and capabilities of the arsenals A and B are presented in Table 1A.1, which shows the numbers and types of individual missiles existing in the arsenals of the two countries. The figures adopted here are by and large in conformity with those given in the description of the US and Soviet arsenals in the SIPRI Yearbook 1974.[1] As far as the hardness of silos, and the accuracy and reliability of missiles are concerned, they are rather subjective approximations, based on the median values of those quoted in numerous sources.[2] The category of the silo indicated in the last column of the table is the same as that used in the text and does not conform to any official classification.

II. Rules for carrying out ICBM reductions[3]

1. Reductions proceed until the total abolition of the land-based ICBM forces of countries A and B has been achieved. These reductions will take place

in 15 subsequent stages over a period of 15 years, starting from the 1974 levels of arsenals.

2. Reductions are designed to keep to a minimum the disparity between the ratio of A and B's forces (the second strike) that survive a hypothetical attack. The most desirable outcome would be to equalize these surviving forces in the latter stages of limitations. This is impossible, however, on account of the enormous disparities in the aggregate values of the offensive and defensive forces of the respective countries.

3. The oldest and the most obsolescent weapons would be liable for reductions first. In some instances other criteria, such as the kill potential of a missile, might alter this rule, as in the case of Titan II which represents substantial destructive potential.

4. The ratio of numbers of missiles and warheads should also be taken into account, especially at the beginning of limitations when they play an important rôle politically, although in practice the differences at this stage are still within the limits of parity of balance.

5. At any given stage the missiles being reduced in numbers should preferably be of the same type, that is, have the same parameters (size). This arrangement would make the process of reductions easier to monitor by national technical means of verification.

6. Numerically and so far as is possible in terms of type of missiles reductions in Scenario I and II should be identical.

Discussion of the rules for reductions

Rule 1 determines the rate at which the limitations will take place. This rate is considered sufficient for maintaining the momentum of reductions, whilst being not so rapid that the process of reductions will become uncontrollable in terms either of verification or management. At the beginning of limitations the number of missiles reduced in a given year represents approximately 10 per cent of the total number. By the end of the process the number per year will amount to a much higher proportion of the total, say some 50 per cent. This proportion may appear excessively high, but to slow down the process of reductions at its conclusion seems dangerous to the security of states. If these ICBM arsenals are maintained at a low level over a long period, their balance could be easily upset in favour of one or the other state by clandestine production of even small numbers of weapons. (On the other hand, because the process of limitations will have been both lengthy and, by definition, successful up to this point, it may be overcautious to suspect the intentions and probable actions of the states involved.)

Many of the initial conditions are both contradictory in character and inextricably interlinked. Thus it is impossible with the aid of a mathematical formula, to arrive at quotas of annual reductions of missiles which would at the same time fulfil rules 1 to 4 above. Such factors as the ratios between A and B's residual second strikes (for a definition, see page 116), the ratios of numbers of missiles and warheads, the relationship between the kill and survival potentials (measured

Table 1A.2. Scenario I: ICBM reductions of countries A and B, 1974–1989 (MRVs counted as single warheads).

Stage or year or reduction	Country	Number and type of ICBMs reduced	Number of ICBMs reduced so far	Number of ICBMs remaining in inventory after reduction	A:B ratio of ICBMs after reduction	Number of warheads after reduction	A:B ratio of warheads after reduction
1974	A	Freeze	—	1 567	1.49	1 567	0.85
	B		—	1 054		1 854	
1. 1975	A	109 SS7	109	1 458	1.48	1 458	0.82
	B	70 MI	70	984		1 784	
2. 1976	A	30 SS7 70 SS8	209	1 358	1.49	1 358	0.79
	B	30 MI 40 MII	140	914		1 714	
3. 1977	A	150 SS11-1	359	1 208	1.48	1 208	0.75
	B	100 MII	240	814		1 614	
4. 1978	A	150 SS11-1	509	1 058	1.48	1 058	0.70
	B	100 MII	340	714		1 514	
5. 1979	A	150 SS11-1	659	908	1.48	908	0.64
	B	100 MII	440	614		1 414	
6. 1980	A	150 SS11-1[a]	809	758	1.48	758	0.58
	B	100 MII	540	514		1 314	
7. 1981	A	150 SS11-1	959	608	1.52	608	0.51
	B	60 MII 54 TII	654	400		1 200	

8. 1982	A	150 SS11-1	1 109	458		458	
	B	100 MIII	754	300	1.53	900	0.51
9. 1983	A	70 SS11-1 40 SS11-3	1 259	308		308	
	B	40 SS13 100 MIII	854	200	1.54	600	0.51
10. 1984	A	20 SS13 38 SS9	1 317	250		250	
	B	50 MIII	904	150	1.67	450	0.56
11. 1985	A	50 SS9	1 367	200		200	
	B	40 MIII	944	110	1.82	330	0.64
12. 1986	A	50 SS9	1 417	150		150	
	B	30 MIII	974	80	1.88	240	0.63
13. 1987	A	50 SS9	1 467	100		100	
	B	30 MIII	1 004	50	2.00	150	0.67
14. 1988	A	50 SS9	1 517	50		50	
	B	25 MIII	1 029	25	2.00	50	0.67
15. 1989	A	50 SS9	1 567	—		—	
	B	25 MIII	1 054	—		—	

[a] This number comprises 50 SS11s in 'soft' silos and 100 SS11s in 'hard' silos. Entries thus — are negligible amounts.

either in lethality (K) values or in kill probability) of a missile and a silo protecting it, vary disproportionately during reductions. Thus, in comparison with country B, country A has a great number of missiles but a smaller number of warheads; furthermore, its residual second strike is inferior to B's second strike. Any attempt at equalizing their respective residual second strikes will result in changing the proportions of numbers of missiles and to a less extent those of warheads in favour of country A. Conversely, an attempt at equalizing the numbers of weapons would result in changing the second-strike ratios in favour of country B. Again, if calculations are made based on K values, the kill potential of certain missiles in relation to the survival potentials of the silos protecting them is disproportionate for the two countries. Thus, if a certain type of missile is reduced, the aggregate offensive potential (KN) value would be disproportionately reduced in comparison to the aggregate survival potential (KS) value reduced, or *vice versa*. For example, if the number of missiles is reduced by 10, say, of the SS-7 type in country A, and the T-II type in country B, then country A's KN values are reduced by 29 and its KS values by 167 (for $P_k = 0.95$). For country B, its KN is reduced by 93 and KS by 386. Any particular reduction adds, therefore, a considerable difficulty to the basic one caused by the overall disproportion in A and B's strategic arsenals, quantitatively and above all qualitatively.

Rule 6, requiring the same numbers and if possible the same types of missiles to be reduced by stages in Scenarios I and II, sets the necessary condition for comparisons between the two scenarios with regard to the impact of technological changes on the security of states and their security requirements. As the only variable factor is the quality of weapons, and not their number, any difference seen in the two scenarios can only be attributed to the technological change in Scenario II.

The ICBM reductions of countries A and B during the years 1974–89 are shown in Table 1A.2. This table presents the number and type of missiles reduced annually; the ratio of A and B's ICBMs; and the ratio of A and B's warheads after reductions. These reductions are shown in Graph 1A.1. As can be seen from Table 1A.2 the pace of reductions, set up in rule 1, ranges from approximately 70 to 100 missiles reduced in the first year, to 150 a year in the intermediate period of reductions, and 25 or 50 at the end of the 15-year period. The majority of annual reductions concern only one type of missile, as was prescribed by rule 5. This number of missiles being reduced annually represents the quantified measure of the direct verification requirement.

The direct verification requirement

As was pointed out in Chapter 2, page 33ff, the basic function of verification is to monitor the degree of fulfilment to the legal norm set up by an agreement on disarmament, and ultimately to ensure a unified implementation of the provisions of such an agreement.

To do this, a verification system should fulfil two sets of requirements. These

Graph 1A.1. Scenario I: countries A and B's reductions of missiles and warheads, 1974–89. This graph corresponds to Table 1A.2,c olumns 5 and 7. A has a non-MIRVed arsenal, so the number of its ICBMs is equal to the number of warheads.

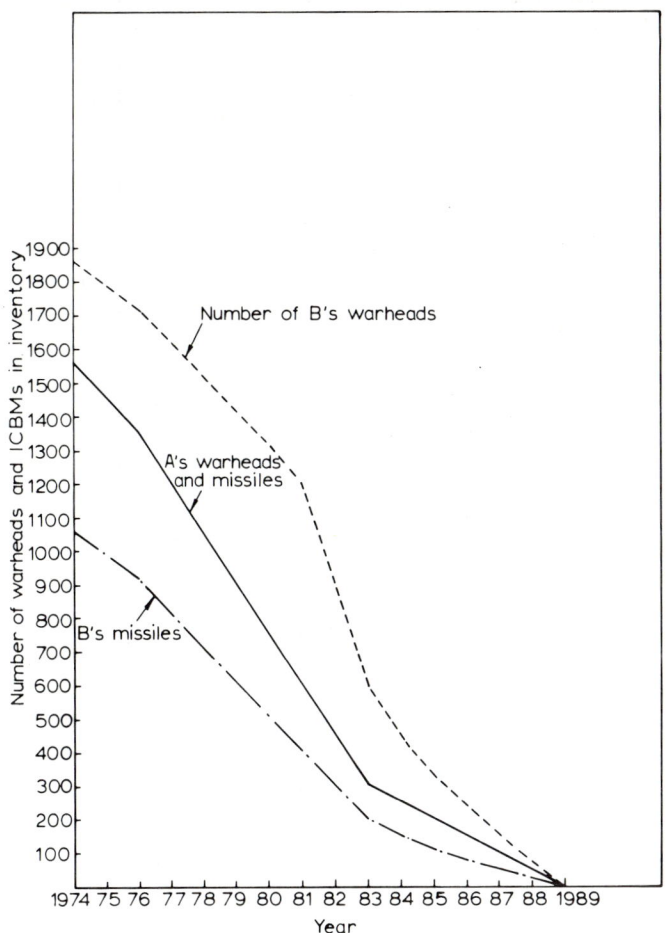

requirements are those related directly to the scope and subject of a treaty itself, and those related to the general security – real or perceived – of states in connection with the implementation of the treaty. The latter is subsequently divided into psychological, political and military security requirements, all of them closely interlinked. This study is concerned only with the military aspect of the general security requirement.

The direct verification requirement, based on the scope and subject of a treaty, is related to the need to verify that states have actually carried out the injunctions of a treaty, namely that they have made reductions of the prescribed numbers and types of weapon, restrained from certain actions, dismantled certain facilities, and so on; and that all these actions were carried out within an agreed period.

Because of the character of this requirement it can also be called the technical verification requirement. As has already been pointed out (Chapter 2, pages 28–30), this requirement is characterized by a number of other secondary requirements, such as detectability, technical feasibility *vis-à-vis* adequacy, continuity and punctuality in communicating the information, the requirement for keeping-pace with new technology and cost-effectiveness. The majority of them can be logically connected with the efficiency of a verification system; efficiency being, however, extremely difficult to measure, and therefore assessed in a completely subjective way, often according to political necessity.

The point of difference between the concepts of direct and security verification requirements lies in the fact that the majority of possible violations of a disarmament agreement do not constitute a threat to the security of the complying state – even though such violations may frequently be invoked by states as threatening their security. Of course the final judgement as to what constitutes jeopardy to a state's security can be made only if the specific circumstances are known. It can be safely assumed that only certain specific, or cumulative violations might be considered dangerous for a complying state's security. However, even if a state is not actually threatened by a violation, it still requires that the letter and spirit of the agreement be fulfilled. The direct verification requirement is thus orientated towards the discovery of those violations which constitute a breach of an agreement, but which are not actually vital for the security of a state.

A verification system designed according to this requirement need be neither very intrusive to the sovereignty of states, nor need it be absolutely watertight. This is in fact technically impossible, in any case. The only way of achieving such a watertight system for the detection of violations would be to establish a national internal mechanism for verification – that is, one operating inside the state's system at all decision-making levels – where the state would be its own watch dog. There exists, obviously, the problem of whether such an internal verification system would then make public internationally the fact that it had discovered such a violation. Even if such a system could be achieved, it is conceivable that some evasions might pass unnoticed.

Having analysed the direct verification requirement, it may now be said that in the case of the strategic disarmament agreement considered in this study the requirement in Scenario I covers: (*a*) actions forbidden as a part of the general freeze on qualitative improvements in strategic arms (such as tests, conversions, and so on); and (*b*) checking the number of ICBMs and SLBMs being reduced, and the number of silos being demolished or incapacitated. (The other stipulation of the agreement, concerning the development, production and deployment of strategic weapons, is covered by the security verification requirement.) The actual state of ICBM reductions in Scenario I is shown in Table 1A.2 in the fourth column and in Graph 1A.2.

The question of how technically feasible it is to meet the direct verification requirement of monitoring the quantities indicated in Table 1A.2 and the quantitative freeze on strategic arms will not be discussed here.

It may be noted that the measurements of the direct and security verification

Graph 1A.2. Scenarios I and II: number of ICBMs reduced by A and B during disarmament, 1974–89. This graph corresponds to Table 1A.2, column 4. It illustrates how disarmament grows, and facilitates understanding of graphs 1A.8, 1A.9, 1A.11, A1.12, 1A.19 and 1A.21, where the same curve of disarmament is used.

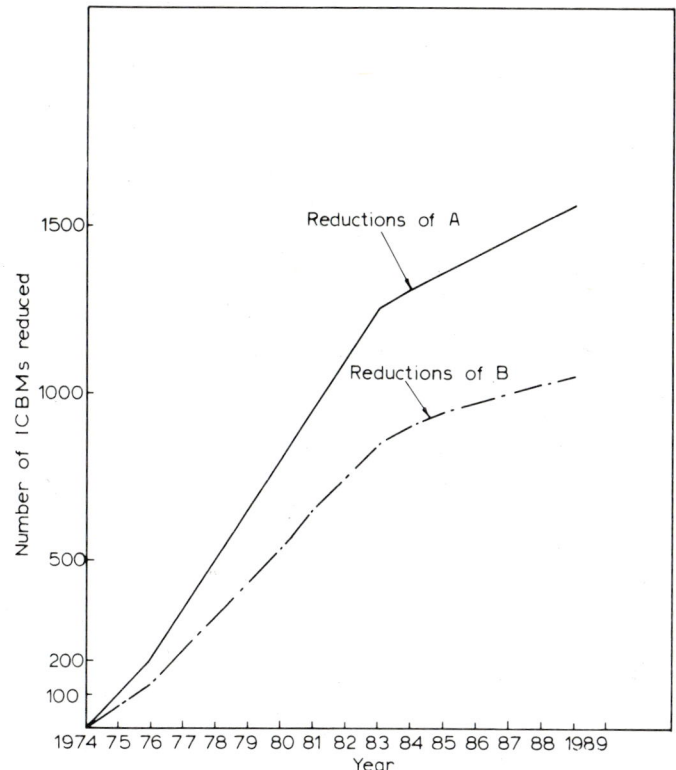

requirements are, at first glance, similar. Both are indications of the number of weapons, and it may happen that they are of the same order, but they are arrived at in completely different ways.

The direct requirement of the verification system has as its starting point the legal provisions of the treaty. Operationally it is therefore concerned with checking the action of states *vis-à-vis* these obligations quantitatively and qualitatively. In terms of the treaty analysed here, the verification system would have to monitor that 25–150 missiles and silos of (preferably) known locations and dimensions were abolished annually at the prescribed time, and that these reductions were carried out in the agreed way. So this verification requirement's quantitative values will be those indicated in Table 1A.2, column three, headed Number and type of ICBMs reduced.

Knowledge of the exact silo locations, before the disarmament begins, would substantially lessen the technical difficulty confronting the verification system in distinguishing the missiles and silos that are being phased out from those remaining in the active inventory.

Qualitatively the verification system would have to ensure that conversion of ICBMs and silos, ICBM flight-tests, and nuclear tests of any kind were not being carried out. Even now, and especially if such activities are on a larger scale, this would not be very difficult.

The security verification requirement

The security requirement of the verification system is also closely linked with the treaty. Operationally it is concerned with monitoring the actions of states *vis-à-vis* the obligations of the treaty, that is, ensuring that the ban on development, production and deployment of ICBMs and SLBMs is observed; but there are eventualities which are as yet unknown, and which constitute the *potential* danger to the security of the state.

Seeing that in this study we have defined the security of states as mutual preservation of the residual second strike, we have calculated the number of ICBMs that would need to be developed, produced and deployed clandestinely at unknown locations and of unknown characteristics in order to be able to threaten this residual second strike. This number constitutes the potential danger, and at the same time it is the smallest number that the verification system should be able to discover. Thus our measure is based not on numbers stipulated in the treaty, but on hypothetical calculations of that number of weapons which would threaten a country's residual second strike.

Hence the two requirements are totally different. Referring to the general observations made in Chapter 2, the difference between these requirements can be exemplified by the difference between verification of 'bonfires', removal, abolition, known actual deployment, non-conversion, and non-testing (direct verification requirement) on the one hand, and verification of non-production, stockpiles, military R&D, non-existence and maintenance within agreed limits (security verification requirement) on the other.

III. Methods

The purpose of the calculations is to find out the quantitative value of the security verification requirements of countries A and B during the strategic disarmament undertaken by them in mutual agreement.

There are two elements to this question. On the one hand one must calculate how many weapons the violating side would need to develop and deploy in order to be assured of complete destruction of the opponent's second strike, that is, of a disarming first strike. On the other hand one must express in a quantified form the efficiency of the verification system in ensuring the security of the complying side. As it is impossible to quantify either 'security' or 'verification' directly, the only measure which remains, is to measure the required efficiency of the verification system needed to discover the clandestine production of this number of weapons. This required efficiency, expressed as the number of weapons which if produced undiscovered, would endanger the security of a complying state, will be called the security verification requirement.

To calculate this number it is necessary first to assess the residual second strike of a country, and then to compute the numbers of missiles needed to destroy this residual second strike.

There are two somewhat related methods available for such calculations. Method I is that in which the kill potentials of warheads and the survival potentials of silos are used to calculate the 'result' of mutual hypothetical attacks of respective arsenals. As the kill and survival potentials are indicated in K values, this method is also called the K method. All theoretical considerations and mathematical formulae used here in connection with K values are based on SIPRI's *Offensive Missiles*.[4] Method II, called the TKP method, uses the concept of the Terminal Kill Probability of the warhead against the hardened target. This method was developed by several scientific and governmental institutions in the United States, and further elaborated and practised by several scientists.[5]

The first method gives the probability of destroying a silo with a one warhead as:

$$P_k = 1 - e - \frac{1}{2}\left\{\frac{Y^{2/3}}{H^{2/3}(CEP)^2\{f(H)\}^{2/3}}\right\} \quad (1)$$

Then K (lethality of the warhead or its kill potential) is defined as:

$$K = \frac{Y^{2/3}}{(CEP)^2} \quad (2)$$

For a missile with reliability ρ, this formula is modified to

$$K\rho = \frac{Y^{2/3}}{(CEP)^2} \cdot \rho \quad (3)$$

and the formula (1) becomes:

$$P_k = 1 - e - \frac{1}{2}\left\{\frac{K(\rho)}{H^{2/3}\{f(H)\}^{2/3}}\right\} \quad (4)$$

From the same equation (1) the formula for K' (the warhead lethality necessary to destroy a silo of a given hardness with a given probability, or in other words, a silo's survival potential) is derived:

$$K' = 2H^{2/3}\{f(H)\}^{2/3}|\ln(1-P_k)| \quad (5)$$

On the other hand in order to calculate by the second method, based on the Terminal Kill Probability (*TKP*) values for a single warhead, the following truncated formula for a single shot kill probability of a nuclear warhead against a hard target will be used:[6]

$$SSKP = 1 - 0.5 \left(\frac{6 \, Y^{2/3}}{H^{2/3} (CEP)^2} \right) \qquad (6)$$

As the actual destruction of a target will depend also on the reliability of a missile, or Overall Reliability (OAR) corresponding to ρ, the terminal kill probability for one warhead will be:

$$TKP = SSKP \times OAR \qquad (7)$$

For n warheads of the same TKP fired at the same target, the kill probability will be:

$$PK_n = 1 - (1 - TKP)_n \qquad (8)$$

Thus, the full formula for the PK of a n warheads of the same parameters and reliabilities is:

$$PK_n = 1 - \left\{ 1 - OAR \left[1 - 0.5 \, \frac{6 \, Y^{2/3}}{H^{2/3}(CEP)^2} \right] \right\}^n \qquad (9)$$

and to find the number of warheads of a given reliability OAR necessary to destroy a silo with a given probability PK the formula (9) will become:

$$n = \frac{\ln |PK - 1|}{\ln \left\{ 1 - OAR \left[1 - 0.5 \, \frac{6 \, Y^{2/3}}{H^{2/3} (CEP)^2} \right] \right\}} \qquad (10)$$

The concept of the residual second strike

The concept of the strategic second strike is conventionally defined as the certain ability of an attacked state, even after sustaining an unexpected and full-scale attack, to inflict on an agressor, in reprisal, damage which is unacceptable to the latter. By 'full-scale' is meant an attack in which all the ICBMs possessed by the striking force are used. The second-strike capability defined in such a way underlines, therefore, the kill or damage potential represented by the missiles which survived an attack. This volume of possible damage inflicted by the second strike in retaliation constitutes the threat which acts as a credible deterrent to a would-be attacker.

In this study, however, the offensive capability of the second strike is disregarded. The stress here is on the preservation of the second-strike capability, that is, on the survival potential of silos, rather than on the retaliatory capacity of the missiles they contain. This second strike will henceforth be called the residual second strike, and its essence is the aggregate survival potential of those silos surviving an attack. Obviously from this aggregate value one could calculate the number of silos and hence the number of missiles in them (for a model of the calculation, see those made in connection with the minimum deterrence threshold, pages 123–127). Such an approach serves the purpose of this study, which is to find the additional number of missiles that would have to be produced in order to destroy this residual second strike.

This concept, underlining the defensive character of the second strike, allows computation of the approximate values of the second strike without specific knowledge about the targeting doctrines of countries A and B. Knowledge of their doctrines would indicate which specific silo is to be attacked by a particular warhead, and consequently the numbers and types surviving an attack. From this could be calculated the particular missiles and numbers to be used in a retaliatory strike. However, such knowledge of targeting doctrines is impossible because it is secret, and for the purposes of this study, irrelevant, if residual second strike as defined here is the object of calculation.

Method I: The K method

If country A has a given number (n) of different warheads (i), where i varies over the number of types of warheads, each type with a different kill potential (K), and these warheads are located on a certain number of missiles (m) then the aggregate kill potential of this country will be:

$$K_1 n_1 m_1 + K_2 n_2 m_2 + \ldots + K_i n_i m_i = \sum_{i=1,2,3,\ldots} K_i n_i m_i$$

If $n_i m_i$ be replaced by N_i (the total number of warheads of country A), then the aggregate kill potential of these warheads will be:

$$\sum_{i=1,2,3,\ldots} K_i N_i$$

and, for simplicity, the KN of country A.

The KN value is, therefore, a multiplication of the kill potentials of the individual warheads by the number of each type of warhead, or in other words, the symbol KN is a measure of the aggregate kill potential of a state's nuclear arsenal against hard targets.

Note that in the case of the non-MIRVed arsenal of country A, the number of warheads equals the number of missiles, $n = 1$. In the case of country B, which possesses a partially MIRVed arsenal, the aggregate kill potential is calculated by multiplying the number of warheads by the number of missiles being MIRVed, $n \times m$ plus the potential of non-MIRVed missiles.

If country A has a given number (S) of different silos of (j) types, each type of different survival potential (K'), then the aggregate survival potential of those silos in country A will be:

$$K_1' S_1 + K_2' S_2 + \ldots + K_j' S_j = \sum_{=1,2,3\ldots} K_j' S_j$$

and for simplicity, it is called the KS of country A. The KS value is, therefore, a multiplication of the survival potentials of the individual silos by their number, or, in other words it is a measure of the aggregate survival potential of a country's nuclear arsenal located in silos.

Thus country A has a survival potential of KS_A and a kill potential of KN_A, and country B has a survival potential of KS_B and a kill potential of KN_B.

Now the aggregate value of the residual second strikes of both countries are computed by subtracting the value of the offensive potential (KN) of one country from the survival potential ($K'S$) of the other country. Thus, the residual second strike of country A after attack will be

$$K'S_A - KN_B = K'S_A'$$

when S' is the number of silos surviving the attack.

In country B the residual second strike will be

$$K'S_B - KN_A = K'S_B'.$$

The question that now arises is how many missiles should either of the two countries develop, produce and deploy clandestinely in order to be able to destroy completely (that is, using 95 per cent as the accepted level of kill probability) the other's residual second strike? It is assumed that a country embarking on clandestine arms production would aim at developing the most efficient of its weapons at that time, that is, those with greatest kill potential per warhead, because of the difficulty in hiding a large number of weapons.[7] Thus for Scenario I such weapons would most probably be SS9s on A's side, and MIIIs on B's side. The security verification requirements, that is, the number of weapons needed for destruction of the other side's residual second strike, will be calculated in terms of the numbers of these missiles.

If the kill potential represented by SS9 and MIII missiles is known for a given reliability (ρ), then the security verification requirement of country A will be:

$$K'S_A'/K_{\text{MIII}} = n\text{MIIIs},$$

when n is the number of warheads of MIII type needed to destroy A's residual second strike $K'S_A'$. As the MIII carries three MIRVed warheads per missile, in order to calculate the security verification requirement in terms of numbers of missiles, one must divide by three. For country B this requirement will be:

$$K S_B'/K_{\text{SS9}} = n\text{SS9s}$$

If a violation of a disarmament agreement on ICBM reductions is to bring about any real military advantage to the violator by giving it the first-strike capability, then it will have to produce clandestinely, or conceal, a number of weapons *no smaller than* that indicated by these numerical values of the security verification requirement.

Conversely, in order for the verification system of a country to satisfy the requirements for that country's strategic military security, it should be efficient enough to detect the clandestine production of no less than that number of weapons.

Method II: the TKP method

To calculate the security verification requirement according to the second method, the Terminal Kill Probabilities (*TKP*s) of all types of strategic missiles possessed by A and B should first be computed. Ideally a calculation of the Terminal Kill Probabilities of warheads attacking a set of different silos requires detailed knowledge of which particular silo is to be targeted and by what warhead. As this is unknown the average hardness of all silos must be reckoned despite the fact that this is an oversimplification of the problem. It then becomes immaterial which silo will be hit by which warhead, because all silos have the same average hardness. The hypothetical strikes considered are of the simplest design. As in method I, no re-targeting, re-programming or sequence of salvoes are envisaged. All warheads existing in the given arsenal are 'used' in one single attack.

The *TKP* value of a warhead indicates the chances that this warhead will destroy a known hardened target. When a certain number of a given type of warheads are used against a known number of silos, the *TKP* value indicates the percentage of these silos to be destroyed.

Thus, if a country has, for example, three types of missiles, say, f, g, h, each with different *TKPs* and of different numbers, a_f, b_g, c_h, then when used against the opponent's silos they would destroy a certain number of the silos according to their *TKP* values (given as a percentage) and to the numbers used:

$$TKP_f \cdot a_f = a_f'$$

$$TKP_g \cdot b_g = b_g'$$

$$TKP_h \cdot c_h = c_h'$$

Therefore, the full-scale attack of this country's missiles against the opponent's silos would then be able to destroy $a_f' + b_g' + e_h'$ of these silos. The difference between the number of silos a country had before an attack and the number of silos destroyed will be the number of silos surviving, that is, the residual second strike of the attacked country. If the attacked side had S number of silos, then after an attack by side A carried out with a, b and c missiles of f, g, h types, the number S will be diminished by $(a_f' + b_g' + c_h') = S'$, where S' will mean B's residual second strike.

Similarly to the calculations used in method I, the security verification requirement can be obtained in method II by solving the question: How many of the best missiles (that is, those with the greatest *TKP*) would a country need to produce to be able to wipe out the opposing country's remaining silos constituting its residual second strike? If the *TKP* of this best missile is known then the simplest way to find out how many of these missiles are necessary to destroy all (100 per cent) silos of the residual second strike is to multiply the number of silos by the *TKP* value as a percentage.

Comparison of the two methods of calculation

To compare the two methods a sample calculation of the security verification requirements at three different stages of reduction of ICBMs will be carried out, say, for the years 1974, 1980 and 1985.

However, to compare the two methods exactly, the same mathematical preconditions must be fulfilled. Method I, using K values, assumes a level of probability of a silo's destruction, $P_k = 0.95$. Method II, based on the TKP, gives the level of a silo's destruction probability, that is, the 'real' destruction probability, reckoned according to the qualities of the missiles used. This real probability in Method II is always smaller than that assumed in the K method.

In order to compare these two methods the two levels have to be made to conform mathematically. Two identical levels of kill probability will be considered in both methods, $P_k = 0.5$ and $P_k = 0.95$.[8]

Consequently, the calculations according to Method II will be carried out in a slightly different way from that described above. Instead of calculating the TKP values of warheads, these TKPs are given, and they are $P_k = 0.5$ and $P_k = 0.95$. Therefore, to calculate the security verification requirement according to the second method, formula (10) must be used. It permits us to calculate the number of warheads of a given type necessary to destroy an opponent's silo of a known hardness and with a given $TKP(P_k)$. Now the total number of warheads of each type in the country's arsenal is divided by this number of warheads necessary per silo. The sum of the results gives the number of the opponent's silos that the attacking country could destroy with the warheads existing in its arsenal. This number of destroyed silos is now subtracted from the total number of the opponent's silos. The difference is the number of silos which have survived an attack, that is, the opponent's residual second strike.

The security verification requirement is, as always in this study, measured in terms of the number of the best missiles possessed by the opponent at a given time. In the case of the sample calculations, as far as Method II is concerned, the best missile is that which can destroy an 'average' silo of the opponent with the smallest number of warheads. Therefore, when the number of silos indicating country A's residual second strike is divided by the number of warheads of country B's best missile necessary per silo, the result will indicate the values of A's security verification requirement. In the case of MIRVed missiles the number has to be divided again by the number of warheads on a missile.

One more note is relevant to the sample calculations. To calculate the security verification requirement by the K method an 'average' hardness for the silos is not necessary. However, as was noted before, in the sample calculations the same values for all the corresponding variables were used. For that reason the same average hardness of silos of A and B, as used in the TKP method, will also be adopted for the K method.

So in order to make the described sample calculations and to compare the two methods it is necessary to know:

in Method I, the K values of individual warheads possessed by A and B, according to their different reliabilities, and K' values per silo (200 and 550 lb/in² respectively for A and B) at $P_k = 0.5$ and $P_k = 0.95$;

in Method II, the number of warheads n, of a given reliability required to destroy the two kinds of silos with the same probabilities. All the values are assembled in Table 1A.3 (average hardness of silos) and Table 1A.4 (K values and number of warheads necessary per silo).

Table 1A.3. Calculation of the 'average' hardness of A's and B's silos (sample calculations)

Type of missile	Number of silos		Pressure per silo, lb/in^2
Country A			
SS7/8 in soft silo	209		100
SS–11–1 in soft silo	500		100
S11–1, 3 and SS13	570		300
SS9 in soft silo	188		100
SS9 in hard silo	100		300
Total	1 567	Average	185.5 = 200
Country B			
TII in hard silo	54		300
MI in hard silo	100		300
MII in hard silo	500		300
MIII in superhard silo	400		1 000
Total	1 054	Average	565.7 = 550

Table 1A.4. Basic values used in sample calculations of the security verification requirement according to two different methods

Type of missile	K method			TKP method	
	K per warhead, ρ	K' per silo 200 pn		n warheads per silo 200 lb/in^2	
	for $\rho = 0.75$	$P_k = 0.5$	$P_k = 0.95$	$P_k = 0.5$	$P_k = 0.95$
SS7/8	2.19			5.2[a]	22.53[a]
SS9	5.53	6.4	27.6	2.2	9.33
SS11/13	0.75			15.1	65.10
	for $\rho = 0.80$	K' per silo 550 lb/in^2		n warheads per silo 550 lb/in^2	
TII	9.34			0.74	3.21
MI	3.20			1.88	8.14
MII	8.89	11.95	60.2	0.77	3.34
MIII	5.90			1.08	4.67

[a] Obviously, in reality, fractions of warheads could not be used. The figures have not been rounded in order to make the comparisons more exact.

The quantified values of the security verification requirements for countries A and B in 1974, 1980 and 1985 reckoned for a kill probability of $P_k = 0.5$ and $P_k = 0.95$ according to Method I and Method II are given in Table 1A.5. To be able to compare the results obtained from the two methods the differences were indicated in percentages.

Table 1A.5. Comparison of the security verification requirement values resulting from the two different methods of sample calculation. (Requirement of A calculated in number of MIIIs, requirement of B in SS9s)

Country	Year	P_k	K method	TKP method	Percentage difference
A	1974	0.5	..[a]	..	—
		0.95	1 747	1 793	2.57
	1980	0.5	..	..	—
		0.95	723	743	2.69
	1985	0.5	..	..	—
		0.95	202	206	1.94
B	1974	0.5	1 762	1 786	1.34
		0.95	10 958	9 306	15.07
	1980	0.5	759	774	1.94
		0.95	5 244	4 440	15.33
	1985	0.5	38	42	9.52
		0.95	997	826	17.15

[a] Two dots indicate that at this P_k the forces of country B can destroy those of A completely, that is, no residual strike is left and therefore the security verification requirement cannot be calculated.

As can be easily noted from the table, the differences between the results are very small (not over 15 per cent). Given the whole range of simplifications and approximations throughout the calculations of the hypothetical attacks by each country on the other, used in both methods, these differences in the results obtained are insignificant.

Thus the logical conclusion of a comparison of the two methods of calculation available is to use either one of them, as they give equivalent results. All the subsequent calculations will therefore be made according to one method only.

Both methods discussed here are simplified. In both of them the physical effects of nuclear explosions, which inhibit the usage of multiple warheads over a single silo in a short period of time, were completely ignored. We assume in the calculations that several warheads are being used against a single silo at the same time. In practice this is not only impossible, because of the fratricide effects, but also uneconomical. The other substantial simplification is the use of only approximate figures: in the K method because all the technical and military intricacies of a real nuclear attack are symbolized in the simple mathematical subtraction of the aggregate kill value of one country from the aggregate survival potential of another. The simplicity inherent in the TKP method derives from the necessity of using an 'average' hardness of silos.

From the theoretical viewpoint the K method seems more useful for our needs. What is being considered here is a theoretical case in which an enemy has forces of the highest efficiency which are used at once, giving him a probability of destroying the country's forces of as high as 0.95. From the security viewpoint this assumption is simply the 'worst case', although we know that this extremely high level of probability is impossible to achieve in practice. What remains from this hypothetical attack is the residual second strike.

The other method operates on real and therefore much lower kill probability levels (for example, for a given set of parameters the TKP of the SS7 is 12, and that of the MIII is 35 per warhead). This lower level of kill probability – although closer to reality – does not allow us the 'worst-case' analysis of the K method.

The minimum deterrence threshold

The security of countries A and B, according to the basic premise of this study is guaranteed when second strikes can inflict unacceptable damage on each other. 'Unacceptable damage' is a subjective term, and differs according to political bias.[9] The classic concept of unacceptable damage as used by, for example, McNamara *vis-à-vis* the USSR, is the possibility of destruction of one-fourth to one-fifth of the Soviet population and one-half to two-thirds of the Soviet industrial capacity.[10]

The criterion of the ability to destroy two-thirds of the 200 biggest urban centres on the territories of A and B has been accepted here as a 'minimum' deterrence threshold that countries A and B want to possess in order to guarantee their security.

In terms of this study such a minimum deterrence threshold is calculated as the overall defensive potentials (KS) minus the offensive potentials (KN) of the opponent. Thus, the values of the minimum deterrence thresholds for countries A and B will indicate their residual defensive potentials after absorbing the first strike. So, before the exchange of strikes begins, the states possess potentials much larger than necessary to destroy two-thirds of the major 200 cities of the opponent. The 'minimum' deterrence assumes, therefore, considerable nuclear overkill capabilities (to be more exact, the ability to destroy those two-thirds of 200 major cities plus a defensive potential which will be destroyed by an attack, and this destroyed potential is equal to the entire KN of the attacking force). Such a high order of nuclear capabilities assumed as a minimum deterrence threshold is equivalent to the nuclear 'overkill' capacity, that is, the ability to destroy an agressor totally by the victim's second strike. It is hardly possible to adopt a higher threshold, because obviously, countries can destroy their enemies only once. Therefore any results obtained in this study will be based on the most extreme and conservative criteria of minimum deterrence and will establish the most pessimistic limits. Seeing that, in reality, countries would be deterred by much lower deterrence capabilities, the situation would be much more optimistic.

What really constitutes a minimum and sufficient deterrent is an open question; and there are numerous and quite contradictory opinions on this matter. It could, for example, be argued that so long as a state possesses even a small number of invulnerable sea-based SLBMs, even without any land-based

ICBMs or other strategic weapons, this force should be regarded as sufficient to deter a nuclear attack on its territory. Presumably this is the rationale behind the existence of French and British nuclear forces. However, such a minimum deterrent would perhaps be regarded by some as not credible enough, and therefore unacceptable.

Furthermore, although it may seem naive, it should be further noted that even one nuclear bomb capable of being delivered and exploded over a densely populated area of a would-be aggressor might be regarded as sufficient to deter the latter from launching a nuclear attack. The high figures proposed below for a threshold of minimum deterrence tally with 'worst case' assumptions, the most pessimistic or conservative from the point of view of arms limitation.

The reductions analysed here start at a very high value of deterrence capabilities, when A and B possess enormous overkill capabilities. Numerical reductions of their ICBMs will cause these military capabilities to shrink. At a certain time the annually diminishing residual second strikes of A and B will have to pass the limits of their minimum deterrence thresholds, and will subsequently diminish until they completely disappear at the end of reductions. The matter of interest is when this point of equality between the residual second strike and the minimum deterrence threshold will come for any country. Having determined this point in time, we shall be able to say that before it arrives, a country enjoys more than minimum deterrence and is completely secure. After this point in time a country's deterrence will shrink and therefore the reductions will begin to influence its security negatively.

We have taken the minimum deterrent to be the ability of a state to damage two-thirds of an aggressor's major cities (conventionally taken to be 200) by means of a retaliatory strike. Let us assume, furthermore, that the overall reliability of missiles used in the second strike will be 70 per cent for both sides considered here.[11] So if a state wishes to have a credible second strike equivalent to the threshold of minimum deterrence defined above, then the necessary number of warheads will be $200 \cdot 2/3 \cdot \frac{1}{7} = 190$.

If therefore at least 190 warheads survive the first attack and can still be delivered against an aggressor, then a state possesses a minimum strategic second strike (minimum strategic deterrent) and can feel secure in terms of strategic deterrence. This assumption is valid with at least one reservation: in the case of a country possessing MIRVed weapons the overlap of the multiple explosions caused by the MIRV could limit the calculation of the number of warheads needed. For simplicity, this factor is not considered here.

In the case of country A with non-MIRVed missiles in Scenario I the figure of 190 re-entry vehicles implies that 190 silos will have to survive the attack. In the case of country B using MIRVed (three warheads) and non-MIRVed missiles the figure of 190 re-entry vehicles implies that the number of silos which have to survive ranges from 190 to $\frac{190}{3} = 64$ silos. Because the residual second strikes of A and B are indicated in KS values, the numbers of silos representing the minimum deterrence must also be translated into K values.

Country A has silos of overpressure resistance to either 100 or 300 lb/in². For a kill probability $P_k = 0.95$ the value of K required per silo (its survival potential) is respectively $K = 16.7$ or $K = 38.6$. There is no way of predicting, without knowing the exact targeting doctrine of the enemy attack, which silos would actually survive the first strike. Most probably a mixture of different silos of 100 and 300 lb/in² overpressure resistance would survive. In this situation only the boundary values can be estimated for the surviving silos: either all the surviving silos are the weakest ones (100 lb/in²) or all of them are the hardest ones (300 lb/in²). The real figure would certainly lie somewhere in between. So, measuring in KS values, the minimum threshold of A's second strike would lie between the lowest figure (only 100 lb/in² silos surviving), that is $190 \times 16.7 = 3\,173\ KS$, and the highest value (only 300 lb/in² silos surviving), namely $190 \times 38.6 = 7\,334\ KS$.

In the case of B all its non-MIRVed missiles are in silos of 300 lb/in² ($K = 38.6$ for $P_k = 0.95$). Assuming that only this type of silo survives A's first strike, then the minimum second-strike threshold, measured in KS values, would be $190 \times 38.6 = 7\,334\ KS$. The MIRVed missiles are all located in silos of 1000 lb/in² overpressure resistance. Such silos require $K = 92.1$ to be destroyed with $P_k = 0.95$. The overall KS values of 64 such silos (containing 190 re-entry vehicles) is $64 \times 92.1 = 5\,894.4\ KS$.

The limits of the minimum deterrence thresholds of countries A and B cannot therefore be clearly defined. These thresholds are confined to the area between $KS = 3\,173$ and $KS = 7\,334$ for country A, and $KS = 5\,894$ and $KS = 7\,334$ for country B.

As the minimum deterrence threshold is of interest here only in terms of interpretating the values of the security verification requirement during reductions, the KS values defining minimum deterrence thresholds must consequently be transformed into the same measurement, namely, the number of an opponent's best missiles needed for the complete destruction of the minimum deterrence threshold. When the values of the security verification requirement are equal to the number of missiles which would be able to destroy completely the minimum deterrence threshold, then the reductions start to diminish the deterrence capacity. Such diminishing credibility of a country's residual second strike can be perceived by its government as a threat to the strategic security of the country. It may then demand more stringent verification in order to ensure that no actual danger exists *vis-à-vis* the opponent's possible clandestine activities. The moment when the two values, that of the security verification requirement and that of the minimum deterrence threshold, are equal will be called point α (see, for example, graphs 1A.3 and 1A.4) and will indicate the point at which a country whose strike has diminished will demand more stringent verification.

The limits of the minimum deterrence threshold are transformed from K values to the number of the opponent's best missiles. The values of the minimum deterrence threshold of A and B are divided by the kill potentials of MIIIs and SS9s. Hence these numbers will be 179–414 MIIIs for country A, and 1 066–1 326 SS9s for country B.

Having discussed the relation between the minimum deterrence threshold and the security verification requirement, we then need to turn to the efficiency of the verification option itself.

Graph 1A.3. Scenario I: country A's security verification requirement and minimum deterrence threshold during ICBM reductions, 1974–89. This graph corresponds to Table 1A.10, column 3. See the values of the security verification requirement of A and points α_A, β_A and also pages 131–136, where the border values of the minimum deterrence threshold and the explanation of points α and β are discussed.

α_A = A's security verification requirement, which equals the upper limit of A's minimum deterrence threshold.

β_A = A's security verification requirement, which equals 100 ICBMs.

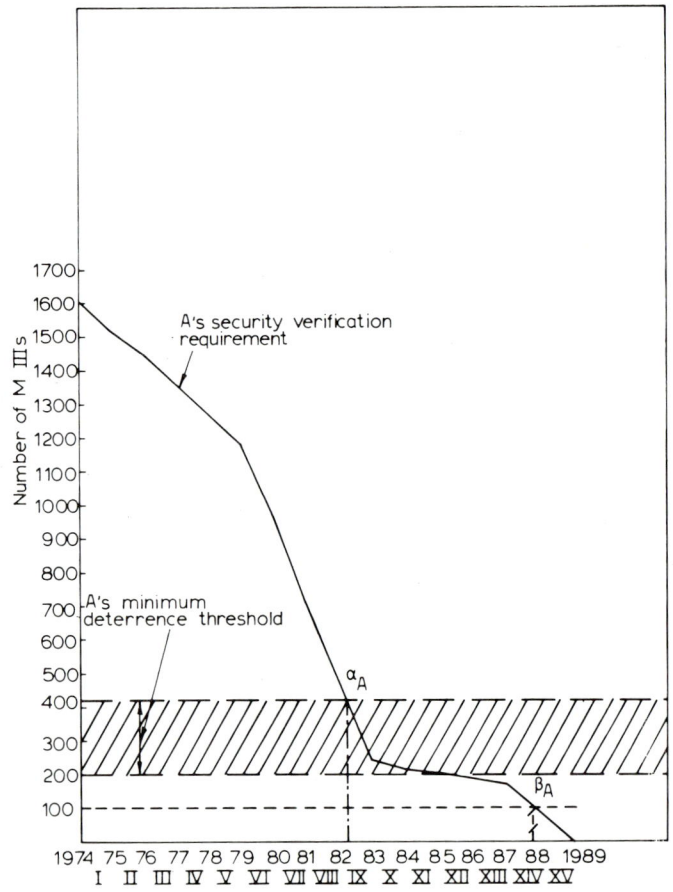

It is obvious that large numbers of strategic weapons developed clandestinely will be easy to discover. Similarly, very small numbers could be produced unnoticed. The problem is that it is impossible, practically and theoretically, to calculate the number of weapons that the verification system could reliably discover. We have thus taken the arbitrary figure of 100 missiles as the borderline beyond which the verification system would need to be strengthened. In reality a borderline of greater or less than 100 could be established according to the

Graph 1A.4. Scenario I: B's security verification requirements and minimum deterrence threshold during ICBM reductions, 1974–89. This graph corresponds to Table 1A.10, column 4 (the security verification requirement of B and points α_B and β_B). See also pages 131–136.

α_B = B's security verification requirement, which equals the upper limit of B's minimum deterrence threshold.

β_B = B's security verification requirement, which equals 100 SS9s.

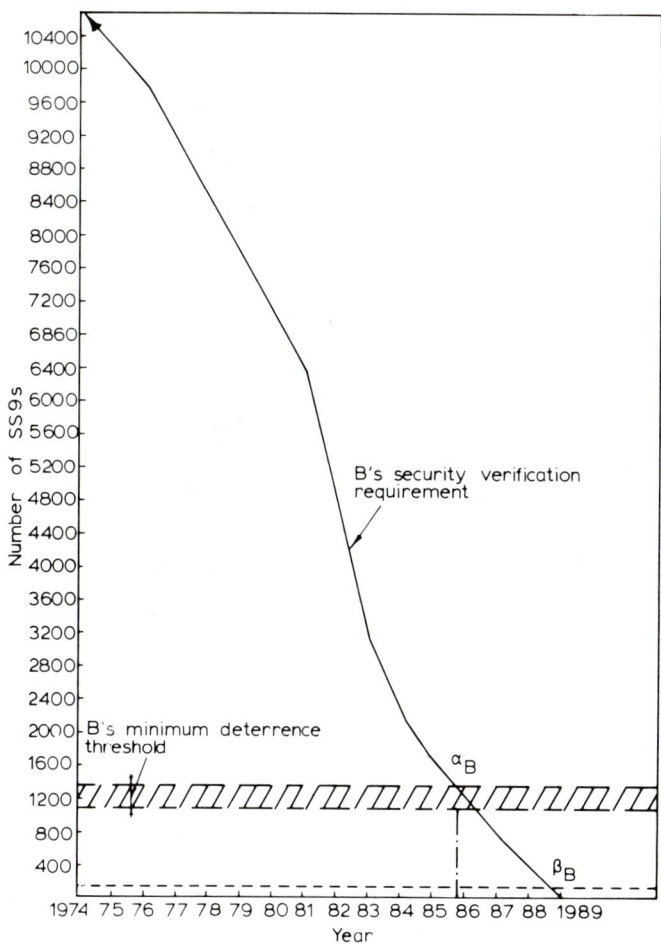

perception of an individual government. The point at which the security verification requirement equals 100 will henceforth be called point β, and it will signal the need for very stringent verification on the part of a country requiring it.[11]

IV. Scenario I: Numerical limitations of A's and B's strategic forces accompanying a freeze in the qualitative arms race

Calculation of the security verification requirements of A and B

A's and B's security verification requirements were calculated according to the K method, as decided. The lethal potentials of warheads (K per warhead with a given reliability) and survival potentials of silos (K per silo with $P_k = 0.95$) used in the calculations are shown in Tables 1A.6 and 1A.7. Lethal potentials of warheads are reckoned according to the characteristics of weapons given in Table 1A.1.

The figures for the total KN and $K'S$ values of both countries, assembled in Table 1A.8, serve as the basis for all calculations of the residual second strikes, and subsequently of the security verification requirements during reductions in Scenario I. The residual second strikes of A and B during all 15 stages of ICBM reductions are shown in Table 1A.9. It has been decided not to load the table with the values of the offensive and defensive potentials of the respective countries.

The final results of the calculations, that is, the values of A's and B's security verification requirements at all stages of reductions are shown in Table 1A.10. For country A these figures are indicated both in numbers of MIIIs and in numbers of MIII warheads. Graph 1A.5 illustrates the figures in Table 1A.10 more clearly.

Table 1A.6. K' required to destroy a given silo with the probability $P_k = 0.95$

H lb/in²	K' per silo
100	16.7
300	38.6
1 000	92.1

Table 1A.7. K per warhead of the missiles of reliability ρ reduced in Scenario I

Type of missile	$\rho = 0.75$
SS7/8	2.19
SS9	5.53
SS11/13	0.75
	0.8
TII	9.34
MI	3.20
MII	8.89
MIII	5.90

Table 1A.8. Total KN and $K'S$ values represented by A's and B's arsenals in 1974

Type of missile	Number of missiles or silos	K per warhead	KN	Silo hardness lb/in²	K' per silo $P_k = 0.95$	$K'S$
A		$\rho = 0.75$				
SS7	139	2.19	304.41	100	16.7	2 321.3
SS8	70	2.19	153.30	100	16.7	1 169.0
SS11 Mod 1	500	0.75	375.00	100	16.7	8 350.0
SS11 Mod 1	470	0.75	352.50	300	38.6	18 142.0
SS11 Mod 1	40	0.75	30.00	300	38.6	1 544.0
SS13	60	0.75	45.00	300	38.6	2 316.0
SS9	188	5.53	1 039.64	100	16.7	3 139.6
SS9	100	5.53	553.00	300	38.6	3 860.0
ΣA	1 567		2 852.85			40 841.9
B		$\rho = 0.8$				
TII	54	9.34	504.36	300	38.6	2 084.4
MI	100	3.20	320.00	300	38.6	3 860.0
MII	500	8.89	4 445.00	300	38.6	19 300.0
MIII	400	3×5.9	7 080.00	1 000	92.1	36 840.0
ΣB	1 054		12 349.36			62 084.4

Table 1A.9. Scenario I: the residual second strikes of A and B during ICBM reductions, 1974–1989, given in $K'S$ values[a]

Year	Country A	Country B	Year	Country A	Country B
1974	28 493	59 232	1982	8 252	25 910
1975	26 896	56 768	1983	4 232	16 812
1976	25 678	54 285	1984	3 710	12 433
1977	24 062	50 538	1985	3 583	9 025
1978	22 446	46 790	1986	3 279	6 539
1979	20 830	43 043	1987	2 975	4 052
1980	17 024	39 295	1988	1 498	2 026
1981	12 262	35 007	1989	—	—

[a] All figures are rounded.

ICBM reductions

In order to facilitate the analysis of results obtained in Scenario I, Graphs 1A.3–1A.12 were drawn. On Graphs 1A.3 and 1A.4 the curves for diminishing values of the security verification requirement of countries A and B respectively are shown together with the values of A's and B's minimum deterrence thresholds. The points of intersection of the security verification requirement curves with

Graph 1A.5. Scenario I: security verification requirements of countries A and B during ICBM reductions, 1974–89. A's requirement is indicated in numbers of MIII warheads and missiles, B's in numbers of SS9s. This graph corresponds to Table 1A.10. As B has a MIRVed arsenal, the security verification requirement of A can be measured either in number of warheads or in number of ICBMs, or both (thus the two lines for A's requirement).

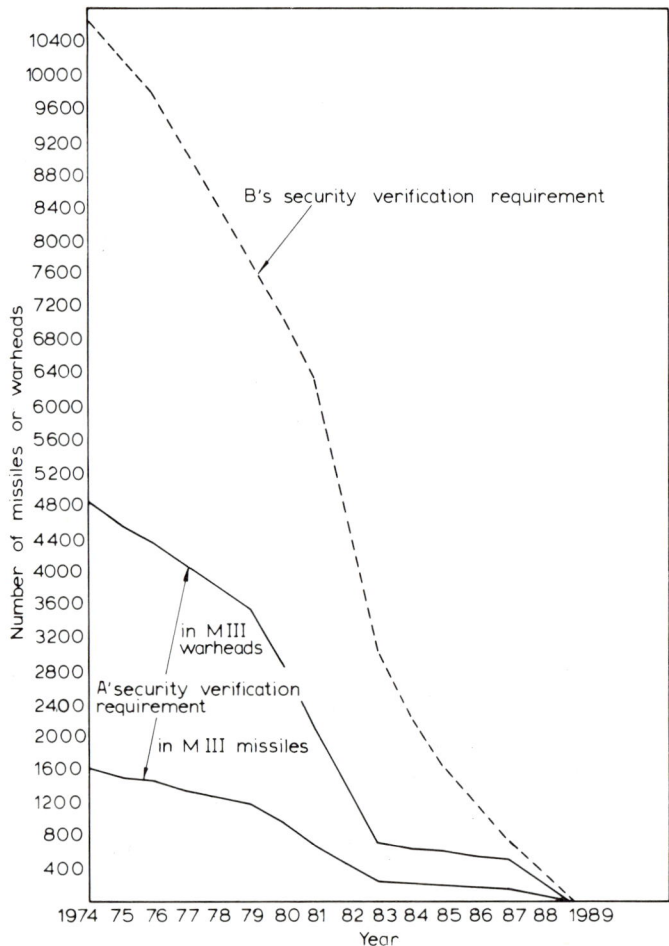

the upper limits of the minimum deterrence threshold (point α) as well as the points at which these requirements equal 100, (point β) are indicated. Country A reaches point α at the beginning of the ninth stage of reductions and point β in the middle of the fourteenth stage. Country B arrives at these points at stages 12 and 15 respectively.

If the value of the security verification requirement expresses the number of missiles to be secretly produced in order to give decisive military advantage to a violator, then it may be observed from Table 1A.10 and from graphs 1A.3–1A.5

Table 1A.10. Scenario I: values of security verification requirements for countries A and B during ICBM reductions, 1974–1989

Year	Security verification requirement of A		Security verification requirement of B
	Number of MIII warheads	Number of MIII missiles	Number of SS9 missiles and warheads
1974	4 830	1 610	10 711
1975	4 560	1 520	10 266
1976	4 353	1 451	9 817
1977	4 077	1 359	9 139
1978	3 804	1 268	8 461
1979	3 531	1 177	7 784
1980	2 886	962	7 106
1981	2 079	693	6 330
1982	1 398	466	4 685
Point α_A	1 242	414	—
1983	717	239	3 040
1984	630	210	2 248
1985	606	202	1 632
Point α_B	—	—	1 326
1986	555	185	1 182
1987	504	168	733
Point β_A	300	100	—
1988	252	84	366
Point β_B	—	—	100
1989	—	—	—

that these numbers are, throughout the process of limitations until the last few stages of reductions, very high. The high figures mean that the actual requirement for verification is low, because the more weapons that are produced clandestinely the easier it is to discover and report on such clandestine activity; hence less stringent verification is needed from the viewpoint of a state's security.

Thus both curves, for countries A and B, shown in Graphs 1A.3 and 1A.4 are divided into three phases: the first, from the outset of reduction until point α; the second, from point α to point β; and the third, from point β down to the end of reductions. The first phase covers the stage of reductions at which the residual second strike of the state concerned is larger than the minimum deterrence threshold. During this phase a state's security is completely assured in terms of strategic deterrence *vis-à-vis* another state taking part in the ICBM limitations. This phase extends for slightly over eight years or stages of reduction, from 1974 to early 1983, for country A; and for 12 stages of reduction, from 1974 to early 1986, for country B.

The second phase of the security verification requirement's curve extends for country A from the ninth to the fourteenth stage; for country B from the twelfth to the fifteenth stage. During this phase it may seem that the security of

Graph 1A.6. Scenario I: three phases of change in A's security during ICBM reductions, 1974–89. The curve of A's reductions is based on Table 1A.2, column 5, and the phasing of this curve is explained on pages 133–135.

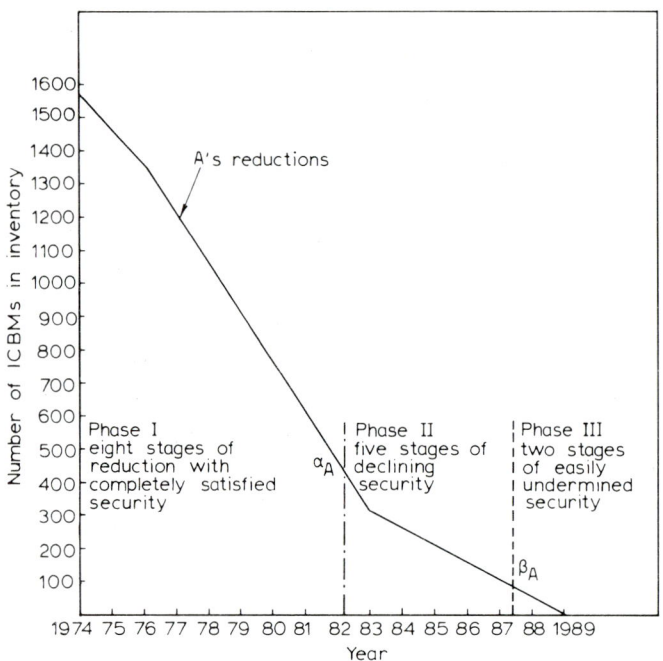

both countries has diminished, owing to the fact that their residual second strikes have sunk below the minimum deterrence thresholds. It may be noted from Graphs 1A.3 and 1A.4 that the shaded areas indicating the minimum deterrence thresholds are quite wide, and that the curves for the security verification requirements pass through them at three subsequent stages of reductions. This means that point α could well be located somewhere below the point indicated on the curves. As we are considering matters of a state's security, the most conservative assumptions should be made; and for that reason we take into consideration the upper limit of the minimum deterrence threshold. All values of the security verification requirement lying between points α and β are greater than 100; in the case of A between 414 and 100, and in the case of B between 1 326 and 100. Thus, although during this period of reduction a state's security could be regarded as diminishing, the numbers of weapons needed to achieve a decisive military advantage are still large, and therefore the actual requirement for verification may still be considered low.

Finally, the third part of the security verification requirement curves are very short; nearly two stages for country A, and a small part of the last, fifteenth stage for country B. During this period even small clandestine acquisitions of strategic weapons by either country might bring about a radical change in their military security, so giving the violator the premium of a first-strike capability. To avoid

Graph 1A.7. Scenario I: three phases of change in B's security during ICBM reductions, 1974–89. The curve of B's reductions is based on Table 1A.2, column 5, and the phasing of this curve is explained on pages 133–135.

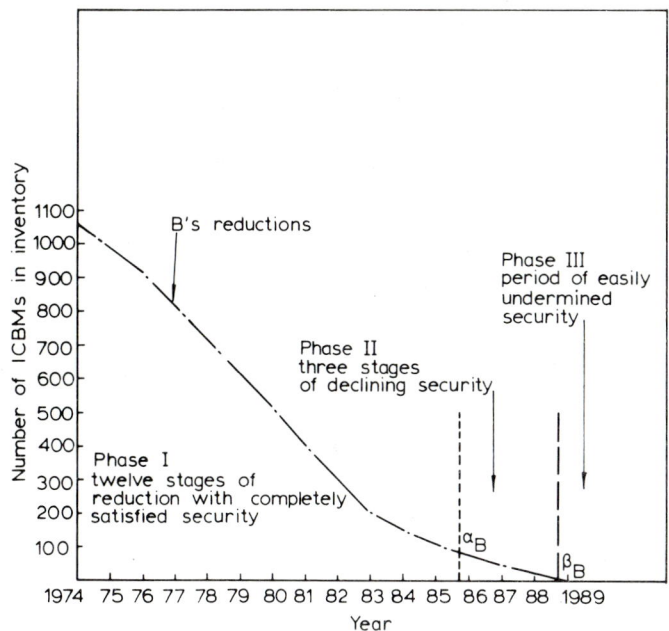

such a possibility the verification system used so far to monitor the agreement would have to be capable of discovering even a small number of missiles being produced clandestinely. At this stage of reductions the verification system would have to be very reliable, comprehensive and stringent.

The above described three phases of change in the security of A and B, engaged in a mutual strategic disarmament agreement, are displayed on Graphs 1A.6 and 1A.7. Here, however, points α and β are indicated, not on the curve of the security verification requirement, but on the curve of the actual ICBM reductions of A and B respectively. The vertical scale used in Graphs 1A.3 and 1A.4 is different from that used in Graphs 1A.6 and 1A.7. For this reason points α and β have been set according to their positions on the time axis.

Thus we can now understand more clearly the way in which numerical strategic limitations influence, or relate to, the security of states engaged in strategic disarmament. The changes in the security of states caused by mutual reductions of their inventories are not, however, measured in any quantitative way, but only as changes in time.

During the first eight stages of reductions when country A has reduced its arsenal by more than 1 100 missiles (from 1 567 to approximately 430) from the start of reductions to point α (see Graph 1A.3, 1A.6 and 1A.8), the security of that state is guaranteed by the fact that its residual second strike exceeds the value of its minimum deterrence threshold. Seeing that in terms of preserving a

Graph 1A.8. Scenario I: relation between disarmament and security of country A during 15 stages of ICBM reductions. The curve of A's ICBMs reduced is based on Table 1A.2, column 4 (see graph 1A.2). The line of A's security is based on the the description on pages 129–134. Points α_A and β_A are located according to their positions on the horizontal axis on Graph 1A.3.

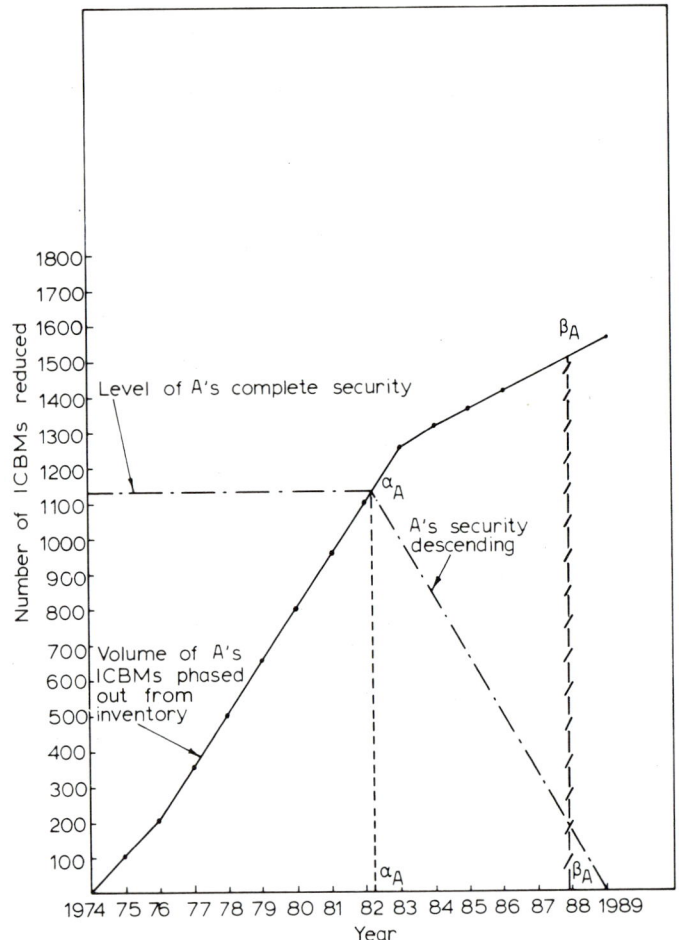

state's security one overkill is as good as many, the need for security is always satisfied so long as that state possesses a residual second strike larger than its minimum deterrence threshold. Any change, up or down, in the residual second strike has no effect on the level of a state's security so long as it does not fall below the level of the minimum deterrence threshold. Hence, during the first eight stages of reduction country A's security declines neither quantitatively nor qualitatively. This is shown on Graph 1A.8 as a straight line extending horizontally from the start of reductions to point α.

Returning to Graph 1A.6 it may be seen that during the next five stages of reductions, from point α to point β, or at stages 9–14, during which country A has reduced some additional 350 ICBMs, its security appears to diminish (though not necessarily so) because its residual second strike is now below the minimum deterrence threshold.

The perception of security is based on the probability of a threat occurring; and even though this probability may be very small, we have to consider it as a real threat to a state's survival. Thus, from point α onwards A's security is declining down to point β and extends to the end of the curve of reductions. This decline in the security of country A is shown on Graph 1A.8. The slope of this security curve at a given moment is impossible to measure. The only known factors are: fully satisfied security up to point α of reductions, and a complete lack of security (as far as ICBMs are concerned) down to the end of reductions.

A similar analysis can be made for country B. The three phases of change in its security are shown on Graph 1A.7. The phase during which security is completely satisfied extends over the first 12 reduction stages; the phase of diminishing security extends through stages 12–15; and the curve of reductions ends when this state's security can be easily undermined by even a small violation, this last phase occurring at the end of the fifteenth stage of reductions. So, during the 12-year period in which country B is reducing its arsenal by about 960 missiles, its security is untouched (see Graph 1A.9). Afterwards its security declines through point β down to the end of the scheme of reductions.

Graphs 1A.8 and 1A.9 give the basis for certain conclusions about the relation of disarmament to the security of the states undertaking it. These conclusions will now be compared with Wiesner's concept of the interrelation between disarmament, security and verification, as exemplified in the Wiesner curve (Graph 6.1, page 76).

It is apparent that during a certain period of reductions the process of strategic disarmament does not influence the security of the state carrying out the disarmament. This period is different for each party to the disarmament agreement, and depends on its military potential *vis-à-vis* the other parties to the agreement. In our model 15-year disarmament agreement this period lasts eight years for country A, and as long as 12 years for country B. The security of states during these reductions is completely satisfied. It does not diminish, as Wiesner asserted, in inverse proportion to the advances in disarmament. Thus, if verification is to be responsive to changes in the security of a state, it can then be assumed, because security remains satisfied during this period of reductions, that the rôle of the verification system in preserving security is negligible, and so the system need not be expanded as advocated by Wiesner.

At a certain point reductions enter a phase where the security of states may be seen to decline because every year smaller violations could endanger the residual second strikes of the countries involved. This decline in a state's security calls for some strengthening of the reliability, stringency and comprehensiveness of verification (though how much, it is impossible to quantify). This perceived need for stronger verification machinery gradually increases over the second phase (lasting five years for A, three for B). In reality, however, the numbers of

Graph 1A.9. Scenario I: relation between disarmament and security of country B during 15 stages of ICBM reductions. The curve of B's ICBMs reduced is based on Table 1A.2, column 4. The line of B's security is based on the analysis on pages 133–135. Points α_B and β_B are located according to their positions on the horizontal axis on Graph 1A.4.

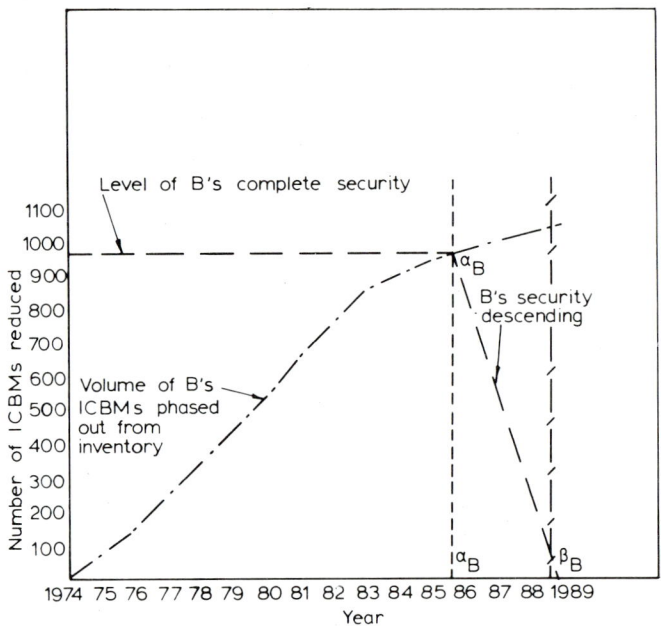

strategic weapons which could endanger the residual second strikes are still very large indeed, and thus any violation of such magnitudes would probably be easily discovered. The need for verification must therefore, even during this period, not be exaggerated. However, at a certain point in time (point β) the numbers of weapons which could become a mortal threat to the complying state become so small that to discover a violation of this magnitude would become difficult for any but the most extensive, reliable and stringent verification system. Although the moment of such a change in the verification requirement may be defined in time, there is no way of quantifying this increase in the requirement for verification. What we have done is to express the security verification requirement in terms only of the numbers of weapons which would need to be discovered by a verification system, and we have no way of measuring the verification itself. It is impossible to give a numerical value to the expressions such as stringency, reliability, comprehensiveness, and so on, which we have used. We have therefore only an impression as to how high a level of verification is required.

At this point it should be remembered that the minimum deterrence thresholds established here are the most pessimistic ones. In reality these thresholds would be likely to be much lower; hence points α_A and α_B would be located much closer to the final stages of disarmament than those considered above.

One proposition which could help in measuring the required level of verification somewhat more definitely is the following. Let us assume that the level of verification – that is, its efficiency, comprehensiveness and stringency – at a time when a state's residual second strike is equal to its minimum deterrence threshold, that is, when its security is fully preserved, is known and equals unity. This means that, at the time when the security of this state is completely guaranteed by its residual second strike, the state would be satisfied with a certain level of verification which we have defined as unity. We have the numerical expression of the security verification requirement for this moment (414 MIIIs for country A, and 1 326 SS9s for country B), as well as numerical expressions for such requirements during all other stages of ICBM reductions. If we divide all the values of security verification requirements by 414 or 1 326 for countries A and B respectively, the result will be an index expressing the relation between (1) the security verification requirement at all stages of ICBM reductions, and (2) the requirement at the time when the security of states is completely satisfied. The index will be a fraction of a unit over point α and a multiplication of a unit below this point. The level of the security verification requirement is inversely proportional to the

Table 1A.11 Scenario I: levels of required verification for countries A and B during ICBM reductions, 1974–1989[a]

Year and stage of reductions	Country A			Country B		
	Security verification requirement SVR	Index (I) of security verification requirement $\dfrac{SVR}{414}$	Level of required verification $\dfrac{1}{I}$	Security verification requirement SVR	Index (I) of security verification requirement $\dfrac{SVR}{1\,326}$	Level of required verification $\dfrac{1}{I}$
1974	1 610	3.9	0.26	10 711	8.1	0.12
1975	1 520	3.7	0.27	10 266	7.7	0.13
1976	1 451	3.5	0.29	9 817	7.4	0.14
1977	1 359	3.3	0.30	9 139	6.9	0.14
1978	1 268	3.1	0.32	8 461	6.4	0.16
1979	1 177	2.8	0.36	7 784	5.9	0.17
1980	962	2.3	0.43	7 106	5.4	0.19
1981	693	1.7	0.59	6 330	4.8	0.21
1982	466	1.1	0.90	4 685	3.5	0.29
Point α A	414	1.0	1.00	—	—	—
1983	239	0.6	1.72	3 040	2.3	0.43
1984	210	0.5	1.96	2 248	1.7	0.59
1985	202	0.5	2.0	1 632	1.2	0.83
Point α B	—	—	—	1 326	1.0	1.00
1986	185	0.4	2.3	1 182	0.9	1.11
1987	168	0.4	2.5	735	0.6	1.67
Point β A	100	0.2	4.14	—	—	—
1988	84	0.2	5.0	366	0.3	3.33
Point β B	—	—	—	100	0.07	13.26
1989	— 0	— $+\infty$	$+\infty$	—	—	$+\infty$

[a] Level of verification required at point $\alpha = 1$.

Graph 1A.10. Scenario I: level of required verification of countries A and B during ICBM reductions, 1974–89. Graph 1A.10 corresponds to Table 1A.11. The vertical axis scale is based on the values in columns 4 and 7 of that Table. The curves extend as high as values 414(A) and 1 326(B), i.e. practically to infinity.

Points α and β are set according to their positions on the horizontal axis (see Graphs 1A.3 and 1A.4). Points α must lie exactly at the level of 1. See also the explanation on page 137.

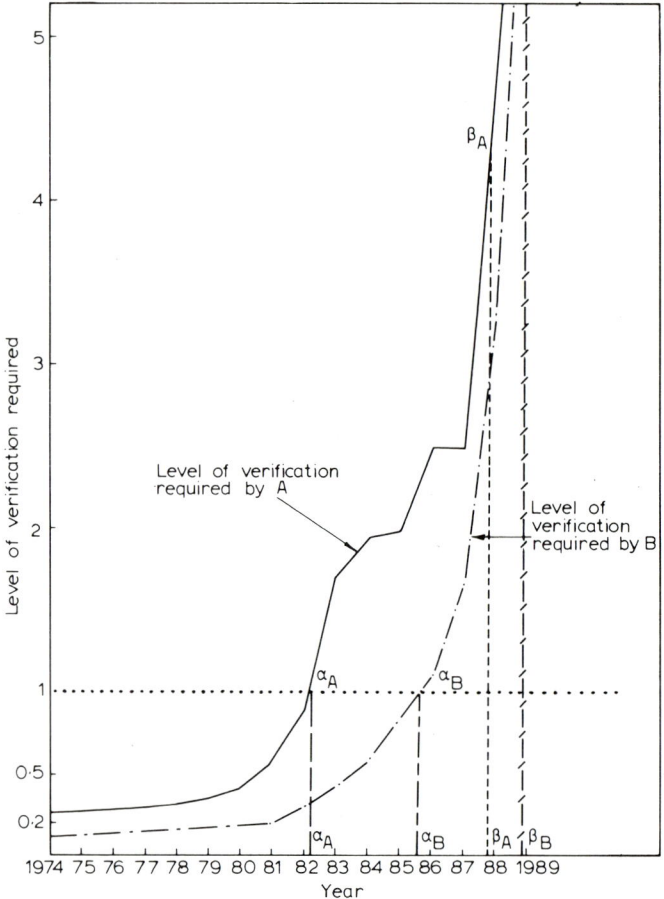

actual need for verification. Therefore to obtain the values of the 'real' need for verification we have to take the reciprocal of the index, that is to divide it into unity. The results of these calculations for Scenario I are given in Table 1A.11 and Graph 1A.10.

What may be seen from Graph 1A.10 is the way in which the level of verification required by either country grows with time, slowly at the outset of the reductions, and after passing point α rising rapidly upwards.

Finally, Graphs 1A.11 and 1A.12 indicate the relation between the variables mentioned by Wiesner, that is, between disarmament, security and verification.

Graph 1A.11. Scenario I: relation between disarmament, security and verification for country A, ICBM reductions. The scale on the vertical axis is for both number of ICBMs reduced and the level of verification required. This is possible owing to the fact that point $\alpha = 1$ of verification required, and at point α_A, in Graph 1A.8, A has reduced ±1 130 ICBMs. (This number is shown on the vertical axis, where a horizontal line is drawn from point α_A). Accordingly all the values of the required level of verification (Table 1A.11 column 4) can be translated into numbers of ICBMs reduced, and all curves on the graphs can be drawn on the same scale. The line of A's security is drawn in the same way as in Graph 1A.8. This graph helps us to compare our values with those shown in Wiesner's graph (see page 76).

The level of verification is shown by boxed numbers on the vertical axis.

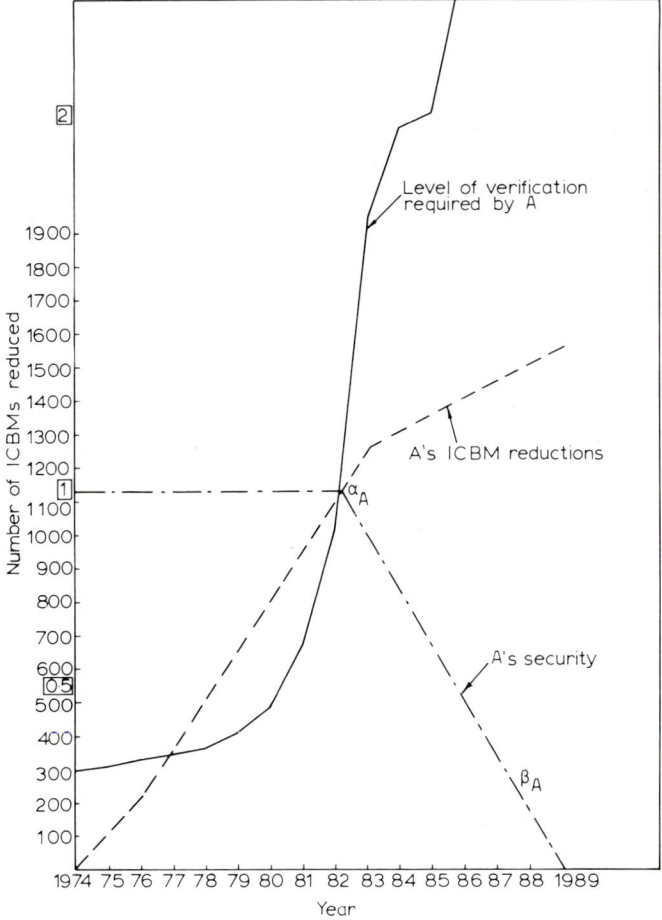

The scale of axis y on Graphs 1A.11 and 1A.12 is in the number of ICBMs reduced. Point α on each graph is found by its position on axis x (time scale). The horizontal line from point α to axis y indicates the level of security and at the same time indicates the level of reductions at which verification equals unity.

Graph 1A.12. Scenario I: relation between disarmament, security and verification for country B, ICBM reductions, 1974–89. The vertical scale is drawn in the same way as in graph 1A.11 (Table 1A.11, column 7) but point $\alpha_B = 1$, of the level of verification required, is now equal to $\pm$ 965 of B's ICBMs reduced. (See the position of α_A on the horizontal axis in Graph 1A.9.) The line of B's security is drawn in the same way as in Graph 1A.9. This graph helps us to discuss Wiesner's assumption of a relation between disarmament, security and verification.

The level of verification is shown by boxed numbers on the vertical axis.

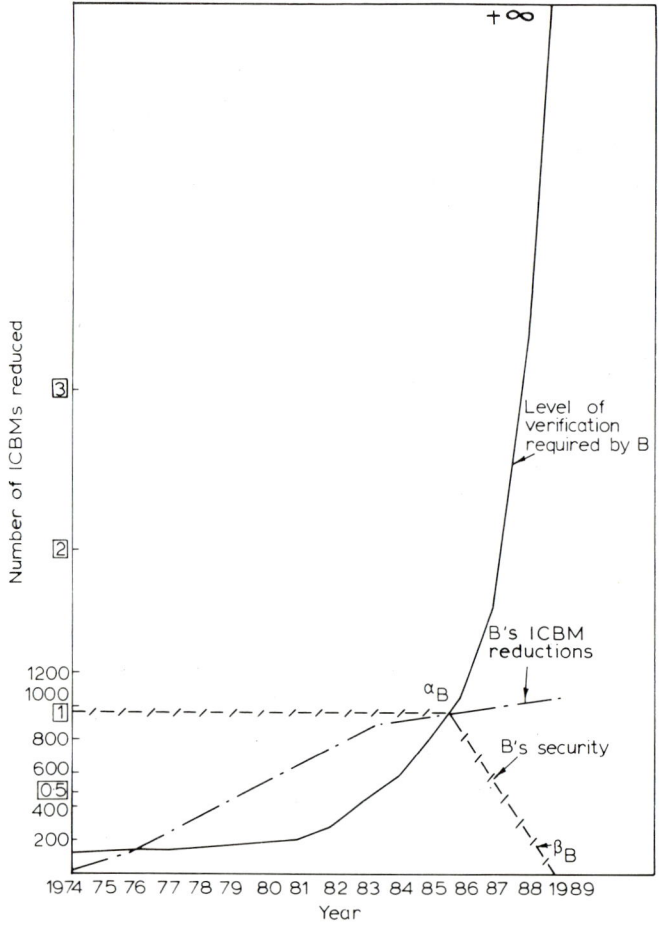

This occurs when A has reduced approximately 1 130 of its ICBMs, and when B has phased out approximately 965 ICBMs.

So it can be said that up to point α verification plays only a negligible rôle, if that, in preserving the security of states, because security is still guaranteed by the remaining weapons. After this point, security diminishes, initially more in perception than in real terms (up to point α), and afterwards rapidly down to zero. During this decrease the need for verification rapidly increases, apparently more rapidly than the diminution of security. In any case these two factors are not related in any directly proportional way.

So far the following conclusions may be drawn from the ICBM reductions in Scenario I:

1. During the long period of reductions, that is, for more than eight reduction stages on the part of country A, and almost 12 for country B, the security verification requirements are very low. Even substantial violations which remained undiscovered would not endanger the opponent's security, so that, practically speaking there is no military or political incentive for violating the treaty on ICBM reductions.

2. During the same period the security of states would remain constantly and completely satisfied in terms of their residual second strikes.

3. During the intermediate period of reductions (the second phase shown on Graphs 1A.6 and 1A.7) the security verification requirement is still very low; over 100 missiles would need to be clandestinely produced by the violating country; and it can be assumed that the level of verification (see its values in Table 1A.11) needed to cope with this requirement would not pose a problem, because its value in comparison with the level of verification when the security has been completely satisfied rises from 1 to 2.5 or 3.3 for A and B respectively.

4. During the intermediate period of reductions the security of states diminishes because their residual second strikes are below the value of the minimum deterrence required for the two countries. At this stage a verification system could be perceived as protecting the security of states to some degree.

5. During the final one or two stages of reductions, for B and A respectively, the security verification requirements become very high, because even a small violation of the order of 1–100 missiles could potentially be very dangerous for the complying state and difficult to discover by this complying state. To discover such small quantities of weapons a verification system would have to be extremely comprehensive and tight, and even if such stringency were possible there would still be limitations to the complete discovery of such violations.

6. Even for the concluding stages of the ICBM limitations the security verification requirement may be considered low if the existence of the substantial number of invulnerable sea-based second-strike missiles (SLBMs) possessed by both A and B is taken in to account. In fact this sea-based deterrent seems to guarantee security more effectively than the comprehensive verification system mentioned above.

7. In the strategic context within which A and B exist the relation between a state's security and verification of disarmament of the kind envisaged by Wiesner does not exist. During the long period of reductions the security of a state involved in strategic weapon limitations is stable and fully preserved, and verification is of little or no importance in maintaining it. At the later stages of reductions the level of verification required grows with the degree of the military insecurity of states, but the exact relation cannot be determined. Moreover, even the highest level of verification cannot give a complete 100 per cent probability of discovery of the small amounts of weapons which could be perceived as a threat to a country's security.

SLBM reductions

Sea-based strategic missiles are not at the present time considered as first-strike weapons.[12] Their primary rôle is seen as an invulnerable deterrence force, able to inflict a punitive second strike on the cities of an aggressor in a so-called countervalue mission. The danger of retaliatory attack on urban centres is essential to the reasoning behind MAD deterrence. It is widely believed that a sea-based deterrent remains permanently invulnerable unless it is endangered by developments in ASW technology. Thus so long as this invulnerability is preserved, the element of a strategic arsenal that is sea-based makes a second strike permanently feasible. So far as MAD deterrence is concerned, it is considered that the security of countries engaged in strategic disarmament is best guaranteed by the possesssion of this sea-based second strike. The presence of SLBM forces during ICBM reductions would therefore have a stabilizing effect on the strategic relationship between states engaged in these reductions, because each side would feel less threatened by even substantial violations of the agreement on ICBM reductions.

This statement about the stabilizing effect of SLBM forces on the military situation of A and B during ICBM reductions must, however, be qualified by the following observation: at the later stages of ICBM limitations, when the numbers of ICBMs remaining in each side's inventory are very low and the residual second strike they represent is small, then the offensive potential of the opponent's SLBMs might be considered a serious threat to the remaining ICBMs. The real situation in this case will depend on the character of the opposing SLBM force. If the offensive potential of this force were based mainly on a larger number of warheads and to a less degree on their megatonnage and accuracy, then its counterforce (countersilo) value would be small, and hence less of a threat to the ICBMs that remained in the opponent's arsenal. Conversely, if one or both sides possessed very accurate and powerful SLBMs, then to preserve the balance of security of these states an ICBM disarmament agreement would probably have to be accompanied by appropriate limitations on SLBM forces.

Although the presence of SLBMs may have a stabilizing effect on the strategic balance of states involved in ICBM reductions, with the reservation expressed above, their existence is connected with all the dangers inherent in any kind of nuclear arsenal: among them the risk of war by accident, miscalculation, or political tension, and above all the danger of proliferation of nuclear weapons to other states. This last mentioned danger could even force the states pursuing ICBM limitations to halt their disarmament.

Ideally, reductions in SLBMs would concern the submarine-launched missiles themselves. In practice it is more convenient to base the analysis on the number of submarines rather than on their missiles. The unit of reductions is dictated here by the nature of the weapons and by the problems they pose to a verification system. It would probably be very difficult to create a reliable verification system, which would not be too intrusive and yet able to check the actual number of SLBMs on submarines being located at sea. Because of the problems connected with verification, the unit to be considered in SLBM reductions will be the submarines themselves.

A complete freeze on qualitative improvements in strategic arsenals at the 1974 level has already been assumed. However, to assume that submarines would continue to be functional during the 15-year period of ICBM reductions without being repaired, overhauled and improved is not realistic. It could then be agreed that some repairs would be excluded from this general ban on qualitative improvements. However, from the point of view of verification this would require additional arrangements to monitor operations in shipyards and docks in order to differentiate between simple repairs on submarines and the forbidden qualitative improvements. So for the purposes of this analysis we ignore the question.

Similarly, for simplicity of argument the difference between the number of submarines on station and the number of all submarines existing in an arsenal will not be taken into account. Again, the question of an SLBM's range, important for any analysis of the sea-based deterrent, is omitted here.

The security verification requirement in the two cases of strategic disarmament considered here, namely ICBM and SLBM reductions, with a prior and complete freeze on qualitative improvements in these weapons has two different yardsticks. The security verification requirement in the case of ICBM reductions defines the demand for the verification system to be capable of discovering the land-based missiles calculated necessary to be secretly produced and deployed (probably over a short time) that would give a violator a real military advantage (preferably a first-strike capability). In the case of SLBM reductions the security verification requirement cannot and need not be quantified, as the danger to security is posed not so much by the characteristics or numbers of the opponent's weapons, but by the opponent's ASW potential of such an order that it would threaten the invulnerability of the other state's missile-carrying submarines. The security verification requirement in this case would therefore be the required capability of the verification system to discover any expansion and intensification of this ASW threat.

The actual disarmament scheme for SLBM limitations, in the light of what was said above about the security verification requirement in SLBM reductions, is therefore quite irrelevant. Any limitation schedule, be it 10 or 15 years, would mean a proportional number of submarines destroyed or incapacitated. As in the case of ICBM reductions it would be advisable from the political point of view to balance the reduced forces according to their offensive capabilities, so that neither country would feel that it was losing the deterrent credibility of its remaining SLBMs. If the methods and locations of these limitations were prearranged, they would be easy to monitor by ordinary national means of verification. The number of submarines being reduced in a given year would constitute the direct verification requirement in SLBM reductions.

At the beginning of the long period of ICBM reductions the security of states is preserved (*a*) by the ICBMs still remaining in their arsenals, and (*b*) by the fact that they still possess SLBM forces capable of a second strike. The security verification requirement is thus fairly low. Even during the final stages of ICBM reductions when the security verification requirement for ICBMs is very high, the existence of these SLBMs represents a sufficient guarantee of a state's security.

The theoretical growth of the security verification requirement at the end of ICBM reductions may thus be disregarded.

It is obvious from the above analysis that a quantified relationship between security and verification during numerical strategic disarmament can be found only when a security verification requirement can be calculated. This is not possible in the case of SLBM reductions, where security-orientated verification is directed at the ASW threat, and not at potential numerical violations. Such numerical violations have no bearing on the quality of the residual second strike represented by the remaining SLBMs.

V. Scenario II: numerical limitations of A's and B's strategic forces accompanying an unrestricted qualitative arms race

With the exclusion of changes caused by the process of technological improvement taking place in Scenario II, the structure of the arsenals in countries A and B is exactly the same in both Scenarios.

Since the K method has been adopted for calculations in Scenario I, the same method will be used in Scenario II.

Country A's ICBM conversions and replacements

Let us assume that, as shown in Table 1A.12, country A will start to MIRV its missiles in 1976. It may begin with SS-17 and SS-19 missiles, both of which types would be armed with five MIRVed warheads, each having a yield of 1 Mt, and an accuracy (CEP) of 0.5 nm. The reliability of these missiles is assumed to be 80 per cent. (Table 1A.13 shows the characteristics of all these newly introduced missiles.) During the first year (1976) the rate of production of these missiles is assumed to be as high as 60 missiles, and 100–120 during the four subsequent years. These missiles will initially replace the SS11-1 model in soft silos, and subsequently those in hard silos as well. A year after beginning this process of MIRVing the SS17/SS19s in arsenal A, another type of missile will be introduced into the arsenal. This is the SS18, tipped with six to eight MIRVed warheads (we have adopted six in our calculations).[13] This missile will have the same characteristics as the SS17/SS19 (see Table 1A.13). An overall production of up to 200 ICBMs annually is assumed, even though this could be regarded as an excessively large figure for the production of a new and very sophisticated ICBM. At such a production rate the SS18 will replace the SS9 type over a three-year period, first from soft and later on from hard silos. The total cumulative production of SS17/19s and SS18s will not exceed the limit of 200 a year. The K values of all missiles considered in Scenario II are given in Table 1A.14.

Table 1A.12. Country A: progress of simultaneous ICBM reductions, replacements and improvements

Year or stage of reductions	Numbers and types of ICBMs reduced	Numbers and types of ICBM improved or replaced	Numbers and types of missiles, silos and warheads (re-entry vehicles (RVs) after reductions and replacements)
1974	—	—	139 SS7s in solft silos[a] 70 SS8s in soft silos 500 SS11–1s in soft silos 470 SS11–1s in hard silos[b] 40 SS11–3s in hard silos 60 SS13s in hard silos 188 SS9s in soft silos 100 SS9s in hard silos
Total	—	—	1567 missiles (1567 RVs)
1975	109 SS7s	—	As above, minus 109 SS7s
Total	109	—	1458 missiles (1458 RVs)
1976	30 SS7s and 70 SS8s	50 SS11–1s in soft silos replaced by 50 SS17/19s (MIRVed with 5 RVs) in very hard silos	450 SS11–1s in soft silos 470 SS11–1s in hard silos 40 SS11–3s in hard silos 60 SS13s in hard silos 188 SS9s in soft silos 100 SS9s in hard silos 50 SS17/19s in very hard silos[c]
Total	100	50	1358 missiles (1558 RVs)
1977	150 SS11–1s in soft silos	100 SS11–1s in soft silos replaced by 100 SS17/19s in very hard silos; 100 SS9s in soft silos replaced by 100 SS18 (MIRVed with 6 RVs) in very hard silos	200 SS11–1s in soft silos 470 SS11–1s in hard silos 40 SS11–3s in hard silos 60 SS13s in hard silos 88 SS9s in soft silos 100 SS9s in hard silos 150 SS17/19s in very hard silos 100 SS18s in very hard silos
Total	150	200	1208 missiles (2308 RVs)
1978	150 SS11–1s in silos	50 SS11–1s in soft silos and 50 SS11–1s in hard silos replaced by 100 SS17/19s in very hard silos; 88 SS9s in soft silos and 12 SS9s in hard silos replaced by 100 SS18s in very hard silos	420 SS11–1s in hard silos 40 SS11–3s in hard silos 60 SS13s in hard silos 88 SS9s in hard silos 250 SS17/19s in very hard silos 200 SS18s in very hard silos
Total	150	200	1058 missiles (3058 RVs)

Year or stage of reductions	Numbers and types of ICBMs reduced	Numbers and types of ICBM improved or replaced	Numbers and type of missiles, silos and warheads (re-entry vehicles (RVs) after reductions and replacements)
1979	150 SS11–1s in hard silos	120 SS11–1s in hard silos replaced by 100 SS17/19s in very hard silos; 88 SS9s in hard silos replaced by 88 SS18s in very hard silos	150 SS11–1s in hard silos 40 SS11–3s in hard silos 60 SS13s in hard silos 370 SS17/19s in very hard silos 288 SS18s in very hard silos
Total	150	208	908 missiles (3828 RVs)
1980	50 SS11–1s, 40 SS11–3s and 60 SS13s all in hard silos	100 SS11–1s in hard silos replaced by 100 SS17/19s in very hard silos	470 SS17/19s in very hard silos 288 SS18s in very hard silos
Total	150	100	758 missiles (4078 RVs)
1981	150 SS17/19s in very hard silos	100 SS18s hardened to 1000 lb/in^2	320 SS17/19s in very hard silos 188 SS18s in very hard silos 100 SS18s in superhard silos
Total	150	100	608 missiles (3328 RVs)
1982	150 SS17/19s in very hard silos	100 SS18s hardened to 1000 lb/in^2	170 SS17/19s in very hard silos 88 SS18s in very hard silos 200 SS18s in superhard silos
Total	150	100	458 missiles (2578 RVs)
1983	150 SS17/19s in very hard silos	50 SS18s hardened to 1000 lb/in^2	20 SS17/19s in very hard silos 38 SS18s in very hard silos 250 SS18s in superhard silos
Total	150	50	308 missiles (1828 RVs)
1984	20 SS17/19s and 38 SS18s in very hard silos	—	250 missiles (1500 RVs) in superhard silos
1985	50 SS18s in superhard silos	—	200 missiles (1200 RVs)
1986	50 SS18s in superhard silos	—	150 missiles (900 RVs)
1987	50 SS18s in superhard silos	—	100 missiles (600 RVS)
1988	50 SS18s in superhard silos	—	50 missiles (300 RVs)
1989	50 SS18s in superhard silos	—	—

Table 1A.13. Characteristics of the new ICBMs introduced by countries A and B during the reductions in Scenario II

Missile	Number of warheads (MIRV) per missile	Y Mt	CEP nmile	ρ per cent
SS17/19	5	1.0	0.50	80
SS18	6	1.0	0.50	80
MIII improved	3	0.3	0.15	85
MIII MARVed	3	0.3	0.03	85

Table 1A.14. K per warhead of the missiles of reliability ρ reduced in Scenario II

Country	Missile	Number of warheads per missile	K per warhead, ρ
A			
	SS7/8	1	2.19
	SS9	1	5.53
	SS11/13	1	0.75
	SS17/19	5	3.2
	SS18	6	3.2
B			
	TII	1	9.34
	MI	1	3.2
	MII	1	8.89
	MIII	3	5.9
	MIII improved	3	13.4
	MIII MARVed	3	87.3

Table 1A.15. Scenario II: hardness (H) and K' values of the reduced silos

H lb/in²	K' per silo, $P_k = 0.95$	H lb/in²	K' per silo, $P_k = 0.95$
100	16.7	500	56.5
300	38.6	1 000	92.1

All these new types of missiles will supposedly be protected by a new type of upgraded silo. At first the new missiles will be located in silos called very hard silos, having 500 lb/in² overpressure resistance. After 1981 the new weapons will be protected by silos called superhard silos, having 1 000 lb/in² overpressure resistance. The process of silo hardening will be completed in 1984 as shown in Table 1A.12. The hardness of these silos and their K' values are indicated in Table 1A.15.

No further improvements have been assumed for country A. The technological capabilities of this country are assumed to be smaller than those of B, and consequently improvements such as MARVing are considered out of A's reach and uneconomical in view of the fact that ICBM reductions will only last until 1989.

Country B's ICBM conversions and replacements

It has been assumed that the first step in upgrading country B's arsenal would be its silo-hardening programme, in which it proceeded to harden silos containing MII missiles to up to 1 000 lb/in^2 overpressure resistance. This process will start in 1976 when the new missiles of country A first appear and will continue until 1978.

In 1978 country B will begin on its next improvement programme by increasing the accuracy and reliability of its existing MIII missiles. These improvements do not have the character of full conversions into different missiles, but rather of certain refinements of critical equipment on board the missiles, such as computers and guidance systems. They may even involve the replacement of the entire re-entry vehicle. This second phase will last from 1978 until the end of 1980, and will be carried out at the rate of 100–150 missiles per year as shown in Table 1A.16.

Table 1A.16. Country B: progress of simultaneous ICBM reductions and improvements

Year or stage of reductions	Numbers and types of ICBMs reduced	Numbers and types of ICBMs improved	Numbers and types of missiles, silos and warheads (re-entry vehicles [RVs]) after reductions and improvements)
1974	—	—	54 TIIs in hard silos^a 100 MIs in hard sillos 500 MIIs in hard silos 400 MIIIs in superhard silos^b
Total	—	—	1054 missiles (1859 RVs)
1975	70 MIs in hard silos	—	54 TIIs in hard silos 30 MIs in hard silos 500 MIIs in hard silos 400 MIIIs in superhard silos
Total	70	—	984 missiles (1789 RVs)
1976	30 MIs and 40 MII in hard silos	50 MII in hard silos hardened to 1000 lb/in^2	54 TIIs in hard silos 410 MIIs in hard silos 40 MIIs in superhard silos 400 MIIIs in superhard silos
Total	70	50	914 missiles (1714 RVs)

Year or stage of reductions	Numbers and types of ICBMs reduced	Numbers and types of ICBMs improved	Numbers and types of missiles, silos and warheads (re-entry vehicles [RVs] after reductions and improvements)
1977	100 MIIs in hard silos	100 MIIs hardened to 1000 lb/in^2	54 TIIs in hard silos 210 MIIs in hard silos 150 MIIs in superhard silos 400 MIIIs in superhard silos
Total	100	100	814 missiles (1614 RVs)
1978	100 MIIs in hard silos	110 MIIs hardened to 1000 lb/in^2 100 MIIIs upgraded to 100 MIIIs improved	54 TIIs in hard silos 260 MIIs in superhard silos 300 MIIIs in superhard silos 100 MIIs improved, in superhard silos
Total	100	210	714 missiles (1514 RVs)
1979	100 MIIs in superhard silos	150 MIIIs improved	54 TIIs in hard silos 160 MIIs in superhard silos 150 MIIIs in superhard silos 250 MIIIs improved, in superhard silos
Total	100	150	614 missiles (1414 RVs)
1980	100 MIIs in superhard silos	150 MIIIs improved	54 TIIs in hard silos 60 MIIs in superhard silos 400 MIIIs improved, in superhard silos
Total	100	150	514 missiles (1314 RVs)
1981	54 TIIs in hard silos and 60 MIIs in superhard silos	—	400 MIIIs improved (1200 RVs) in superhard silos
1982	100 MIIIs improved	100 MIIIs MARVed	200 MIIIs improved 100 MIIIs MARVed (900 RVs)
1983	100 MIIIs improved	100 MIIIS MARVed	200 MIIIs MARVed (600 RVs)
1984	50 MIIIs MARVed	—	150 MIIIs MARVed (450 RVs)
1985	40 MIIIs MARVed	—	110 MIIIs MARVed (330 RVs)
1986	30 MIIIs MARVed	—	80 MIIIs MARVed (240 RVs)
1987	30 MIIIs MARVed	—	50 MIIIs MARVed (150 RVs)
1988	25 MIIIs MARVed	—	25 MIIIs MARVed (75 RVs)
1989	25 MIIIs MARVed	—	—

Country B is assumed to be technologically superior to A. It is therefore capable of making more than basic improvements in its MIIIs, making it possible to deploy the technologically superior terminal guidance system on these missiles. Its three MIRVed warheads will then in effect have been MARVed. With these

Graph 1A.13. Scenario II: illustration of A's and B's reductions of missiles and warheads, 1974–89, concomitant with an unrestricted qualitative arms race. This graph corresponds to Tables 1A.12 and 1A.16. See the totals, and the last column of these Tables. See also pages 144–149.

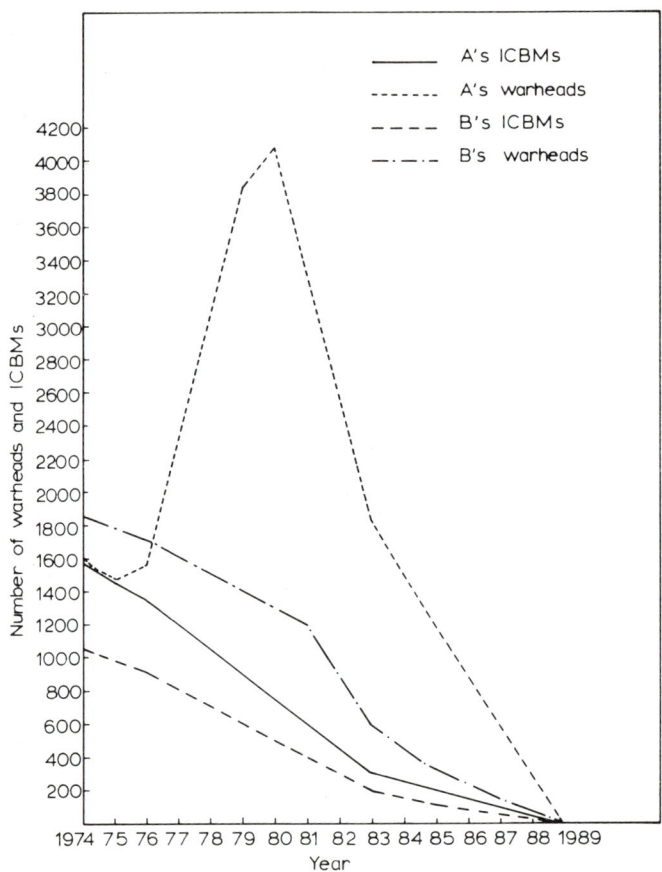

advances the MIIIs will acquire a countersilo capability limited only by its reliability figure. The characteristics of these improved and MARVed missiles are shown in Table 1A.13, and their K values in Table 1A.14.

The process of MARVing is rapid (100 ICBMs a year). As only 200 MIIIs improved are left in B's arsenal, the whole programme will be accomplished in two years (see Table 1A.16), on the surface a rather too short period. What is being visualized here, however, is only the period of actual deployment, not the long process of research and development prior to this deployment. Moreover, in terms of the scheme of improvements linked to the ICBM reductions considered here, the process must be concluded very rapidly if it is to have any rationale at all.

All weapons of country B in the process of being improved or MARVed are protected by silos of 1 000 lb/in² overpressure resistance. Further substantial upgrading of the resistance of these silos seems to have no effect on their survivability, and therefore has not been considered here.

None of the conversions and improvements in A's and B's forces described above changes the structure of their arsenals so far as numbers of ICBMs are concerned. Numerically the reductions in ICBMs envisaged in Scenario II are exactly the same as those for Scenario I. This is not the case with warheads. In Scenario II country A's technological expansion means that it embarks upon a programme of MIRVing its missiles. The number of warheads (or re-entry vehicles) deliverable against country B is thus substantially expanded as can be seen from Tables 1A.12 and 1A.16 and Graph 1A.13. In this graph the lines indicating the numbers of A's and B's missiles and warheads are exactly the same as those in Graph 1A.1, Scenario 1. The only difference between the two graphs is the line showing A's warheads (in Graph 1A.13), which shoots up to a peak in 1980. This graph illustrates how the introduction of technology makes it difficult to apply the same rule of numerical proportionality in numbers of ICBMs and warheads to both Scenario I and II. In Scenario II, though proportionality is maintained in the numbers of reduced ICBMs, the difference between the numbers of A's and B's warheads remaining in the inventories is enormously in favour of A. Such a disproportion, though simplified and therefore not a true picture of the relation between the two arsenals, nor of the two countries' military capabilities, could create difficulties in getting such a scheme of reductions accepted, because on paper at least, the discrepancy is overwhelming.

From this it can be inferred that the rule of proportional security between A and B during ICBM reductions, which was the basic premise in Scenario I, cannot be applied fully to Scenario II, because of the unrestricted technological arms race.

Graph 1A.13 also shows A's and B's military efforts carried out to the full extent of their technological capabilities, both quantivatively and qualitatively. As will be seen later, such an effort may be in vain for one country if the technological capabilities of its competitor are uncontrolled and substantially different.

Maximum limits of the K value

The technological improvements in Scenario II, especially those of country B, expand the accuracies and reliabilities of ICBMs, creating a situation where the kill probability of the missile used is limited only by its reliability figure. In such a situation the *CEP* of a weapon is equal or smaller than the crater radius (which is a function of yield). At this point the value of *K* as a measurement of a weapon's lethality becomes questionable. From the moment when the radius of a crater created by a weapon is equal or larger than the *CEP* of the weapon there is a limit to the growth of the *K* value. The formula for *K* is:

$$K = \frac{Y^{2/3}}{(CEP)^2}$$

When $CEP \leqslant r_c$, where r_c is the radius of the crater, the formula will be

$$K = \frac{Y^{2/3}}{r_c^2}$$

Notice that $r_c = \lambda\, Y^{1/3}$, where λ is a constant (19 metres per kiloton, or 0.107 nm per Mt for dry soil).

Thus the

$$K_{\text{limit}} = \frac{Y^{2/3}}{\lambda^2 \cdot Y^{2/3}} = \frac{1}{\lambda^2},$$

therefore the K_{limit} is independent of yield and CEP, once the CEP goes below the value of r_c. Because λ varies with the soil, the harder the soil the larger will the K maximum be. Calculating for dry soil the maximum K value will be

$$K_{\text{limit}} = \frac{1}{0.107^2_{\text{nm}}/\text{Mt}} \simeq 87$$

This is the maximum K value for any weapon whose $CEP \leqslant r_c$ in the case of dry soil. Any number larger than this is meaningless. The maximum value of $K = 87$ will be used to calculate the lethality of the most modern weapons introduced in Scenario II, that is, of country B's MARVed MIII missiles.

The minimum deterrence threshold

The calculation of the minimum deterrence threshold for Scenario II is somewhat more complicated by the fact that new weapons protected by new silos are constantly being introduced. The actual calculations are made in exactly the same way as those for Scenario I, and their results are shown in Tables 1A.17 and 1A.18. It is clear that the values of the threshold fluctuate according to technological changes in the arsenals. The apparent rise of the threshold's upper value in 1978–79 for both countries is caused by the process of strengthening the silos protecting the non-MIRVed missiles still existing. As we are measuring the threshold values in terms of the K' values of the certain number of silos that must survive if a state is to retain its minimum second strike, the expansion of a silo's qualitative characteristics augments their survivability, and consequently causes the value of the minimum deterrence threshold to increase accordingly. To give one example of the calculation: in 1978 country B has in its inventory 54 TIIs in silos of 300 lb/in², 260 MIIs in silos of 1 000 lb/in², 300 MIIIs in silos of 1 000 lb/in², and 100 improved MIIIs in silos of 1 000 lb/in². In the case of only non-MIRVed missiles surviving an attack B's minimum deterrence threshold (assuming that 190 missiles must survive) will be 54 TIIs and 136 MIIs. Their silos have K' values of 38.6 and 92.1 respectively. Multiplying and adding together these figures gives a value of 14 610 $K'S$, which is the highest possible limit of B's minimum deterrence threshold in 1978. In the same way the limits of A's and B's minimum deterrence thresholds were calculated. The fluctuations of A's and B's minimum deterrence threshold are given in Tables 1A.17 and 1A.18. They are indicated

Table 1A.17. **Fluctuation of the minimum deterrence threshold of A during ICBM reductions in Scenario II, given in** $K'S$ **values and in numbers of the opponent's best missiles needed to overcome these** $K'S$ **values** (same measurement as for the security verification requirement)

	Country A				
	$K'S$ value		Number of the opponent's missiles needed		
Year	Lowest limit	Highest limit	Lowest limit	Highest limit	Type of missile
1974	3 173	7 334	179	414	MIII
1975	3 173	7 334	179	414	MIII
1976	2 147	3 173	121	179	MIII
1977	1 808	3 173	102	179	MIII
1978	1 808	7 334	45	182	Improved MIII
1979	1 808	7 334	45	182	Improved MIII
1980	1 808	1 808	45	45	Improved MIII
1981	1 808	2 947	45	73	Improved MIII
1982	1 808	2 947	7	11	MARVed MIII
1983	1 808	2 947	7	11	MARVed MIII
1984–88	2 947	2 947	11	11	MARVed MIII

Table 1A.18. **Fluctuation of the minimum deterrence threshold of B during ICBM reductions in Scenario II, given in** $K'S$ **values and in numbers of the opponent's best missiles needed to overcome these** $K'S$ **values** (same measurement as for the security verification requirement)

	Country B				
	$K'S$ value		Number of the opponent's missiles needed		
Year	Lowest limit	Highest limit	Lowest limit	Highest limit	Type of missile
1974	5 894	7 334	1 066	1 326	SS9
1975	5 894	7 334	1 066	1 326	SS9
1976	5 894	7 334	368	458	SS17/19
1977	5 894	7 334	307	382	SS18
1978	5 894	14 610	307	761	SS18
1979	5 894	14 610	307	761	SS18
1980	5 894	9 913	307	516	SS18
1981–88	5 894	5 894	307	307	SS18

Graph 1A.14. Scenario II: fluctuations of A's and B's minimum deterrence threshold during ICBM reductions, 1974–89, concomitant with an unrestricted qualitative arms race. This graph is based on Tables 1A.17 and 1A.18, columns 4 and 5 (highest and lowest limits). See also this Appendix, pages 158–161.

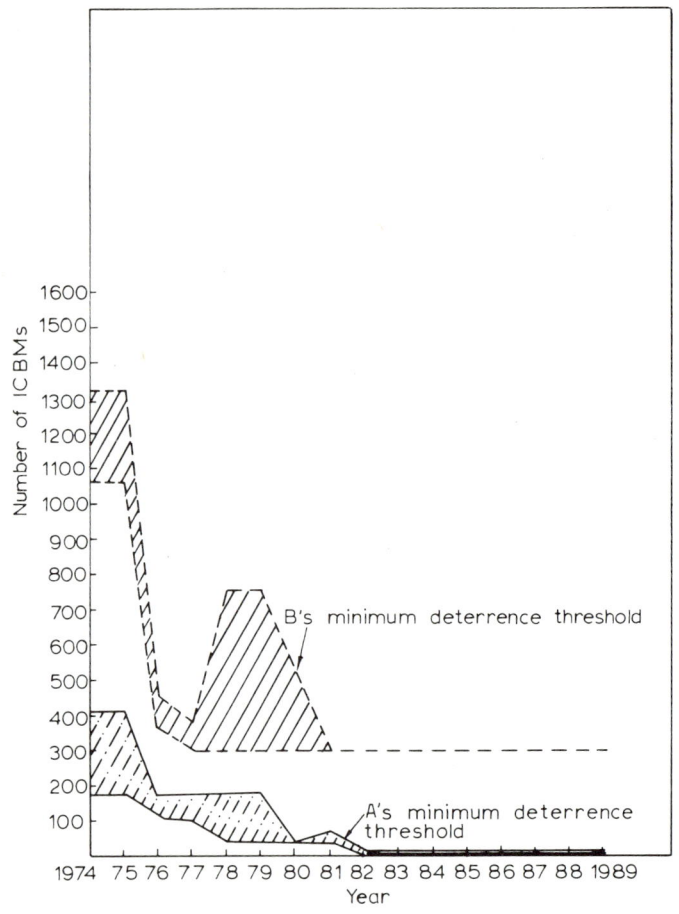

both in KS values and in numbers of the opponent's best missiles which would have to be clandestinely produced in order to overcome this minimum deterrence threshold. This second measurement makes it possible to draw the highest limits of the threshold, using the same scale as for the security verification requirement, in order to find the location of points α and β in Scenario II. Thus the fluctuations of the thresholds of A and B are shown together on Graph 1A.14, where both the lowest and highest limits were shown. Subsequently, in the following graphs only the highest limits are indicated.

It is clear from Tables 1A.17 and 1A.18 that the $K'S$ values of the minimum deterrence threshold are, despite their fluctuations, of a quite high order, and do not differ so radically from those in Scenario I. However, when these values are measured in numbers of the opponent's best missiles existing at the time, then the limits of the minimum deterrence threshold have a tendency to decline sharply, because the newly introduced missiles have much greater accuracy and reliability (greater kill potential). For country A which has greatly expanded the survivability of its silos, so that, for example, in 1984 its minimum deterrence threshold is equal to $K'S = 2\,947$, this value can be matched by as small a number of B's MARVed MIIIs as 11. This same $K'S$ value in Scenario I would imply that about 196 MIIIs would need to be built clandestinely in order to threaten this minimum deterrence. The difference in these situations has serious consequences for the whole concept of the minimum deterrence threshold and hence the considerations about security that are linked to this concept. In Scenario I the threshold has apparently been established to such a high, even excessive, level that a country possessing it could rest assured that its verification system would probably easily cope with finding any clandestine production aimed at the acquisition of such a number of weapons which could destroy this minimum deterrent. In the case of Scenario II a country possessing a minimum deterrent of a certain value cannot be assured that even a small number of the opponent's best weapons, extremely difficult to be discovered by any system of verification, will not endanger the very existence of a major part of this minimum deterrent on account of the rapid expansion of military technology in the accuracy, communication and reliability of weapons.

These considerations are confined, however, only to the ICBM arsenal and to the deterrent based on ICBMs. This is too narrow a perspective from which to draw sound conclusions about a state's overall military security, and such conclusions will therefore be avoided until the whole Scenario has been considered.

Calculation of the security verification requirements of A and B

The security verification requirements of A and B in Scenario II were calculated with the K method described on pages 117–118. The basic figures for KN and KS potentials in 1974 are exactly the same for Scenario II as for Scenario I. From these basic figures the appropriate KN and KS values represented by the reduced numbers of ICBMs and their silos were subtracted. The values of the residual second strikes of A and B being reduced annually during ICBM reductions in Scenario II are given in Table 1A.19. The security verification requirements are based on these values.

Only two additional operations are involved in the calculations for Scenario II; they are required because of the need to add the additional KN and KS values brought in by the introduction of the new weapons into the reduced arsenals. The resulting figure shows that in consequence of the process of technological expansion in the arsenals their military capabilities, measured in KN and KS values increase substantially, despite the reductions in ICBMs. Another complication in the calculations in Scenario II is the need to quantify the security verification requirement in numbers of different types of missiles as new missiles enter the arsenals. Thus until 1977 the requirement of country A is calculated in

Table 1A.19. Scenario II: the residual second strikes of A and B during ICBM reductions concomitant with an unrestricted qualitative arms race, 1974–89, given in $K'S$ values[a]

Year	Country A	Country B
1974	28 493	59 232
1975	26 896	56 768
1976	27 668	56 198
1977	34 012	54 908
1978	36 748	54 154
1979	32 195	42 023
1980	25 709	31 401
1981	21 832	26 190
1982	3 267	19 380
1983	—	12 570
1984	—	9 015
1985	—	6 290
1986	—	4 487
1987	—	2 684
1988	—	1 277
1989	—	—

[a] All figures are rounded.

Table 1A.20. Scenario II: the security verification requirements of A and B during ICBM reductions concomitant with an unrestricted qualitative arms race, 1974–89

	Country A		Country B	
Year	Number	Type	Number	Type
1974	1 610	MIII	10 711	SS9
1975	1 520	MIII	10 266	SS9
1976	1 563	MIII	3 512	SS17/19
1977	1 922	MIII	2 860	SS18
1978	914	MIII improved	2 821	SS18
1979	801	MIII improved	2 189	SS18
1980	640	MIII improved	1 635	SS18
1981	543	MIII improved	1 364	SS18
Point β_A	100	MIII improved	—	—
1982	15	MIII MARVed	1 009	SS18
Point α_A	11	MIII MARVed	—	—
1983	—		655	SS18
1984	—		470	SS18
1985	—		328	SS18
Point α_B	—		307	SS18
1986	—		234	SS18
1987	—		140	SS18
Point β_B	—		100	SS18
1988	—		67	SS18

Graph 1A.15. Scenario II: country A's security verification requirement during ICBM reductions, 1974–89, concomitant with an unrestricted qualitative arms race, and A's minimum deterrence threshold during these reductions. This graph is based on Table 1A.20, column 2. The level of A's minimum deterrence threshold is similar to that in Graph 1A.14, country A.

α_A = Point at which A's security verification requirement equals the highest limit of A's minimum deterrence threshold.

β_B = Point at which A's security verification requirement equals 100 ICBMs.

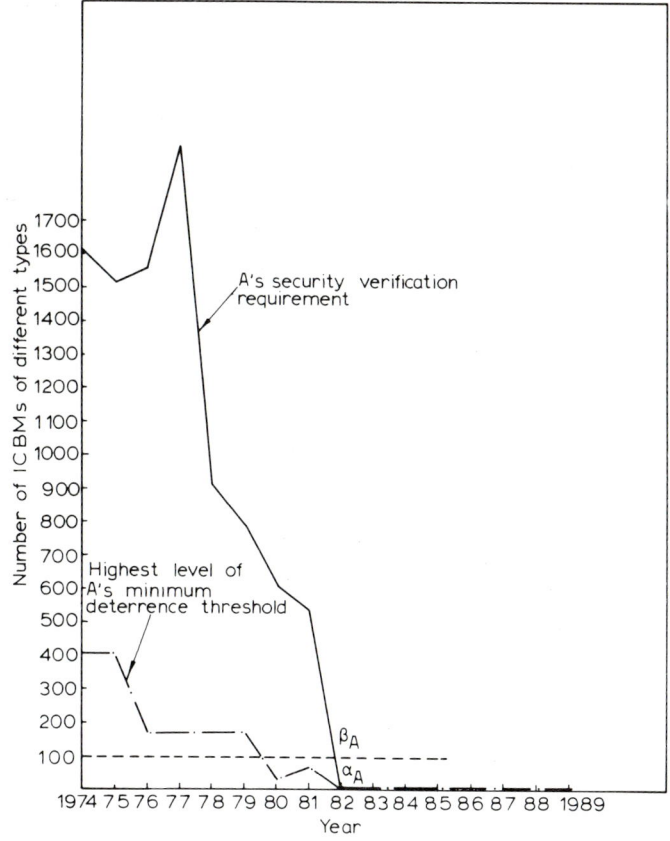

numbers of MIIIs, from 1978 to 1981 in numbers of improved MIIIs and subsequently in numbers of MARVed MIIIs. The security verification requirement of B is reckoned in SS9s until 1975, then in SS17/19s in 1976, and subsequently in SS18s as being the most advanced weapon in A's arsenal.

The final results of the calculations of A's and B's security verification requirements at all stages of ICBM reductions in Scenario II are shown in Table 1A.20. For both countries the figures are indicated in numbers of missiles. The same figures are shown also on Graphs 1A.15 and 1A.16 (the continuous line indicating the security verification requirement).

Graph 1A.16. Scenario II: country B's security verification requirement during ICBM reductions, 1974–89, concomitant with an unrestricted qualitative arms race, and B's minimum deterrence threshold during these reductions. This graph is based on Table 1A.20, column 4. The limit of the minimum deterrence threshold of B is as in Graph 1A.14.

α_B = Point at which B's security verification requirement equals the highest limit of B's minimum deterrence threshold.

β_B = Point at which B's security verification requirement equals 100 ICBMs.

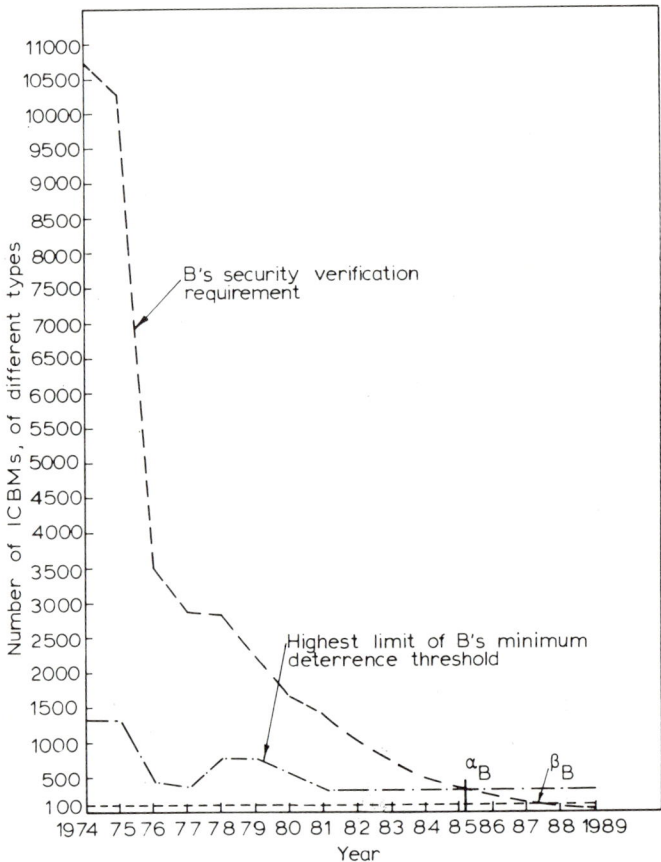

ICBM reductions

The main difference between Scenarios I and II is that, whereas in Scenario I, ICBM reductions are made when there is an overall freeze in strategic weapons development, in Scenario II ICBM reductions are made against a background of an unabated technological arms race. By comparing the two scenarios we can determine the impact of this technological arms race on a disarming state's security, and hence its need for verification. This impact, as can be seen from Tables 1A.19 and 1A.20 and Graphs 1A.15 and 1A.16, is enormous.

Countries A and B start out from very different technological capabilities. Even before the ICBM reductions were begun, country A was somewhat behind B in the quality (but not quantity) of its arsenal. Hence the extent of its initial effort to introduce new weapons and expand its forces exceeds that of B. Despite this, however, the initial disproportion between the two countries continues; A's effort cannot match the new technological developments of its opponent, because of the time lag. As a result of the fact that the strategic disarmament agreement discussed here contains no provisions restraining the qualitative arms race, the balance of security which had existed at the time the treaty was concluded will be rapidly destroyed. As Table 1A.19 shows, even if country A had made large qualitative and quantitative improvements in its strategic arsenal much earlier, B would anyway quickly acquire a capability even larger than A's second strike, and would thus gain the first-strike capability. In terms of the ICBM reductions considered here this point would be reached at the eighth stage of reductions, so that whatever expansion country A had undergone by that point, country B would have acquired such powerful MARVed MIIIs that A's residual second strike is extremely small, or disappears completely. This situation continues throughout the period of reductions.

This enormous offensive potential on the part of B is the result only of vast improvements in the accuracy and reliability of its warheads. Consequently, the comparison between A's and B's defensive and offensive potentials made for Scenarios I and II – in both cases by subtracting KN potential from KS values – is much more realistic in the case of Scenario II. With the high accuracy of its warheads B's all-out attack will require fewer retargeting operations, and the rate of attrition of A's silos will be much higher in the first salvo than in Scenario I, where an analysis of the worst case was based on sheer numbers, rather than on accuracy.

The vast strategic superiority of country B in Scenario II in its ICBMs, its first-strike capability, and in its possession of a substantial land-based second strike right up until the last stages of reductions, has two implications. The first is that it is unlikely that the two countries could enter into such an agreement, because A could never accept such a position of inequality. The second and even more important implication is that, even if the two countries did enter into an agreement of this kind, the loss by country A of its land-based residual second strike would leave it without security in terms of the major part of its deterrent force; a situation in which verification would play absolutely no part. In other words, the fact that B has superiority in ICBMs and still has a strong second strike, means that it has no incentive to 'cheat' by producing more ICBMs clandestinely. Similarly, A's position is so bad that even if B did cheat, it would make no difference. Verification therefore has no rôle in ICBM reductions in Scenario II.

This can be seen clearly from Table 1A.20 and Graph 1A.15. During the first eight stages of limitations the numbers needing to be produced clandestinely by A (the security verification requirement) are expressed in such large numbers (1 610 to 543) that there would be no need for B to have a tight verification system. At the next stage the requirement becomes very high for a short period

Graph 1A.17. Scenario II: phases of change in A's security during ICBM reductions, 1974–89, concomitant with an unrestricted qualitative arms race. The curve of A's ICBMs in its inventory is according to Table 1A.12, column 4, or Table 1A.2, column 5. The phasing of A's security is described on pages 144–148, especially page 144. The asterisk on the curve of A's ICBM reduced is point α_A from Scenario I (according to its position on the x axis in Scenario I) indicating the moment when A's security in Scenario II is assumed to be still fully satisfied. This asterisk is necessary for making Graph 1A.19.

Points β_A and α_A in Scenario II are placed on the curve of ICBM reductions according to their location on the x axis in Graph 1A.15. The three vertical lines run through point β_A first, then through point α_A. The last one marks the moment when A completely loses its second strike.

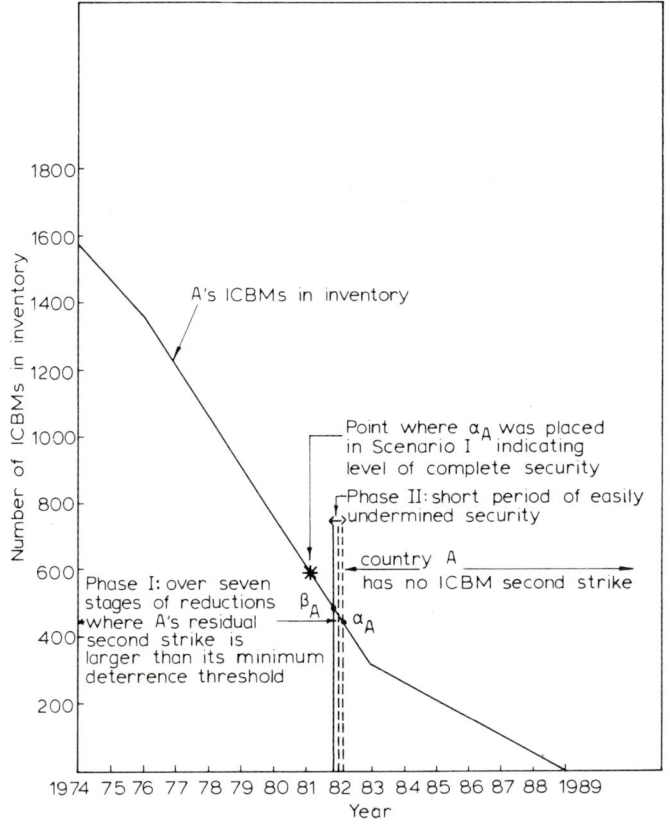

(equal to 15 ICBMs), after which A loses its residual second strike because of developments in country B. Verification of ICBMs hereafter becomes irrelevant. Whatever security A may have depends on its SLBMs, come what may with its ICBMs.

The technology factor introduced in Scenario II creates a situation in which the security verification requirement of A approaches point β_A (number of 100 ICBMs) earlier than point α_A (the requirement equal to that on the minimum

Graph 1A.18. Scenario II: three phases of change in B's security during ICBM reductions, 1974–89, concomitant with an unrestricted qualitative arms race. For B's ICBMs still in the inventory and simultaneously the scale of the vertical axis see Table 1A.16, column 4, or Table 1A.2, column 7. The phasing of B's security is described on pages 148–151. Points α_B and β_B are the same as in graph 1A.16 (horizontal axis).

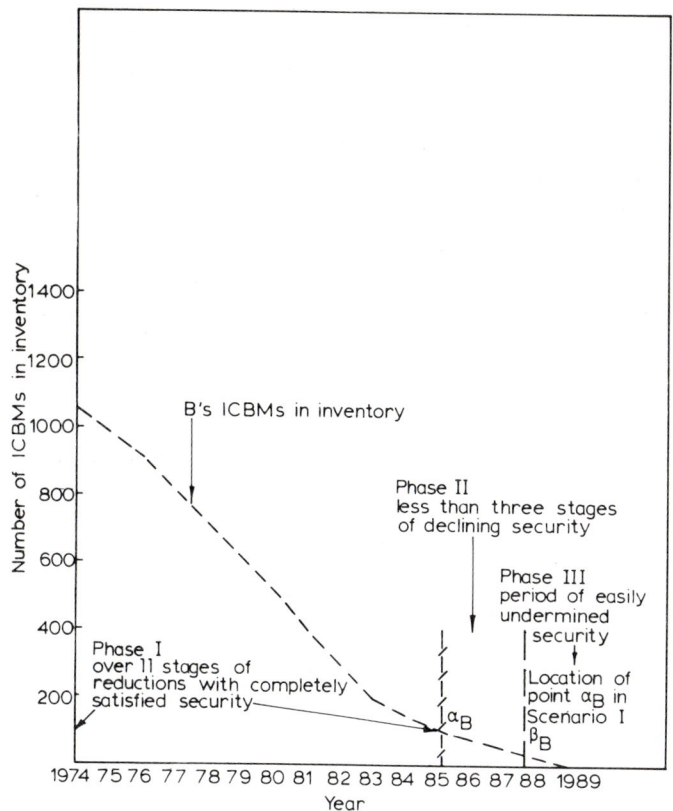

deterrence level). This situation is completely opposite to that in Scenario I, as can be seen by comparing Graphs 1A.3 and 1A.15. It means that, although A still possesses a residual second strike able to destroy 190 of B's cities, this second strike may be incapacitated by less than 100 of B's best ICBMs. So in order to be credible, A's second strike would have to be protected by a strong verification system much earlier than is required in Scenario I, that is, even before its residual second strike approached the level of its minimum deterrent.

As seen in Table 1A.20, at point α_A only 11 of B's MARVed MIIIs are needed to undermine A's minimum deterrence threshold. This threshold could hardly be called minimum in Scenario I, and could be overcome only by a large number of ICBMs (over 400). In Scenario II, although its $K'S$ value is still considerable, the existence of only a small number of B's extremely sophisticated weapons is a threat to it. Even if A possessed a verification system accurate

161

enough to monitor such a small number of weapons, this system could not prevent country A from losing its residual second strike anyway through B's technological expansion. Shown graphically, as on Graph 1A.17, we can see that phase I of the security verification requirement curve in Scenario I, namely, the period during which a country enjoys complete security, cannot be applied equally to Scenario II. Although A's residual second strike is also larger than its minimum deterrence threshold, it cannot be assumed that this second strike is secure, because only a very small number of weapons developed clandestinely by B could undermine it. This phase of complete security is thus shorter than in Scenario I. To make this comparison between the two scenarios easier, point α_A from Scenario I has been marked (an asterisk) on the curve of ICBMs being in A's inventory (Graph 1A.17).

From the above analysis it can be seen that where the factor of unabated technology is added, the security of A is not completely assured by its own deterrence capabilities, though these may be large. Much more important are the developments taking place in country B's arsenal, especially those increasing the accuracy of B's weapons. Where these numbers to be produced clandestinely are large, A's verification system may be able to monitor them, but this would not be the case when even a very small number of B's best missiles (say 10–15) could threaten its residual second strike. Furthermore, from the ninth reduction stage onwards, B's technological advances will have brought it into a position such that A will have been completely deprived of its second strike.

Turning now to the security verification requirement for country B, it is clear that the situation is not very different from that for Scenario I. As may be seen from Table 1A.20 and Graph 1A.16, the three phases of change in B's security during ICBM reductions concomitant with an unrestricted qualitative arms race are almost exactly identical in timing as in Scenario I (compare Graph 1A.18 with Graph 1A.7). B's requirement will be very low throughout the period of reductions until the last two stages, when the number of weapons having to be produced secretly by A in order to threaten B's second strike would be lower than 100. (At this stage B would still possess a formidable SLBM force, so that its ICBM security verification requirement, though numerically high, can be disregarded.)

It has already been said that phase I in the scheme of A's reductions is, unlike that of Scenario I, no longer characterized by complete security, even though A's residual second strike is larger than its minimum deterrence threshold. This is because during the eighth stage of reductions only a very small number (15) of MARVed MIIIs is able, if developed clandestinely and added to the existing legitimate stock of B's ICBMs, to undermine A's land-based residual second strike completely. Such a small number would probably be quite easy to produce clandestinely, because the technology would then be well known, and they could perhaps be assembled without additional R&D or tests. We have, therefore, arbitrarily taken A's level of complete security to be the point at which A's residual second strike is very large and its security verification requirement high. We have taken this point to be α_A from Scenario I where the values both of $K'S$ and of number of B's ICBMs necessary to destroy it were high. This point is

Graph 1A.19. Relation between disarmament concomitant with an unrestricted qualitative arms race and the security of country A during ICBM reductions. The graph is based on: firstly, the curve of A's ICBMs reduced as in Table 1A.2 or 1A.12 or Graph 1A.2; secondly points α_A from Scenario I, α_A from Scenario II and β_A from Scenario II which can be found in Graph 1A.17; thirdly the fact that A's security line is horizontal to point α_A from Scenario I, and marks (on the vertical axis) 980 ICBMs reduced at this point. This number of ICBMs reduced is a measure of verification required and equal to unit 1. Thus, 1 = 980 on the vertical scale, 0.5 of verification required = 490 ICBMs, and so on.

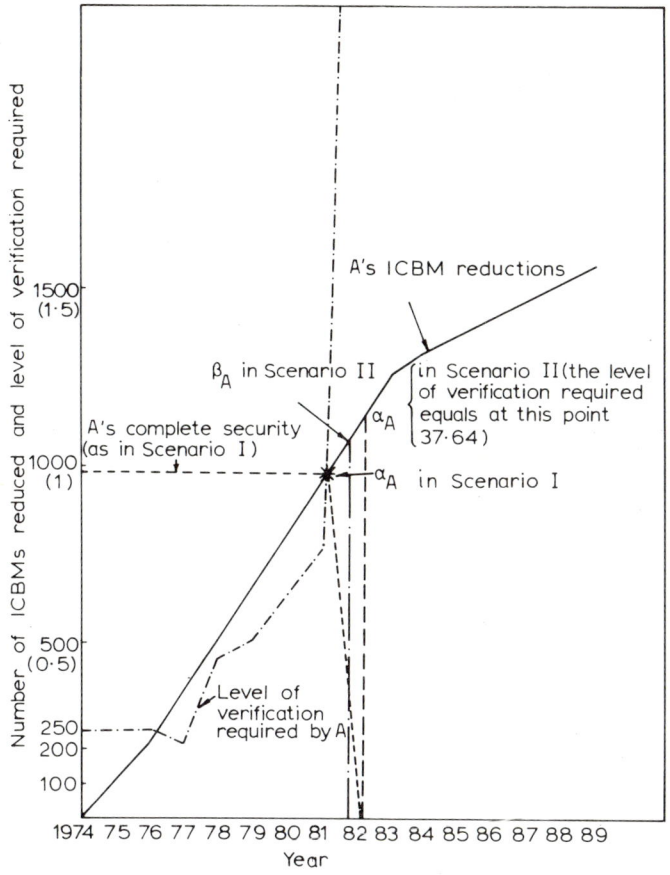

marked by a star on the curve of the number of ICBMs remaining in A's inventory (Graph 1A.17) and on the curve of A's reductions (Graph 1A.19). In Scenario I this point α_A lies immediately after early 1981, which corresponds roughly to 980 ICBMs reduced from A's inventory. This horizontal line drawn from the y axis to the same point as that of α_A in Scenario I will then be the level of A's complete security in Scenario II. At this point the security verification requirement of A is about 500 ICBMs and its residual second strike is also very large.

Table 1A.21. Scenario II: levels of required verification for countries A and B during ICBM reductions concomitant with an unrestricted qualitative arms race, 1974–1989[a]

Year or stage of reductions	Country A			Country B		
	Security verification requirement SVR	Index (I) of security verification requirement $\frac{SVR}{414}$	Level of required verification $\frac{1}{I}$	Security verification requirement SVR	Index (I) of security verification requirement $\frac{SVR}{1\,326}$	Level of required verification $\frac{1}{I}$
1974	1 610	3.9	0.26	10 711	8.1	0.12
1975	1 520	3.7	0.27	10 266	7.7	0.13
1976	1 563	3.8	0.26	3 512	2.7	0.38
1977	1 922	4.6	0.22	2 860	2.2	0.46
1978	914	2.2	0.45	2 821	2.1	0.47
1979	801	1.9	0.52	2 189	1.7	0.61
1980	640	1.6	0.65	1 635	1.2	0.81
1981	543	1.3	0.76	1 364	1.0	0.97
Point β_A	100	0.2	4.16	—	—	—
1982	15	0.04	27.62	1 009	0.8	1.32
Point α_A	11	0.03	37.64	—	—	—
1983	—	—	—	655	0.5	2.04
1984	—	—	—	470	0.4	2.86
1985	—	—	—	328	0.3	4.00
Point α_B	—	—	—	307	0.2	4.32
1986	—	—	—	234	0.2	5.56
1987	—	—	—	140	0.1	9.09
Point β_B	—	—	—	100	0.08	13.26
1988	—	—	—	67	0.05	20.00
1989	—	—	—	—	—	—

[a] The level of verification is assumed to be equal to unity for the same values of the security verification requirement as in Scenario I, that is, for A = 414 ICBMs and for B = 1 326 ICBMs. In this way the required levels of verification in Scenario I and II will be comparable. The values of points α and β in Scenario II are indicated in the Table for A and B respectively, according to the time at which they appear.

The figures for the required level of verification for the subsequent years of ICBM limitations are given in Table 1A.21 and Graph 1A.20. The method of calculating these are exactly the same in Scenario II as that for Scenario I (see Table 1A.11 and pages 136–138). Using these figures the curve of the required level of verification has been drawn (see Graphs 1A.13 and 1A.21), and shows the relationship between disarmament, verification and security for both countries. For country A this curve ends at a specific point immediately after point α_A, when A lost its land-based residual second strike completely and the security verification requirement could therefore not be calculated. For country B the same curve grows *ad infinitum* (that is, at the end of the limitations, it reaches 1 326, an extreme level which has no practical meaning).

Graph 1A.20. Scenario II: levels of required verification for countries A and B during ICBM reductions concomitant with an unrestricted qualitative arms race, 1974–89. This graph is based on Table 1A.21, columns 4 and 7. The level 1 for the verification requirement is taken from Scenario I and equals 414 for A and 1 326 for B. It is done in this way because in Scenario II point α_A no longer shows the point of fully assured security for country A, and thus verification required for this moment would have to be much more stringent than 1. Acceptance of the level of 1 from Scenario I, although somewhat misleading, is the only way of measuring the level of verification in Scenario II. Moreover it permits a comparison of the levels required in the two scenarios. Points α_A and α_B indicated at the line of 1 are the real points α in Scenario II. Note how widely the curves of the required verification miss these points. This indicates how much the technological factor increases the demand for verification. (At level 1 from Scenario I, $\alpha_A = 37.64$ and α_B 4.32).

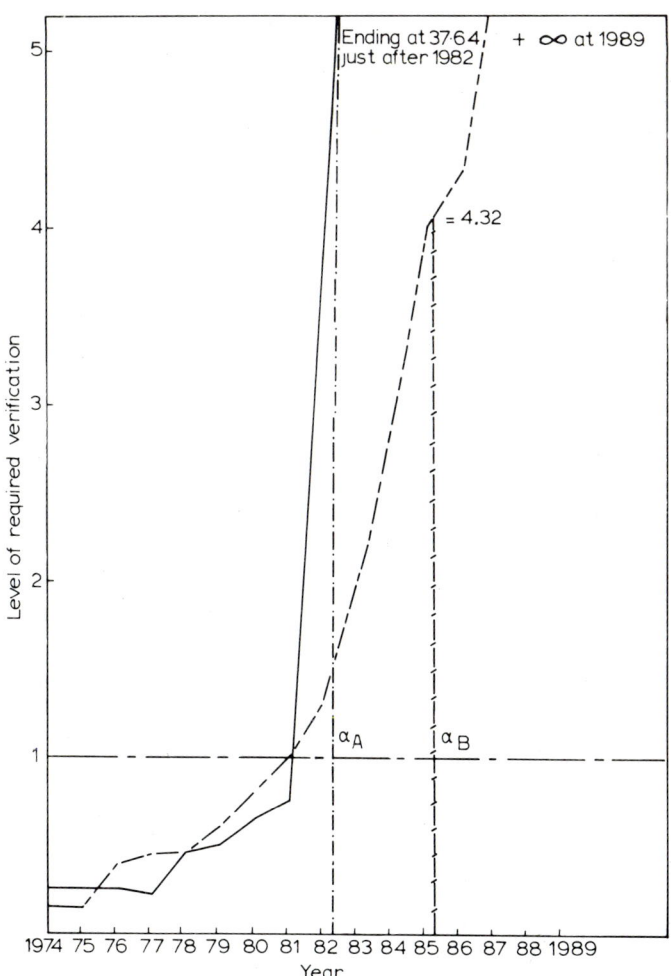

Graph 1A.21. Relation between disarmament concomitant with an unrestricted qualitative arms race, and the security of country B during ICBM reductions. The line of B's ICBMs reduced is based on Tables 1A.2 and 1A.16. The line of B's security is horizontal to point α_B from Scenario I, found according to its position on the horizontal axis and then cut into the curve of ICBMs reduced. The value at this point $= \pm 920$ ICBMs reduced. This is thus the measure of unity (verification required in Scenario I, or 4.32 in Scenario II). According to this, the vertical scale is: $1 = 920, 0.5 = 460$, and so on. The line of verification required is based on Table 1A.2, column 7.

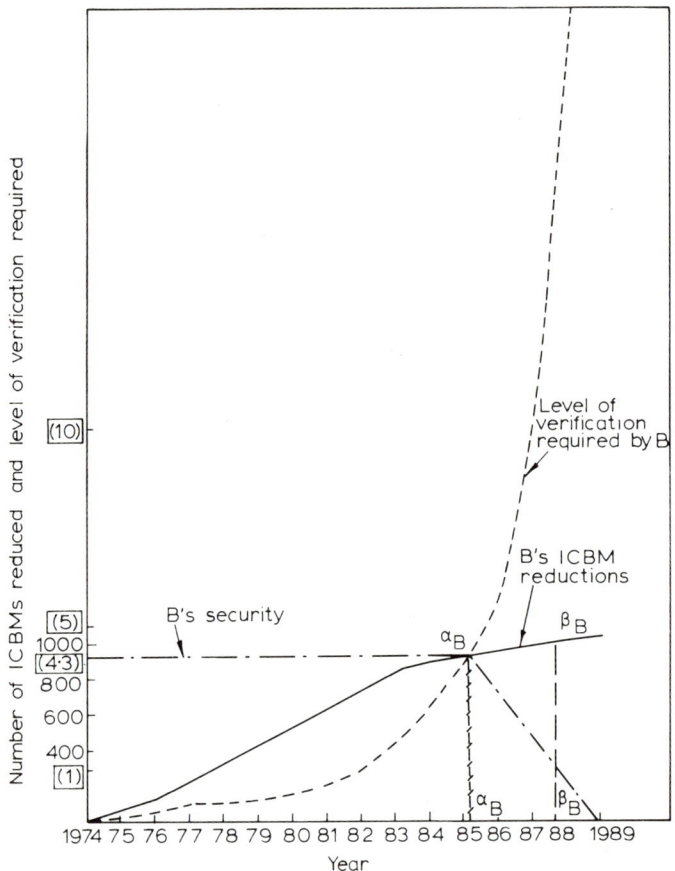

Graphs 1A.19 and 1A.21 illustrate once more the fact that if security and verification are plotted in a quantified way, then the relation between them is not inversely proportional during ICBM limitations. For a long period, and so long as the residual second strike is larger than the minimum deterrence threshold, a country's security is stable and the demand for verification is correspondingly small. After passing point α verification responds to a decline in security and rapidly rises. However, if the rôle of the sea-based deterrent is taken into account and is adopted as an additional guarantee of security during ICBM reductions, then we can assume that despite the ICBM limitations the security curve does not

Graph 1A.22. Scenario II: comparison between the required level of verification of countries A and B in Scenarios I and II. Level 1 is equal to verification's efficiency at points α_A and α_B in Scenario I, where the security of both countries has been completely satisfied. The lines of A's and B's level of required verification for Scenario I are based on Table 1A.11 and Graph 1A.10. The lines of A's and B's level of verification required for Scenario II are based on Table 1A.21 and Graph 1A.20.

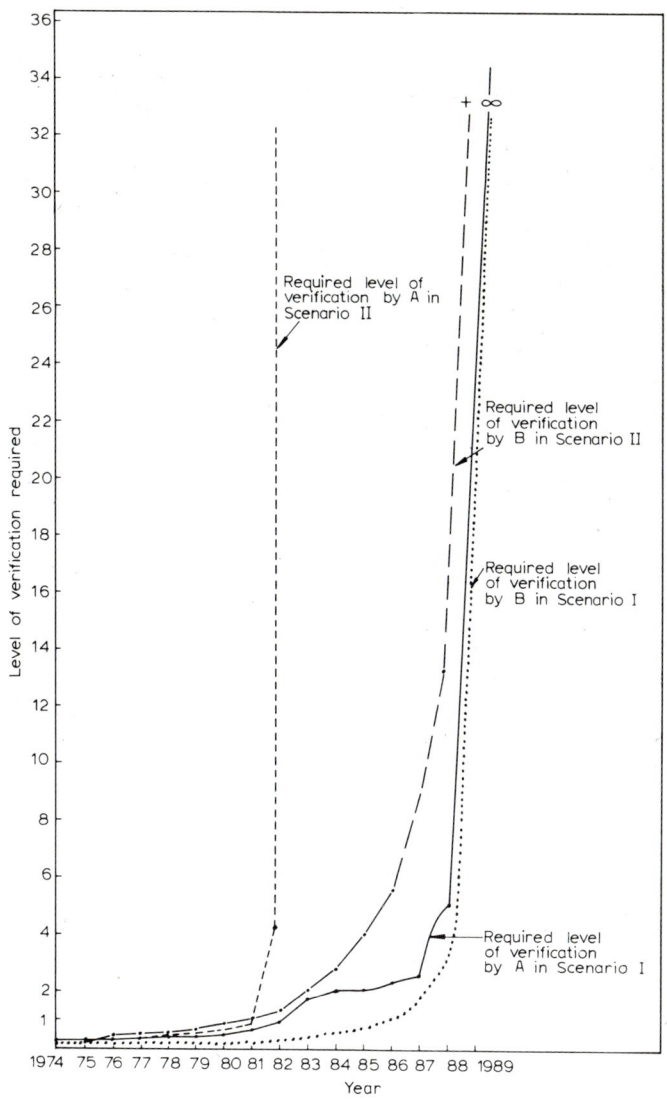

descend at all. The relationship between disarmament and security, and that between verification and security are thus not linked to each other in the strategic context we have analysed.

This is especially true in the context of country A's strategic situation in

Scenario II. As far as the ICBM component of its security is concerned, after only eight years of ICBM limitations country A loses its security and hence its need for verification; but this does not necessarily imply a breakdown of the ICBM limitation agreement. So long as A has large SLBM forces that are invulnerable to the developments in anti-submarine warfare of country B, it can largely rely on this component for its security.

Finally it can be seen from Graph 1A.22 that the level of required verification rises at an earlier stage in Scenario II than in Scenario I. In other words, because of the technological advances occurring in Scenario II, the need for verification arises sooner and therefore becomes an important issue in the strategic arms limitation agreement earlier than was the case in Scenario I.

SLBM reductions

Future developments in SLBM technology are even more unpredictable than those in the field of ICBMs. Nevertheless, it can be assumed that during the years 1974–89 unrestrained technological developments in strategic sea-based arsenals would create a situation to some extent resembling that described below.

By 1989 country A could be in possession of 62 missile-carrying submarines, 33 of which would be 'Y'-class carrying 528 SLBMs and 29 'D'-class submarines with 324 SLBMs. This would give a sum total of 852 missiles. If, say, half of the entire fleet of SLBMs were to carry MIRVed missiles (15 'Y'-class and 15 'D'-class submarines with MIRVs), each missile carrying six MIRVs of approximately $K = 1.5$, then the total offensive potential of this force would be $KN = 5\,496$.

By 1989 country B would probably possess about five 'Trident'-class submarines, each carrying 24 C-4 missiles, each missile with 10 re-entry vehicles (RVs) of approximately $K = 8$ per RV. The total KN value of these five submarines would equal 9 600. These weapons would be of much higher accuracy than those of the mid-1970s. In addition it can be assumed that if B had undergone an intensive technological expansion, then about five 'Polaris'-class submarines would by that time be fitted with the new C-4 missiles instead of B-3s. Their KN value would then be 6 400. The rest of the 31 'Poseidon'-class submarines would possess a KN potential of about 7 440. The sum total of B's SLBM offensive potential after this technological expansion would be as large as $KN = 23\,440$.

Moreover, country B would be capable of making further improvements in its SLBM arsenal, namely, to introduce MARV technology. In this case the offensive potential of B's SLBMs would expand in a dramatic way. Assuming a K value of a single MARVed re-entry vehicle to be the maximum $K = 87$, this would give a total kill potential of one Trident submarine amounting to $KN = 20\,880$. Having used MARV technology on its ICBMs in the past, B will be able to draw upon its experience and complete its MARVing of the C-4 missile rather rapidly.

No actual calculation of the numbers involved in SLBM reductions has been worked out. So far as the proportions between old and new submarines are concerned, Scenario II's SLBM limitations may proceed in a different way from those in Scenario I, because the qualities of submarines and their missiles will have changed. It may however be assumed that numerically the rate of reduction could be quite similar; and when, say four to six submarines are phased out annually, then these reductions could be accomplished after a ten-year period. The numerical value of the direct verification requirement is equal to this rate of reductions.

References and Notes to the Appendix

1. Report of the Secretary of Defense, James R. Schlesinger, to the Congress on the FY 1975 Defense Budget and FY 1975–79 Defense Program, 4 March 1974; Statement by Admiral Thomas H. Moorer, USN, Chairman, Joint Chiefs of Staff before the House Armed Services Committee on US Military Posture for FY 1975 Authorization for Military Procurement, Research and Development and Active Duty, Selected Reserved and Civilian Personnel Strengths, Hearing before the Committee on Armed Services, US Senate, 93rd Congress, 2nd session, Part 1. Authorizations, 5 February 1974; US–USSR Strategic Policies. Hearing before the Subcommittee on Arms Control, International Law Organizations of the Committee on Foreign Relations, US Senate, 93rd Congress, 2nd session on US and Soviet Strategic Doctrine and Military Policies, 4 March 1974; *World Armaments and Disarmament, SIPRI Yearbook 1974* (Stockholm, Almqvist and Wiksell, Stockholm International Peace Research Institute), pp. 106–107; *World Armaments and Disarmament, SIPRI Yearbook 1976* (Stockholm, Almqvist and Wiksell, Stockholm International Peace Research Institute), pp. 24–27.
2. See among other sources: Luttwak, E., *The US–USSR Nuclear Weapons Balance, The Washington Papers*, Vol. II, No. 14, (Beverly Hills, SAGE Publication, Center for Strategic and International Studies, Georgetown University, Washington, 1974;) Military Record of CBR, Atomic Happenings, Report WS 087/75, *Aviation Studies Atlantic*, March 1975, p. 25; *Offensive Missiles*, Stockholm Paper No. 5, (Stockholm International Peace Research Institute, 1974); Simons, H. T., Problems and Prospects for a SALT II Arms Control Agreement, *Interavia*, Vol. XXX, No. 8, 1975; *World Armaments and Disarmament, SIPRI Yearbook 1972* (Stockholm, Almqvist and Wiksell, Stockholm International Peace Research Institute), p. 10.
3. A number of other approaches were applied in calculating the quantitative ICBM reductions, among which were:
   –reductions aimed at the common ceiling in numbers of missiles or in numbers of independently targetable warheads,
   –reductions irrespective of number of weapons (whether missiles or warheads), guided only by limitations of kill potentials, that is, according to the proportional yearly reductions – numerical or by percentage – of the respective KN potentials.

   It can be noted, however, that the security verification requirements are insensitive to a particular arithmetical approach unless they: (*a*) are continuous and uniform, and (*b*) preserve the condition of undiminished security (proportionality of the second strikes).
4. *Offensive Missiles, op. cit.*

5. Bellany, I., Controversy About MIRVs, *Nature*, Vol. 242. No. 5395, 23 March 1973, pp. 237–39; Davis, L. E. and Schilling, W. R., All You Ever Wanted to Know About MIRV and ICBM Calculations But Were Not Cleared to Ask, *Journal of Conflict Resolution*, Vol. XVII, No. 2, June 1973; Nacht, M., The Vladivostok Accord and American Technological Options, *Survival*, Vol. XVII, No. 3, May–June 1975; Luttwak, E., *The US–USSR Nuclear Weapons Balance, op. cit.*
6. Davis, L. E. and Schilling, W. R., All You Ever Wanted to Know About MIRV and ICBM . . ., *op. cit.*, p. 213.
7. This assumption is another example of the 'worst case' analysis accepted in this study. In the case of any other, less lethal missile being secretly produced the requirement would be proportionally less stringent because the violating side would have to develop an accordingly larger number of these missiles than in the case of the requirement measured in the most lethal and accurate weapons.
8. We use $P_k = 0.5$ and $P_k = 0.95$ because they are at two different and distinct regions of the P_k versus K curve. With small probabilities of kill ($P_k = 0.5$) the curve grows slowly with K, and when P_k is large, approaching unity, the curve grows asymptotically with K.
9. The K_n of any existing single warhead is substantially lower than the K_s of a well hardened silo. It would, therefore, be necessary to use more than one warhead in order to destroy the silo, speaking in terms of simple arithmetic. The aggregate number of KN values does not mean that this value would be wholly 'functional' during the nuclear attack against a silo (see on this point, pp. 10–14 and 24–25 of *Offensive Missiles, op. cit.*). This is particularly the case when the aggregate value of KN of a strategic arsenal is created mainly by the sheer number of warheads and not by their individual K_n values (yield and accuracy). The equivalence of KN and KS values of the opposing arsenals would not, therefore, necessarily mean that every silo would be destroyed in an attack. The real number of missiles necessary to overcome a state's residual second strike would probably be higher than that indicated by the security verification requirement. It must be admitted, therefore, that certain inaccuracies in the calculations based on a comparison of KS and KN values will arise. This does not, however, impair the validity of the concept of the security verification requirement for general theoretical study.
10. Statement of Secretary of Defense, Robert McNamara, before the Joint Sessions of the Senate Armed Services Committee and the Senate Subcommittee on Department of Defense Appropriations on the FY 1968–72 Defense Program and 1968 Defense Budget, 23 January 1967, pp. 38–39.
11. The calculations by Tsipis are based on $\rho = 1$ (100 per cent reliability of missiles), but in the case of the minimum deterrence threshold outlined above ρ was taken to be 0.7 (OAR = 70 per cent). The reason for this disparity is that the concept of the security of states demands that all calculations be based on the most pessimistic values, according to the well known practice of the military planners. The 'worst case' approach, which seems justifiable in many cases, is however open to abuse and exaggeration. It follows that when the calculations refer to weapons used offensively, diminishing the residual defensive potential of the 'attacked' state, KS, then a much more pessimistic figure is adopted, namely $\rho = 0.75$ or $\rho = 0.8$ (Scenario I) and even $\rho = 0.85$ (Scenario II). See Tables 1A.1 and 1A.16.
12. Ball, D., Déjà Vu: The Return to Counterforce in the Nixon Administration: (Or, the Politics of Potential Nuclear Castration), Appendix in O'Neil, R. ed., *The Strategic Nuclear Balance. An Australian Perspective*, (Canberra, Strategic and Defence Studies Centre, Australian National University, 1975), p. 205; the same

point may be exemplified in the following way: For a silo of, for example, 500 lb/in²-hardness, which has a probability $P_k = 0.99$ of being destroyed, as many as 58 Poseidon C-3 warheads or 44 SS-N-6 warheads are required (see Table 6 of the SIPRI paper *Offensive Missiles*, *op. cit.*, pp. 24–25). Such numbers of warheads could not in reality be used. Moreover, besides the low K values of the old and contemporary SLBM missiles, they are generally believed to be of much smaller reliability than ICBMs and not all of them are permanently on station.

13. This number of MIRVs is taken quite arbitrarily, and is open to objection. This and all other assumptions could differ substantially without influencing the outcome of the paper. The numbers used here should be treated only as theoretical examples.

Index

ABM (Anti-Ballistic Missile) 69, 70, 94, 101
ALCM (Air-Launched Cruise Missile) 102
ASW (Anti-Submarine Warfare) 68, 83–86, 92–95, 100, 142–144
Afheldt, H. 62, 64, 66, 69, 70, 94
Antarctic Treaty (1959) 14, 23
Arms control 57, 58
Arms limitation 11, 12, 94, 124
— —, strategic 74 ff
— —, —, terminology 78
Arms race 48, 57, 64 ff, 84, 85, 87, 91, 92, 95, 100, 101, 144 ff
Atomic energy 15
Australia 52

Balance of power 40, 64, 70, 81, 83, 91
Barnett, R. 34–36
Baruch Plan 96
Berg, O. 57
Biological Weapons Convention 18, 19
Bloomfield, L. P. 18
Bohn, L. C. 17
Bombers 65, 68, 79, 82, 86, 89, 93, 94, 102
Brooks, H. 101
Bureaucracy 45
Burton, J. 52

CBW (Chemical and Bacteriological (Biological) Warfare) 28, 47, 76
CCD (Conference of the Committee on Disarmament) 22
CEP (Circular Error Probability) 151, 152
Commission for Conventional Armaments (1948) 13
Control 11, 12
Control of armaments, Agency of the Western European Union 16
Cruise missiles 65, 79, 103
Cuban crisis 8

Deterrence 3, 61 ff, 80, 81
—, stability 66, 69
—, strategic nuclear 61 ff, 100
Disarmament 2, 3, 11, 57, 58, 75 ff, 98
— agreement 92, 102
— —, compliance 43 ff
— —, impact 4 ff
— —, implementation 40 ff, 98, 103
— —, public opinion 44
— —, violation 46 ff, 69, 102
—, national security 56, 99
—, strategic 7, 64, 78, 80 ff, 95, 99–101, 103–171
— subcommittee 16
—, verification 8, 10, 80 ff
—, —, agreement 24 ff
—, —, definition 12 ff
—, —, means 15 ff, 20
—, —, methods 15 ff, 20
—, —, types 15, 21 ff

Egypt 14
Eisenhower, D. D. (President) 16

FLR (Flexible Limited Response) 63–65, 67, 68, 82, 83, 90, 94
Falk, R. 76, 77
Feld, B. 17
France 124
Frankel, J. 51, 55

GCD (General and Complete Disarmament) 17, 26, 104
Geneva Conference (1955) 16
Great Lakes 32
Gromyko, A. 96

Halperin, M. H. 34
Henkin, L. 18
Holsti, K. J. 51

IAEA (International Atomic Energy Agency) 14, 15, 16, 22

172

ICBM (Intercontinental Ballistic Missile)   48, 65, 66, 68, 70, 81, 82, 86, 88–91, 93–95, 102, 105–171 *passim*
Institute of Defense Analysis   13
International Court of Justice   44
International law   43
Israel   14

K (Kill potential)   117, 151–155

Lauterpacht, H.   43
League of Nations Covenant   43
London Declaration on the Sanctity of Treaties (1871)   43

MAD (Mutually Assured Destruction)   62 ff, 82, 83, 86, 88, 90, 94, 142
MARV (Manoeuvrable Re-entry Vehicle)   90, 105–171 *passim*
MIRV (Multiple Independently targetable Re-entry Vehicle)   66, 70, 82, 102, 103, 120, 144, 152
MRV (Multiple Re-entry Vehicle)   66
McNamara, R.   63, 123
Marshall, C. B.   18
Melman, S.   16
Military R & D   24, 28, 42, 47, 76, 82, 83, 102, 114
Military security   100, 118
— —, verification requirement   105
— technology   42, 81, 83, 91, 95, 98, 101, 102, 103, 105
Minimum deterrence threshold   62, 63, 123–127
Missiles   108, 109, 118, 168

NPT (Non-Proliferation Treaty)   14, 22, 36, 43
National interests   99
— —, definition   51 ff
— —, formulation   54 ff
Norway   32
Nuclear explosions (including underground)   29, 32, 122
Nuclear Test Ban Treaty   32
Nuclear tests   16, 17

Outer Space Treaty   23, 24

Partial Test Ban Treaty   8, 21

Paris Peace Conference (1919)   10
Public opinion   44

Robinson, T. W.   51
Rosenau (Professor)   51
Rush-Bagot Agreement   32

SALT (Strategic Arms Limitation Talks)   13, 19, 79, 103
SALT I   7, 14, 35, 36, 48
—, Standing Consultative Commission   6, 35
SLBM (Submarine-Launched Ballistic Missile)   65, 66, 82–86, 89–95, 105–171 *passim*
SLCM (Submarine-Launched Cruise Missile)   102
Safeguards   13, 14, 28, 40, 58, 59, 101
Schelling, T. C.   34
Sea Bed Treaty (1971)   19, 22–24, 36
Security   2, 3, 8, 31, 33, 45, 46, 51 ff, 56 ff, 69, 74 ff, 80 ff, 95, 99, 101
—, calculable   80
—, strategic   105
—, —, military   61 ff
—, verification   114, 115, 118, 120 ff, 155 ff
Sinai   14, 22
SIPRI publications, *Offensive Missiles*, (1974)   115
— —, *Yearbook 1974*   106
Snyder, G. H.   66
Sonntag, P.   62, 64, 66, 69, 70, 94
Stassen, H.   96
Submarine   83–85, 91–93, 95, 102, 142, 143, 168, 169
Sweden   32

TKP (Terminal Kill Probability)   118, 119
Titan II   107
Treaty of Tlatelolco   14

United Kingdom   52, 56, 57, 124
United Nations   10, 19
— — Charter   43
— — Commission for Conventional Armaments (1948)   28
— — Security Council   19, 22

USA 8, 14, 16, 17, 19, 22, 29, 32, 34, 36, 52, 65, 74, 79, 94, 106
US Congress debates 7
US Department of Defense 88
US Joint Chiefs of Staff 13
USSR 8, 16, 19, 29, 36, 62, 75, 79, 106, 123

Verification 2, 3, 12 ff, 58, 64, 69, 74 ff, 80 ff, 95, 96, 99, 101–103
—, efficiency 115
—, functions 33 ff, 58 ff, 101
—, requirements 28 ff, 103, 155 ff

Vienna Convention (1969) 43, 44

Wainhouse, D. W. 18
Weapons, strategic 79, 81 ff, 100
Wiesner, J. 75–77, 86, 101, 135, 138–141
Woods Hole Summer Study (1962) 13, 17, 19
World War I 10
— — II 7, 10, 12, 15, 57
Wright, M. 17, 26

Zorin-McCloy Agreement (1961) 75, 103, 104